"*Emotional Medicine Rx* is an eminentl   practica   manual fo
creating health in mind, body, and sp   it. I highly recommend it."

Christiane Northrup, MD, author of *Mother-Daughter Wisdom, The Wisdom of Menopause*, and *Women's Bodies, Women's Wisdom*

"How wonderful to find a book that connects so intimately with readers, where the author is as deeply concerned about how her words might affect us as she is in delivering her message. She anticipates our hopes and fears, describing *wisdom tools* to ease our lives while gently prompting us to deepen our self-knowledge. Reading this book is an experience of love."

Hal Zina Bennett, author of *Write From the Heart: Unleashing the Power of Your Creativity*

"Penelope Young Andrade is a wise, compassionate and deeply committed professional with a strong, compelling vision of emotional healing. She helps us see and experience how changing our innermost feelings will cause our thoughts and actions to follow suit and our lives to change for the better. This is an important book that can help people heal and grow in meaningful ways."

Jeremy Geffen, MD, author of *The Journey through Cancer: Healing and Transforming the Whole Person*

"So much wisdom here, so much heart, so much knowledge. And so accessible and practical. This book is a treasure. *Emotional Medicine Rx* shows readers clearly and precisely how our emotions can be portals to well-being. I highly recommend it. Listen to the doctor and take your Emotional Medicine. It will help you have more happiness in your life."

Diana Fosha, Ph.D., creator of AEDP (Accelerated Experiential Dynamic Psychotherapy), author of *The Transforming Power of Affect* and coeditor of *The Healing Power of Emotions: Affective Neuroscience, Development, and Clinical Practice*

"*Emotional Medicine Rx* is a wonderful book, beautifully written. The synthesis of the author's many years of work as a therapist, meditation practitioner, and her commitment to deepening relationships translates into a profound understanding of emotions. In this book, she offers an elegant, simple and effective way of using attention to rapidly relieve emotional pain and restore well-being. I highly recommend Emotional Medicine."

> Nicolee McMahon, MFT, American Zen Teacher, originator of Practice of Immediacy

---

"*Emotional Medicine Rx* has greatly helped my Science of Mind practice. I've learned to name and embody the physical sensations that accompany any emotional upsets. Further, I've learned to trust that experiencing my emotions this way leads to feeling *really* good. With this embodied and peaceful perspective my affirmative prayers are now more effective – Recognition and Unification steps flow effortlessly. My fondest wish is that all Science of Mind Practitioners have access to this healing book."

> Evelyn Eads, Human Resources Executive, Science of Mind Practitioner (RscP)

"Written from the heart, this book connects with many of the processes research is showing are helpful to human growth and the alleviation of human suffering. Facing the challenge of difficult feelings and thoughts is important for every human on the planet and this book is an aid in that process."

> Steven C. Hayes, University of Nevada, author of *Get Out of Your Mind and Into Your Life*

"I was engaged from the first sentence. Making and integrating all the personal examples from your own life connects me instantly to you. I feel as though you have written the book just for me."

> Doretta Winkelman, Director of Binational Education, San Diego Natural History Museum

---

"This book is a gift – a gift of love, experience and an enduring belief in the healing power of the mind/body. Thank you, Penelope, for your focus on the body and on the movement of emotions through the body. This is a wonderful contribution to the evolution of personal healing and psychotherapy."

"Reading this book was a pleasure. It is excellent – didactically sophisticated, scientifically informed and based on grounded experience. As your reader I trust you, the author, because while you are 'selling' me an extremely simple method for attaining well-being, it becomes clear that your concept of well-being is not a superficial happy-go-lucky one. Emotional Medicine offers peace and integrity in the face of difficult experiences, even facing one's own process of dying."

Margit Loemeda-Lutz, Dr. Dipl. Psych., author of *Intelligente Emotionalität – vom Umgang mit unseren Gefühlen (Intelligent Emotionality – How We Deal with Our Emotions)*, Trainer for the International Institute and the Swiss Society for Bioenergetic Analysis and Therapy IIBA/SGBAT, and coeditor of *Bioenergetic Analysis*

"Penelope Andrade shows us the too-often-ignored approach to natural healing – our emotions. It's time we pay attention to her words, and to this rich, information-filled source of living and healing naturally."

Barry Vissell, MD and Joyce Vissell, RN, MA, authors of *The Shared Heart* and *The Heart's Wisdom*

"As we confront accelerating global crises, with wide-spread destruction and suffering, many of us are experiencing an increased sense of fear, anger, and grief. These emotions are healthy responses to these crises, reminders that we are all connected through the web of life and that all life is under threat today. Penelope Young Andrade's approach to emotional health can help us to transform these emotions, allowing us to respond creatively and compassionately to the challenges we are all facing today."

Molly Young Brown, author of *Growing Whole: Self-realization for the Great Turning* and co-author of *Coming Back to Life: Practices to Reconnect Our Lives, Our World*

"Our original psychological staff at Sanoviv Medical Institute had the benefit of being trained by Penelope. The tools shared in this book are now used every day in our work with clients, helping them recover a healthy relationship with their body and find their inner wisdom as a way of improving well-being. Emotional Medicine is a natural and effective path towards self discovery and healing that I recommend for everyone."

Jonas G. Chong Curiel, Head of Psychology and Spirituality Programs, Sanoviv Medical Institute, Baja California, Mexico

"Penelope Young Andrade is a master of emotions. This book offers in-depth insight into dealing with the emotions that course through our daily lives. A must-read for those desiring to know how to live in harmony with themselves with a fulfilling sense of peace and equanimity."

Jaqueline Lapa Sussman, M.A., author of *Freedom From Failure: How to Discover the Secret Images that Can Bring Success in Love, Parenting, Career, and Physical Well Being* and *Images of Desire: A Return to Natural Sensuality*

"Everyone can benefit from Penelope Young Andrade's practical wisdom as she guides us on the path toward emotional healing and balance, nourished by our inner truth."

Halé Sofia Schatz, author of *If the Buddha Came to Dinner: How to Nourish Your Body to Awaken Your Spirit*

"Emotional Medicine has been life-changing for so many of my clients and for me! For readers who already love their emotions, Penelope adds fresh insight into letting the body lead quickly back to bliss. For those who have not yet befriended their emotions, this book reveals in simple and practical detail just what a remarkable resource they are. *Emotional Medicine Rx* is highly recommended!"

Shana Stanberry Parker, Sc.D., psychologist and editor, *Fearless Nest: Our Children as Our Greatest Teachers*

"Emotional Medicine's unique approach combines Penelope's heart-felt personal experience, her 30-plus years of clinical experience along with scientific information to support her theory. As in Feldenkrais, readers discover how to cooperate rather than coerce what is happening in the present moment to restore functional living. *Emotional Medicine Rx* offers the reader numerous easy ways to practice healthy emotional expression, thus creating a healthy lifestyle."

Donna Ray, MFT, Feldenkrais Trainer

12 STEPS TO HAPPINESS, VITALITY AND INNER PEACE

Emotional MEDICINE

CRY WHEN YOU'RE SAD, STOP WHEN YOU'RE DONE, FEEL GOOD FAST

R_x

*Darla and John
I send you love
and support for.
Your Hearts healing*

Penelope

Penelope Young Andrade
LCSW

TENACITY PRESS

ISBN-13: 978-0615517087

ISBN-10: 0615517080

TENACITY PRESS

Visit www.emotionalmedicine.com and download your free audio versions of two awareness processes described in this book. Penelope has recorded these personally to support your *Emotional Medicine Rx* healing journey.

Disclaimer

This book is a first-aid kit for the ordinary emotional upsets experienced in daily life. It is not intended to be a substitute for psychotherapy or medical treatment of mental or emotional distress. If you have any reason to fear that your state of mind or mood is unstable or if you feel too frightened to read this book or try this method, please seek the help of a clergyperson, counselor or qualified therapist. If you have any concerns that you might harm yourself or others, find professional help immediately.

It is entirely appropriate to seek professional help to support yourself while learning Emotional Medicine. You can request your therapist, minister and/or coach to use the methods described in this book as an adjunct to their standard treatment protocols.

For my beloved Arturo
I can feel you to the center of the earth

CONTENTS

Introduction

All my life I've been figuring out how people could be happier, starting with me. I set out on this quest for transformation not only to heal myself, but because as long as I can remember, I've had a deep longing to help others. Twenty-five years ago in the midst of a personal crisis I discovered something that changed my life and my clients' lives forever. I'm eager to share my discovery with you.

I've found a way to restore an experience of self-confidence, well-being, and spiritual peace in minutes. This has been so profound that I'd like to shout it from the roof tops: If you've been numbed out by too much pain, scared off from your emotions by too many bad examples of what you've mistakenly labeled "emotional hysteria," help is on the way. Let me take you gently by the hand and show you how to safely feel emotionally alive, happy, well again.

Disaster Precedes Discovery

Twenty-five years ago my first husband, David, announced he wanted to end our 14-year marriage. My heart was broken. We had a three-year-old son, Adam, whom we had waited eleven years to conceive. We had just designed and built our dream home on a rural mountainside. I felt like I was dying. My life as I knew it was over.

Before you consider David a villain, let me say this was something he needed to do. I might quibble with his timing and wish for a few more years of full-time mothering, but I've thanked him many times since for enabling me to find my beloved husband, Arturo.

However, in those first days and weeks after he left, I was devastated. It took all of my personal, professional and spiritual resources and training as well as my ongoing faith in the evolution of my being to get through this crisis. Ultimately, I believed there had to be some wisdom in this breakup, and that I would one day understand and appreciate why it happened. I held onto this faint prospect with my fingernails, as I tried to keep myself from falling into an abyss of despair.

One afternoon, I was having a bodywork/healing session with Jane, a medical intuitive reputed to be a gifted healer. Shortly after our session began, the familiar waves of grief crashed in with full force. I sobbed as anguish coursed through my body. I felt as if I'd never stop crying. After some time Jane said something which altered me forever. Her simple observation began a process of healing and revelation which continues to this day.

So what did Jane say? I'll tell you in just a bit. First, though, I want to tell you more about what my emotional life had been like up to that point. Tears have always come easily for me—but knowing when or how to stop crying? That's been a big mystery.

As an Irish extravert with a history of childhood abandonment, I'd been moving through vales of tears much of my life. I figured I was just too "emotional" as a result of my childhood trauma. Amazingly, what I was about to learn enabled me to see that the problem was not with my emotions at all.

Emotions are Not the Problem

Up until this discovery, the only way I'd known to handle deep emotional distress was to cry until I was too tired to cry any more. On some other occasions, I'd had to use my will to suppress my feelings and stop the process. Neither had ever seemed organic. Though I didn't know it, this time was about to be different. I was on the verge of a breakthrough.

Even today, I can still see myself on Jane's massage table, writhing in agony. A barrage of breakup images is flooding my brain. I can't stop thinking how Adam's happy, secure life is now irrevocably changed. I can't stop thinking of how we are no longer a family, of how we now have to sell our home and live separate lives. I sob and sob.

After some time (I don't remember how long . . . just that it was the perfect amount), Jane said the words that opened the door to a new way of being.

She said, "I think you're done now."

What did she mean by that? I searched my experience for the answer. As I searched, however, I noticed that at that very moment, I *was* done. I didn't feel sad, mad, glad, scared. I felt peaceful and complete. Though my mind struggled for a moment wondering if she was judging me, telling me I "should" be done grieving, the sense of completion I felt in my body was palpable, nourishing, restorative. As I lay there enjoying this respite, I found myself dropping deeper and deeper into peaceful wellbeing. It certainly seemed I was done with grieving. There was no discussion. No more questions. Just feeling good.

I drove home feeling more happy and resourceful than I had in months. Of course, my mind tried to make sense of what had just happened. Was I permanently done with grieving? I didn't think so, for just the slightest thought of our breakup brought a slight swell of emotion again. Fortunately my sense of well-being was so pervasive it didn't restimulate grief in any big way.

I kept pondering. OK, what was done, who was done? As I continued to scan my experience, I realized that my *body* was done for that moment. My *emotions* were done with grief for that moment. Something organic within me was complete and thus I felt complete.

Jane and I never did discuss what she meant that day. I didn't need to. I knew I had received a gift which would transform my life. I was off and running. By God, my body knew when I was done crying and it knew when to stop. I could drop my awareness into my body any time I chose and get information about what needed to happen – more tears, or time to rest and restore.

Learning to Let My Body Lead

After my experience on Jane's table, I realized that what typically happens in the midst of what we call an "emotional upset" is we focus attention on our endless *stories and thoughts*, rather than our body's *brief emotional experience*. In my case I'd been trapped in an endless wheel of misfortune. Each miserable thought of our broken home would trigger a new wave of crying until I was wrung out, depleted.

This time, on Jane's table, I cried, I stopped and I felt good even though my situation hadn't changed. Because of this breakthrough, I decided to keep looking to my body to determine whether I needed to cry or not, *not to my thoughts about any situation.* I began noticing whether a blip or wave of grief was stimulated by upsetting thoughts of my marriage ending or whether there was a ripeness of feeling in my body waiting to be plucked and released.

If sad thoughts entered my mind, I'd check in with my body. If it was *predominantly* peaceful, I'd let those sad thoughts go by like clouds. When it seemed my body was full of emotion and needed discharge, I'd cooperate and let feelings flow. I also tried to tune in to what specific gestures or sounds my body needed to do to fully express and release the emotion. I began to develop a practice I now call Emotional Medicine.

Emotional Medicine is Different from Other Methods

Using my own life as a laboratory to explore Emotional Medicine, I began to ponder the difference between what I was doing and the emotional catharsis work featured by methods I'd studied such as Bioenergetic Analysis and my personal experience with a helpful neo-Reichian therapist.[1]

Although there were many similarities, I soon realized that the essential guideline for my emotional release process was different.

My focus was not analysis or attention to characterological issues or upsetting thoughts about any life problem, but rather moment-by-moment attention to the organic movement of emotion through the body in a natural cycle of building, discharging, releasing. This was followed by an intentional focus on the resulting good feelings. No matter what beguiling narrative beckoned, I would brake for my body. I would drop thoughts, incomplete issues, intriguing insights the moment they were no longer supporting or in line with the body's experience.

I was continually intrigued by how *quickly* my emotions would shift. When I let my body lead, waves of emotional distress often morphed in minutes to an increasing state of calm and peace. Timing was everything. This was very different from narrative-driven venting.

When my body was "done," I was deposited on the shores of well-being. I then had to make the choice to dwell on my fascinating analysis of how David's leaving was a mirror of my early abandonment experiences, or focus attention back on the restorative process happening in my body.

As weeks and months post-breakup passed, I was interested to see the number of times I would be peacefully attending to some activity when thoughts of the breakup would intrude out of nowhere. If I wasn't mindful of checking in with my body immediately, before I realized it my emotions would be triggered, full force. I began to gently pull myself back into the calm of the present moment, rather than head into the sad past or fearful future.

Living Emotion Meditation

Now, staying out of your head to stop recreating misery is classical mindfulness process. Since I'd been a meditator for years, I knew about this. As a matter of fact, it was because of my meditation practice and my years of Psychosynthesis training that I had developed the awareness skills to notice what was happening to me on Jane's massage table.

I knew how to focus awareness on the stream of thoughts, images and sensations that travel endlessly through my mind. That's standard operating procedure for most mindfulness practices. However, I had not been trained to notice the flow of emotion during its *embodied expression* through a cycle of buildup, discharge, release and completion. I hadn't been explicitly trained to use mindfulness practice during the active (noisy, messy, often fluid-filled) process of emotional release. As a result, I hadn't learned to stop when my body was done and I certainly hadn't learned to focus my attention on the pleasure that ensued.

Letting my body lead expanded my awareness in accord with my earlier training in Psychosynthesis: being present for my experience while also distinct from it. This required me to focus part of my awareness on the moving *dynamic* of emotion through the chest, legs and arms of my body's experience in the present moment.[2] *At the very same time* another part of my awareness needed to focus on *observing* my embodied emotional experience. Without full-bodied participation, I couldn't cooperate with my body's needs for particular types of physical expression. Without careful observation, I wouldn't know when my body was done.

I realized Emotional Medicine was not about letting the body (or emotions) rule. We'd already been there and done that in our human evolution. No, this was about letting the body lead, being ever mindful that *who it is that lets this body lead is our evolving, multimodal awareness*, our big "S" Self.

Feel Good Fast

See one, do one, teach one. I applied this time-honored medical tradition to my own psychotherapy practice. As I was experimenting in my own life, I began inviting clients to let their bodies lead. I soon saw to my dismay that after just a taste of embodied relief, people (myself included!) would tend to move on very quickly to the next life issue to be resolved. In worse cases, if mindful awareness wasn't focused on relief for at least a few minutes, it was easy to get pulled back into restimulating the whole upset over again.

For most postmodern people, staying present, even indulging in good feelings, is not going to happen if you don't have a specific intention to do so. I learned to help people *actively* look for and stay focused on the body sensations that felt good, thus giving our busy minds a job to do to avoid getting derailed by negative thoughts. I developed a guided, interactive body meditation to help prolong this peaceful presence. I invited clients to speak out about what felt good in terms of body sensation. I helped them feel the pulsing, warm, tingling energy that spread through hands, feet, shoulders.

I encouraged clients to use the words and images that would most authentically reflect their body's experience. I asked people to see what color this energy was if it were a color. I guided people into taking this healing, pleasurable energy into every muscle, joint, cell, molecule and atom.

I discovered that it took about three minutes of focusing on pleasurable, healing energy before the inner thoughts/self-talk would automatically become positive. Clients who had come in with feelings of desperation, worthlessness, and inadequacy would soon be saying: "I am OK," "I am confident," "I feel God's presence."

As a matter of fact, clients would so continually end up with spiritual experiences I thought I might have stumbled upon a law of nature: Cry when sad, stop when done, experience God. I saw again and again that crying when sad and stopping when done increased the potential for connection with a divine force, a limitless presence. For some this was God. For others, this deepened an experience of Jesus, Buddha, Mohammad, Zoroaster, nature spirits, Wicca, or the Great Mystery of native spirituality.

Personally, I consider myself a quasi-Christian, Buddhist, mystic, New Age Unitarian. I believe there exists a divine force, a limitless presence of awareness, love, light, being and will propelling all humans into ever-increasing capacities for being kind, cooperative, creative, sensually alive people. I was delighted to discover that one simple, easy way to connect with this inherent divine energy is through fully experiencing brief, embodied emotions.

Using Good Feelings to Facilitate Transformation

Although knowing that you are always just minutes away from feeling good is a boon to happy living, I knew as a therapist this knowledge wouldn't automatically translate into transformation. I needed to help people use good feelings as a conduit for healing and loving wounded parts of themselves as well as appreciating, loving and aligning with their strong, capable core Selves.

Self-love is the foundation for all change. If you love yourself enough (good, bad and ugly), it's easier to make the healthy choices required for a fulfilling life. While loving relationships, therapeutic and otherwise, are immeasurably important in helping people love themselves, it's also crucial to generate self-love experiences that originate with you.

My Psychosynthesis background came in handy again here with its emphasis on integrating various "parts" or "subpersonalities" into an experience of wholeness guided by the consciousness, love and will of Self. I personally taught clients to use affirmation, parts work, role play, setting and aligning intentions, etc. to facilitate behavior change fueled by feeling good.

I spent the next 10 years developing, refining and teaching these techniques. I was pleased to discover the work of Gerda Boyesen, Clover Southwell and the Biodynamic community in England. I integrated Boyesen's "Emotional Cycle" diagram with its simple depiction of the buildup-discharge-release flow. I thought I had it all figured out.

Soon life showed me I didn't. Dragged kicking and screaming into a new series of profoundly painful crises, I didn't know I was about to discover an entirely new adjunct to the process of letting the body lead.

Murder, Menopause and MDMA

In the early 90s I faced three crises. A dear friend and her daughter were murdered by a serial killer, I went into early menopause, and I had a bad experience with MDMA, the drug known on the street as "Ecstasy."[3] As a result of all this, I developed a panic disorder which I couldn't fix with Emotional Medicine. That was because I couldn't feel any emotions at all! I was numb.

My panic disorder was exacerbated by the estrogen replacement patches my doctor suggested I use, which seemed to be increasing my anxiety. Months later, this doctor discovered new research indicating estrogen affects the parasympathetic nervous system in a similar way to MDMA. I was, unwittingly, redosing myself with an MDMA-like substance every day. Every day I faced some variation of the panic and anxiety I'd felt on that drug. How I longed for some familiar grief or anger. Not to be.

Six months after taking MDMA, I found mention of Dr. Peter Levine in a footnote and began learning about Somatic Experiencing. Peter was just then writing his first book on trauma, *Waking the Tiger*. Many personal sessions and many workshops later, I not only healed my anxiety disorder, but also gained the insight needed to modify my emotional healing protocols to the special situation of panic and anxiety.

Seeking Safety

I learned how to be on the lookout for numb, frozen physical energy states and to stop any narrative or emotional process in myself or my clients until everyone felt safe, embodied, and resourced enough for emotions to flow again. Where Peter described a beautiful method for "titrating" the trauma and restoring resources, I incorporated some of this into a brief body-led protocol, which I call VIVO, to achieve a similar result. (I describe this process in detail in Chapter Five, "Learning the Language of your Body.")

I started asking clients whether they felt safe enough to continue moving into the center of emotional experience whenever we entered upsetting territory. When they didn't, I taught them how to use VIVO to gently restore resourcefulness and strength before proceeding into any embodied emotional release. I encouraged clients to always make a decision to seek safety, first and foremost.

Another aspect of seeking safety was taking responsibility for being sensitive to others' needs during any emotional expression. Several painful lessons involving my own blind spots highlighted for me the importance of eliciting the support and agreement of anyone present before taking any Emotional Medicine.

Finally, in the last year of writing this book (2010), I found another therapeutic approach which makes my heart sing and makes me know once again, quite happily, that I don't have it all figured out. This has led to more training, more learning. Three cheers for life as an ongoing exciting classroom.

My latest training has been with Diana Fosha and the Accelerated Experiential Dynamic Psychotherapy (AEDP) community. Diana's clarity and commitment to the *Healing Power of Emotion* (the title of her latest book) helped me articulate even more explicitly the importance of feeling loved and valued in any transformational journey. Although AEDP is focused predominantly on clients feeling safe and cherished within the psychotherapy relationship as they work through intense emotions to reach "core states" of well-being ("core states" being Diana's term for states I sense are similar to the profound "feel-good states" I've been discussing), I've spotlighted the importance of using good feelings specifically to generate and strengthen our inner experiences of *self* love. When you feel good, it's much easier to love yourself. It's also much easier to love others.

Dear reader, this is what I now offer you. This book is the result of my unending quest to find the simplest, easiest methods to enable you to live the life you long for. These are home-tested recipes. This book offers you a moment-by-moment guide for using your emotions to restore a sense of happiness, confidence and peace, *fast*.

What's the Science of Emotional Medicine?

Nobody in the laboratory knows exactly how the interplay between emotions in brain and body works to shift biochemistry and change behavior. James J. Gross, head of Affective Neuroscience at Stanford University and editor of *The Handbook of Emotional*

Regulation, quotes Churchill to describe the current understanding of emotions: "A riddle, wrapped in a mystery inside an enigma."[4]

Furthermore, as I write this introduction, there is a sharpened focus on disturbing problems with scientific research in general. Many dramatic results (for example, fats are bad for your heart, estrogen is good for your heart) haven't held up over time.[5] Important soul searching is taking place in all fields of research about how the drive to publish dramatic data first has skewed research away from conducting the more mundane studies that will produce enduring results.

The hard data concerning whether emotional expression is good for physical and emotional health covers the whole spectrum—yes, no, and in-between. I believe the reason these results are so varied is that researchers are not making the distinctions between narrative-driven "venting" and brief, body-led emotional expression. As long as these two vastly different types of emotional expression are lumped into one concept, it won't be possible to open the doors of our inner Emotional Medicine chests in the laboratory.

Over the years, I have written many of the leading neuroscience researchers offering to demonstrate my Emotional Medicine process at their labs. While no one has yet taken me up on this, I know it is just a matter of time. Someday, somewhere, someone will run the MRI scans, draw the blood, and test the saliva to quantify what I've see in my therapy office and my life for over 25 years: *Brief embodied emotional release followed by focus on good feelings creates experiences of subjective well-being and observable vitality and health.*

Soon everyone will know the truth about and avail themselves of our gift of human resilience—the ability to cry when sad, stop when done, and feel good fast. In the meantime, dear reader, you're ahead of the crowd on this one.

Interestingly, research describing the outcomes of psychotherapy and parenting styles incorporating emotional expression is clear. Emotional expression helps people recover.[6] These studies are not using blood draws to determine the changes in cortisol and dopamine levels (some of the markers used to measure stress and well-being), but are focusing on whether or not people benefited from emotional expression in counseling situations.

Susan Johnson's Emotionally Focused Therapy (EFT) research demonstrates an 86 percent improvement rate in distressed couples using EFT. Leslie Greenberg and colleagues are engaged in a multitude of EFT research projects validating the usefulness of emotional expression in promoting fulfilling relationships as well as increasing mental and physical health.

Studies at the Gottman Institute in Seattle found that using emotional expression as an opportunity for intimacy and teaching gave parents an opportunity to raise "emotionally intelligent" children capable of regulating, calming and self-soothing emotions. Children raised to value emotional expression had fewer infectious diseases, focused attention better, related better to others, and had higher levels of academic performance.[7] (Although it hasn't been tested, I'm sure this goes for your inner child as well!)

In another vein, Dr. Richard Davidson's (Director of the University of Wisconsin-Madison Laboratory for Affective Neuroscience) and Jon Kabat-Zinn's (University of Massachusetts Medical School) meditation and mindfulness research programs are especially relevant for Emotional Medicine, because crying when sad, stopping when done, focusing on feeling good *requires* mindfulness to work. Davidson and colleagues have demonstrated that mindfulness practice reduces stress, increases cheerfulness and changes the structure of the brain for the better.[8]

Throughout this book you'll find reference to some of the research that I believe is the foundation for future experiments with Emotional Medicine. Keep in mind that I am describing case studies drawn from my clinical practice and my own life. Everything you read in these pages actually happened to a real person.

How to Use This Book

This book is full of Action Tips and experiments to try out these new concepts one by one. I am very interested in the insights and gifts *you* discover in the laboratory of your life. Let me know via email, penelopeyandrade@gmail.com how Emotional Medicine works for you. Even though I'm describing a method for using emotions to feel good fast that will work when you're alone, another good way to use this information is to find a "feel good fast friend" (FGFF). If possible, find someone with whom you can share this book. This could be your spouse, your lover, friend, or neighbor. You will always get more bang for your emotional buck if you take your Emotional Medicine with a loving, supportive ear/shoulder/helping hand present.

If you can't find someone, read and master this method yourself and then teach those who love you to be the emotionally supportive presence you need. They don't need to read the book. You can show them how it works. After they've seen you move through mad, sad, scared feelings in minutes and feel good, they'll be relieved to know they can just be with you ... they don't have to fix you. They'll get fringe benefits just from watching it happen.

The latest research about mirror neurons indicates that if you go through a healing emotional process in someone's presence, his/her brain will experience a similar benefit. It's as if your companion were having the same experience him/herself. When you cry, stop, and focus, you'll *both* feel good fast!

This book could also be a helpful adjunct to any therapy you're experiencing. If you're not in therapy, but the processes in this book open you to deeper levels of self-awareness for which you'd like therapeutic help, that's great. Finding an unconditionally loving and supportive therapeutic relationship is a boon to healing and growth.

ONE

Emotional Medicine

What would your life be like if every time you felt sad, mad, or scared you could relax into knowing you were only minutes away from feeling good again? How much easier would your life be if even after crushing disappointment you could release the pain you were feeling and feel self-confident in minutes? And how would it feel if you could encounter life's inherent fears knowing they would guide you to effective, empowering action?

This is all possible. Here's what you need to know to make it a reality.

No Such Thing as a Negative Emotion

There is no such thing as a negative emotion. Of course, there are emotions that don't feel good – emotions you don't like experiencing. But primary emotions, those feeling experiences of sadness, anger, fear, happiness, surprise and disgust are *positive, purposeful* parts of your human makeup. It's all good. Without emotions your rational mind can't function – you're not able to make wise decisions. Without emotions your organism would have no way of relaying information crucial for your survival. Without emotions there would be no great art, great music, great books, great thought, or great sex, just to name a few.

Your emotions are your body's first line of defense against the insults and injuries you experience in life. Scientists now understand one of the main reasons you have emotions is that they propel you to take action to survive. This means your emotions are *designed* to serve you. They move you, teach you, guide you, and I say, they heal you.

Believing emotions are negative is the number one myth preventing people from benefiting from the feel-good "medicine" emotions are designed to deliver.

What is Emotional Medicine?

Emotional Medicine is the term I've invented for my discovery that a few minutes of brief, body-based emotional release followed by a few more minutes of focusing on the subsequent relief brings profound well-being. Sadness, anger, fear, happiness ... these emotions appear to change your body chemistry and open your body's medicine cabinet to dispense a personalized prescription of well-being just for you. And what's more amazing, they do it in just minutes when you know how to use them.

The number two myth that keeps people from using their emotions to thrive is the belief that humans have conscious control of *initial* emotional responses. Not so! Your conscious thoughts are just the tip of the iceberg of your human beingness. Your thoughts and rationales for your behavior follow your organism's emotional response to events – for very good reasons.

Emotions Come First!

Your emotional responses *precede* your conscious thinking responses by about five hundred milliseconds. As leading neuroscientist Dr. Antonio Damasio puts it, "We are always hopelessly late for consciousness and because we all suffer from the same tardiness no one notices it."[1]

The reason your emotions come first is practical. By the time you've entered the pros and cons about an action plan into the eter-

nal debating squad of your mind, your emotions have already figured out what's up, sent you signals via sad, mad, scared, glad (dis-
gusted, surprised etc.) responses to guide your actions, and gotten
back to the business of regulating your well-being. A tiger might
already be digesting you if you had to rely on "thinking it through"
to handle an impending attack.

A Caveat: You Still Need to Take Responsibility!

Hmmm. So if emotions come first, before you're even conscious
of them, does this mean you're not responsible for emotional responses that do spill out? Or that you can now use scientific valida-
tion to justify a classic victim stance: "It's not my fault. My emotions made me do it!"? Not hardly. You are tardy for the party of
consciousness – i.e., late in noticing how you are actually reacting.
But once you get to awareness, what you do *is* under your aegis.
You have to take responsibility for your responses – whether you
like them or not, whether they feel good or not, whether you think
you *should* feel them or not.

This is the hardest thing to get. No matter what someone does
to hurt you, what you do in the moments after that first response
remains your responsibility now and forevermore.

If you're like most of us, you've probably thought that controlling and suppressing emotional experience *was* taking responsibility. That's likely what you were taught. You may now be realizing, however, that although you've been successful in controlling
your emotions, the fact that you no longer feel them doesn't mean
they're not there.

The truth is they *are* still there, and they are still your responsibility. Someone hurts you and you get sad, mad or scared, yet *you*
have to handle it. It doesn't seem fair, does it? Furthermore, your
body's physiological response to being sad, mad or scared is set in
motion before you're even aware of it. You not only have to take
responsibility for how you handle emotions outside yourself in relationship, but inside yourself in your body and mind.

This isn't fair. But taking responsibility for your emotional responses is the *only* way you'll have the mastery to create the life you deserve. You cry when you are sad, you stop when you are done, you focus on feeling good. You do this in a way that is responsible to you and others around you. And you transform yourself and your life. However, there's yet another area of confusion about emotion that needs to be cleared up in order to get on with your transformation.

Calling an Emotion an Emotion

You need to get very precise about what the word *emotion* means. Whenever I talk about emotions, I mean *only* the cross-culturally accepted big six: sadness, anger, fear, happiness, surprise and disgust.[2] And for the purposes of Emotional Medicine, I am condensing this even further to cover just what I call the four horsemen of the apothecary: sad, mad, scared, glad. Before we had pharmacies we had apothecaries – places where healers mixed up remedies from natural substances. Sad, mad, scared, glad *are* the natural substances that constitute Emotional Medicine.

This is an essential distinction. Emotional Medicine does not include depression, resentment, guilt, anxiety, worry, worthlessness, inadequacy, pride, envy or jealousy. These are *states of mind* that usually involve repetitively disturbing thoughts: I am worthless, I am inadequate, I am undeserving. These thoughts are not emotions. They make up the stories you tell yourself when you're trying consciously or unconsciously to avoid feeling sad, mad, scared … and glad. Yes, strange as it sounds, people do avoid even their joy when they are caught up in sad stories.

You may have grown up thinking that most of these states of mind *are* emotions. And, though they are considered *secondary* emotions by some students of human nature, they are not primary emotions. Let's give this a test. If I ask you what you are feeling right now, what would you answer? If you're like most people, it would be something you're thinking about yourself. I can tell you from years of experience that most people have little idea what emotions they are actually *feeling*.

Inadequate or Scared?

I was taking a walk along the beautiful San Diego Bay at sunset the other day with a friend, Mary. We had reconnected after a couple of years and discovered we were both writing books. Mary was attempting a very ambitious, highly complex literary thriller, and having the hardest time getting to the writing. I asked her what she was feeling when she sat at her computer.

She replied, "I felt insecure."

I said, "I meant, what are you feeling?"

She answered, "Inadequate."

Since we are close enough to talk straight to each other, I said, "Well, girlfriend, those are the labels you are putting on yourself, but they are not your emotions."

She was silent for a moment and then said, "I'm scared. Aha!"

We both laughed out loud at the appropriateness of this underlying emotion. Of course Mary was scared; this was a big project she was attempting. We also both knew of plenty of times when I, too, was scared. We were in this together. We walked in silence for a few moments.

Neither of us tried to do anything to fix her fear nor make it go away. As we walked, we stayed present so she could feel her fear. We both could feel it easing and almost dissolving as we did so. Mary was trembling slightly as she explored what she was most scared of – her ignorance about the setting for the novel. Her fear was trying to help her, to point her in the direction of the action she needed to take – more research. When I talked to her later in the week, Mary was happily planning a trip to explore some of the backdrop locales in her novel.

Scared is something you can take action about right now. Scared is something that moves through you. Scared, as a body experience, is *fleeting*. And scared is Emotional Medicine for feeling threatened. Scared moves you to take action to help you survive and thrive. Interestingly, one of the things the body gets ready to do when you're scared is move your legs to get away from a threat. The fact that my friend and I were walking briskly was actually helping her move through her scared feelings.

When Mary was caught up *thinking* how inadequate she was, she was immobilized. When she looked for what she was *feeling* beneath those negative thoughts, she could free herself, then shift from paralyzed to powerful. Of course, there are other ways to shift moods, but mad, sad, scared and glad emotions are a direct route to your body's remarkable ability to help you change the way you feel and think about yourself.

If you're alive, you've probably had firsthand experience being stymied by negative thoughts or comparisons. This comes with the territory of being a 21st century human. It may even be the reason you've picked up this book. This book is about how to get out of your mind misery and back into your body to experience emotions in the brief, healing way they were designed.

ACTION TIP

Try this. From now on, whenever you're not happy, don't waste a minute *thinking* about what's wrong with you. Just ask yourself, what am I feeling emotionally? Write the following sentence on a piece of paper: "Am I sad, mad, scared or glad right now?" Put that sentence up on your bathroom mirror as a reminder to include it in your self-talk.

Just the act of naming a basic emotion such as mad, sad, scared begins to relieve stress. Try it! If you go beyond that label and allow yourself a safe, private minute to actually allow emotion to move through your body and then focus on the relief that ensues (for another few minutes) you not only relieve your stress, you soon feel truly good – happy, confident, and peaceful.

Emotional Medicine requires you to shift focus from how you are thinking to how you are feeling *in your body* in this moment. That means whenever you're not thinking happy thoughts, you look to your body to see what you can do to change the way you feel, especially to change the way you are feeling or not feeling your emotions.

If You Change the Way You Feel, You Can Change the Way You Think

For years, self-help books have told you that if you change the way you *think*, you can change the way you feel. And some of that has certainly been very useful. However, *Emotional Medicine Rx* is different. This book turns that adage on its head to tell you, *If you change the way you feel, you can change the way you think.* Here's what I mean by that.

If you change the *way* you experience your emotions – crying when you're sad, stopping when you're done, and focusing on the relief that follows – you'll naturally change the way you *think* about yourself and your life.

Emotions work to change your thinking by changing what is happening in your body. This is similar to the way drugs, alcohol and other psychotropic drugs work – they change what is happening in your biochemistry, which changes the way you feel in your body, and voila – they change the way you think.

Why do you think cocktail hour is called "Happy Hour"? Alcohol, like marijuana, cocaine and other drugs, floods your biochemistry with some of the neurochemicals associated with pleasure and relief. You take a drink, toke, sniff and it changes the way you feel. All of a sudden everything is all right in the world. You think happy thoughts. You feel confident – temporarily anyway. "Happy Hour" is aptly named, not only because you get happy, but also because that happiness just lasts for an hour or so. The unhappy side effects of alcohol/drug dependency may last a lifetime. Alcohol and drugs work on the "play now, pay later" plan.

Emotional Medicine, on the other hand, works via a "pay now, play later" plan. I cannot lie to you – when sad, mad, scared emotions arise they do not initially feel good. You may experience some or all of the following: accelerating heart rate, rapid shallow breathing, tightening throat and jaw, biceps and/or fists clenching, knees/legs buckling, shoulders slumping, eyes filling with tears. You pay the price of (temporary) discomfort right up front.

However, once you know how to let your body lead, you can cooperate with the body movements for which your emotions are primed – eyes releasing tears, shoulders heaving as your throat and lungs release sobs or yells, fists pumping, feet stomping or kicking, whole body trembling – and you'll feel better fast. In minutes your body will be done and ready to luxuriate in the biochemistry of relief. You'll have created your own naturally induced Happy Hour.

Whenever you resist allowing those sad, mad, scared emotions to *move* briefly through your experience, you substitute that initial acute discomfort with ongoing anxiety, irritability, and/or numbness. You can end up having a bad day, week, month...or life.

Of course you don't want to sob or stomp around in front of people when it is not safe, appropriate or supported. This is behavior best saved for your parked car, your spouse/lover's compassion, your best friend's couch, your own bedroom, your massage therapist's table, or your therapist, counselor, or pastor's office. You need to feel safe to take Emotional Medicine properly.

Balance Sheet

Let's compare the effect of using emotions versus substances to change your mood. You take alcohol and drugs; they quickly change the way you feel and think about your self and your life. You feel better fast but coming down is a drag, your liver may take hours or days to detox, and you run the risk of addiction and a ruined life. You start living for the drug rather than living for your life.

Conversely, with Emotional Medicine, you choose to feel your painful emotions for a few minutes and focus on the ensuing relief. This also quickly changes the way you feel and think. You feel happy, confident and peaceful. No side effects. You no longer fear the painful emotional responses that life inevitably entails. You know you can handle them.

Here's something else to remember. Even when you choose not to feel your emotions, your body still has to cope with the physiological and neurobiological changes emotion arousal evokes. When you don't cooperate with your emotions in a healthy way, you become a sitting duck for increased stress, as well as physical and mental disease.

Of course, Emotional Medicine, like alcohol and drugs, is also a temporary fix. You'll need to take it again and again to feel good - maybe even on a daily or weekly basis. But the long-term results couldn't be more different than the long-term effects of drugs. You'll be healthier, happier, and more confident. You'll be connected to your vitality in a way that enables you to take care of yourself and your life. You'll exude well-being. And ... you'll have an emotional life which is the greatest gift of all.

You Have Within You Everything You Need to Feel Good Fast

Your body is a great alchemist; it knows how to make happiness and well-being from emotions, just as it knows how to generate well-being from other organic aspects of life – food, sleep, sunlight, sex, relationships, nature, etc. Of course your body also knows how to create "medicinal" delight from music, art, dance, prayer and meditation. Your body knows how to do this all by itself, without relying on anything but its own nature-given, God-given, Spirit-given intelligence.

This is big. This means you are designed to feel good naturally in all the ways you can think of and even some you can't. Your brain knows inherently how to produce happy, safe, confident feelings ... and it doesn't need alcohol or drugs to do so.

A caveat: I am the therapist people come to when they want to handle anxiety, depression, and other emotional disorders without drugs of any kind. I know first hand, personally and professionally, that it is indeed possible to handle even severe mental/emotional distress without drugs, *if* a person is able and willing to make healthy choices in nutrition, exercise, hydration, sleep and stress reduction, as well as taking Emotional Medicine. These make it much easier to cooperate with your body's effort to get you back to feeling good as quickly and naturally as possible.

Sometimes, however, when misery is too strong and inner resources too weak, I refer clients for antidepressant medication. It can be humane to use medication to remind yourself what it's like to feel good again. If, for whatever reason, you don't feel capable or ready to make the kinds of changes necessary to live without medication, by all means take the meds. No blame!

Everything you are learning here can be tried even if you are currently using prescription medication. You'll begin to see possibilities you hadn't seen before. In any case, do not stop using prescription or non-prescription drugs, or alcohol, without a careful plan and a doctor's support for making these alterations in your life. Withdrawal from these substances puts your body as well as your mind through some pretty serious changes. Don't take them lightly.

A Special Plug for Food

Proper nutrition is essential for feeling good under any circumstances. If you are not eating the foods your unique body needs to thrive (that means vegan for some, low carb for others, macrobiotics for still others), you won't feel good. And do you know what happens when you don't feel good? Your thinking changes! Just as feeling good leads to happy thoughts, feeling bad – tired, achy, bloated, hungry – leads to unhappy thoughts. Whenever you're thinking unhappy thoughts, ask yourself first, Who or what am I sad, mad or scared about? Then ask yourself, What did I eat?

How Emotions Heal

Here's what I've discovered about how emotions deliver healing. Emotions are about movement. The word emotion comes from the Latin words for "move" and "out." Emotions build up, discharge, release and are done. Emotions are designed to move you to action. They are brief and *temporary*. A typical emotional response moves through your body in an incredibly orderly and *brief* cycle. Up – out – done!

As a body experience, emotions move through this cycle in minutes. I know this from personal emotional experience and because I've watched the clock during my therapy sessions for years. Not because I am bored, far from it, but because I am my mechanical engineer father's daughter.

Over the years in sessions, I've noticed that people typically spend 20 to 40 minutes of a therapy session avoiding emotions that were building up or stuck on simmer. When they finally feel safe enough to experience emotion, it takes only about three minutes of expression for the feelings in their body to subside. Three minutes! And then they feel better. Three minutes of a messy emotional experience can lance a chronic boil of stuck resistance. Furthermore, when they focus on the relief for another few minutes, confident resourcefulness is restored.

If you've ever spent time with very young children, you know they instinctively know how to do this. They cry when they're sad, stop when they're done. They may have tears still fresh on their chubby little cheeks, when suddenly they burst into a radiant smile at the sight of mother, the offer of a lap, or a loving hug. You knew how to do this then, and you can learn again how to do this now. It's like riding a bicycle. Once you learn, you never really forget. Remember, your body is designed to feel your feelings briefly and efficiently and get you back to experiencing how resourceful you really are.

ACTION TIP

The next time you are fortunate enough to be actually feeling and/or expressing sad, mad or scared feelings, watch the clock. If you are not feeling some relief in your body in three minutes or so, you have probably left your body and are back up in your thoughts. That's OK. Just notice what is actually happening in your body. If you catch that pattern soon enough, you may still be able to feel some of the release and relief. And if you don't catch it in time, and find yourself back in an emotional buildup ready to cry or rage again … just set the timer, again. The good and bad news is that life is guaranteed to present many opportunities to practice crying when you're sad and stopping when you're done.

Babies can cry when they're sad and stop when they're done because they haven't learned yet how to put the brakes on their *initial* emotional response to the world. They also haven't learned to wrap thoughts around what they feel. Babies are still operating from their natural human design in which emotions are primary.

But What If I Start Crying and Can't Stop?

Now, as I'm inviting you to experience your emotions, you may be feeling some resistance to this suggestion because you remember a few times when you did feel your emotions, and it wasn't pretty. You may even be recalling some rare moment you got caught in a feeling of emotional despair so piercing it cracked your facade of rationality. If you were like me, you then plummeted into a swirl of pain so huge you had to hold on for dear life. You couldn't stop crying. You were terrified that you were out of control, as you found yourself throwing things, pounding and sobbing until you were too exhausted to feel anymore.

Like most of us, that experience probably did little except leave you exhausted. You may have vowed once again to do everything you could to avoid ever getting so "emotional." As you're reading this now, you may be wondering: if you risk opening the door for your emotions, will this happen again?

Fear not. The change we are talking about guarantees this will not happen again. Why? Because the problem has never been the endless crying or raging, *it's been where you've focused your attention during the crying or raging.* Make a note of this.

Hysteria Isn't an Emotional Problem, It's a Mental Problem

Most of us were taught early in our lives that emotions were the cause of wallowing in hysteria and other problems – yours or others. They were not! Your body was most likely done moving through that sad or mad energy in literally a few minutes. If you are like many, the reason you kept crying until you were depleted is that you were focusing your attention on the story of your loss or violation as it played over and over again in your *mind,* like an endless loop. You were unintentionally prolonging and recreating your own misery by focusing on your *thoughts* – yes, I said "thoughts" – about the terrible upset you experienced. Here's a real-life example.

Lillian came to see me because she couldn't make peace with her terrible history. Her health was deteriorating, and she wasn't able to relax or get a good night's sleep. Lillian was a mid-level executive at a large company. She continually experienced subtle and not-so-subtle lack of respect from her male superiors. Her current work situation kept triggering memories of being abused by her father and unprotected by her depressed mother.

Lillian had been working on her issues for years and was quite able to access her sad and mad feelings. Every time these feelings came up, she would identify and express them; then, just as her body would begin to settle into relaxation and resolution, she'd remember some other horrible thing her boss, father or mother had done to her. These thoughts would trigger another round of emotion. Lillian was not protecting *herself* from bad memories; in a way, she had become her own ineffective mother, subjecting herself to painful experiences over and over again without taking action to get away from the abuse.

As Lillian learned to notice how she was replaying victim moments in her mind and shift focus to her body, she realized that her body was truly done emoting in minutes. Once Lillian learned to change the way she felt by refusing to allow thoughts to keep her continually agitated, she began to calm down. She started sleeping better, enjoying life more, and was able ultimately to interact with her bosses in a way that garnered respect and appreciation.

Changing the *way* you feel means changing *where you put your awareness during emotional expression.* You shift your attention away from your thoughts to your sad, mad, scared, glad emotions. Once you do this you'll see how quickly emotions move through your body. You'll also discover that cooperating with emotions enables you to think more clearly.

Thinking Clearly!

Dr. Candace Pert, a neuroscientist and pioneer in the study of what she calls the *bodymind* connection, tells us in no uncertain terms that our thinking brains *require* emotional flow to function properly. This is particularly true for the part of our brain called the frontal cortex, which gives us our advanced abilities to evaluate, strategize and make decisions to change our lives.

She writes, "[I]f our emotions are blocked due to denial, repression or trauma, then blood flow can become chronically constricted, depriving the frontal cortex, as well as other organs, of vital nourishment. This can leave you foggy and less alert, limited in your awareness and thus your ability to intervene into the conversation of your bodymind, to make decisions that change physiology or behavior."[3] The jury is in on the fact that suppressing emotions is bad for your thinking, bad for your health and bad for your relationships.

I Feel, Therefore I Am

The French philosopher René Descartes" famous dictum, "I think, therefore I am," was a guiding principle for humans long before he articulated it in 1637. *It is only in the last 50 years* that emotions have emerged as profound proponents of human well-being, worthy of scientific time and attention. And what science is just beginning to discover about emotions has led to a new mantra for the 21st century – "I feel, therefore I am."

I knew a girl in high school, Marva, who looked and acted tough as a gangster. Marva dressed like a biker chick, with spiky metal jewelry, dark eyes and a perpetual scowl. Most of us kept our distance. When I happened to run into her years later, I was amazed at how normal she seemed, how happy and successful she had become. Over a cup of herbal tea, Marva, now wearing an appealing ensemble of fine linen and wool, told me the gangster style was just for show, an identity she assumed to survive the horrors of high school. The whole time she looked so "bad," she told me, she was actually a virgin who never drank or did drugs. Her "bad girl" act was just that. Underneath she was innocent and pure.

Emotions have a similar bad reputation. Look at the words most often used to describe them – "toxic," "negative," "destructive," "bad." Like most of us, you may have been scared away from the healing nature of your emotions by the stories your head (and culture) told you. You weren't taught how important it is to distinguish between what you think about any emotion, and the healing experience of that emotion.

Living Emotion Meditation

Distinguishing between emotions and stories about your emotions is your essential first step in taking responsibility for your feeling responses. The practice of shifting your attention from your thoughts and letting your *body* lead you to cry when sad, stop when done, and feel good fast is mind blowing and brain building. Using your awareness as a tool, you weave threads of cooperation between body and mind. Rather than trying to dominate your emotions, you enter into partnership with them and your body, and you become whole.

Stretching your awareness to observe and cooperate with the moving *feeling* of any emotion through your body is actually very similar to meditation practice. I call it a *living emotion meditation* practice because it requires you to stay focused in your awareness while you simultaneously stay engaged in your emotional life – sad, mad, scared and glad. I believe science will ultimately discover that this kind of living emotion meditation actually *creates* new nerve pathways to the part of your brain that enables you to think and feel at the same time.

Dr. Richie Davidson, the innovative director of the Laboratory for Affective Neuroscience at the University of Wisconsin, Madison, has already discovered that experienced meditators' brain activity gravitates toward the part of their brains responsible for happy, cheerful states of equanimity and spiritual peace. Increasing awareness, whether through classical mindfulness or the living emotion meditation I've just described, is good for you!

Your emotions provide a direct route to clarity, consciousness, and spiritual experience. This is no longer burning heresy. It is your present and it is your future – your evolutionary destiny. When you slow down and use your awareness to distinguish between what emotions you are feeling and what thoughts you are thinking, you are rewiring your brain as you heal yourself. You are changing the *way you feel AND the way you think*. You are actively cooperating with the advancement of human consciousness, cocreating a new way of being. I believe this ultimately means more grey matter, more brains, more Emotional Medicine and the fringe benefits of power, pleasure, and peace.

Twelve Steps to Feeling Good Fast

In the pages ahead you'll learn the 12 steps enabling you to cry when you're sad, stop when you're done, and feel good fast.

- **Step One: Find Resources Inside and Out.** You'll discover how resources you didn't know you had help you master Emotional Medicine.
- **Step Two: Get Out of Your Head.** You'll learn what it means to be in your head and then how to get out of it.
- **Step Three: Make Friends with Your Body.** You'll be amazed to discover that your body is your "best friend forever" (bff) once you welcome it as your ally.
- **Step Four: Learn the Language of Your Body.** You'll see the essential role sensations play in signaling true needs as you learn the elemental language of your body.
- **Step Five: Attend to Anxiety and Depression.** You'll discover natural methods for soothing anxiety and depression as well as learning how the immobilization response impacts these states.
- **Step Six: Cultivate MultiModal Awareness.** You'll have your consciousness thoroughly raised when you discover how powerful it is to practice multimodal awareness.
- **Step Seven: Align with Your Big "S" Self.** You'll learn how connecting with your biggest, best, deepest Self gives you the strength to make healthy choices.
- **Step Eight: Accept Your Shadow.** You'll learn how to love and accept yourself – even your darkest parts.
- **Step Nine: Let Your Body Lead.** You'll learn how efficient your body is in moving you briefly through sad, mad, scared emotions.
- **Step Ten: Stop When You're Done.** You'll see how to take responsibility for cooperating with your brilliant body's signals for emotional completion.

- **Step Eleven: Focus on Feeling Good.** This is the most fun step of all – learning how to give in to and maximize the healing power of feeling good.
- **Step Twelve: Take it Back to Daily Life.** Feeling good is a great time to reappraise any upsetting situations as well as look within for guidance about how best to integrate good feelings into self-love, healthy choices and well-being.

TWO

Find Resources Inside and Out

Zoe Bell has been a death-defying stuntwoman for action stars like Lucy Lawless, Uma Thurman and Sharon Stone. When director Quentin Tarantino tapped *her* to be the star in his film *Death Proof*, she had to face her biggest fear of all: feeling her feelings. In an *LA Times* interview she said, "I had to get over that fear of showing emotion. Doing the butt-kicking stuff was no problem. But crying? That's scary!"

You may have had a similar reaction to crying yourself. When you're not familiar with Emotional Medicine, emotions can seem scary even in private. Your first step in taking Emotional Medicine is to find resources of safety and support inside and outside yourself for this new journey. This chapter is designed to help you do exactly that.

Most likely, Zoe Bell had to work through fearing her emotions without the information you now have. She probably didn't know emotions were brief, orderly, and designed to help her feel good fast. However, I'll bet she soon discovered one resource she could turn to for at least a modicum of relief regardless of what else was happening. That resource is awareness.

Your Number One Resource: Awareness

Awareness gives you a sense of connection and control no matter what is happening. Awareness provides essential information about what is happening *inside* your body, emotions, mind and spirit and *outside* in your relationships and world at large. Without this vital input from your awareness you'd react to stimuli, inside or out, without a sense of personhood. Without awareness you might as well be a puppet on a string.

To give you a firsthand experience of the information awareness provides, let's try a little experiment. Take a moment to focus awareness on the fact that you're reading now. You might have a book in your hands, a digital reader on your lap or a computer screen on your desk. Notice the font and size of the letters, the shade and texture of the page in your fingers, or the brightness of the screen in front of you. Is the text easy to read? Notice how you are sitting or reclining as you are reading. Are you comfortable in your chair? Do you need to make an adjustment? Notice how you are feeling in general – OK, blah, or in between.

Take a moment to become aware of what you think so far about what you've been reading – intrigued, confused, wanting more information? Finally, take a look around the room you're in. Are others present? Notice the temperature of the air, the sights and sounds around you. Check whether you're comfortable in the setting.

These questions just scratch the surface of the essential information awareness gives you – information which enables you to know what's happening and what you need at any given moment, and helps you maximize positive, supportive, healthy experiences inside and out.

Awareness gives you access to the most important relationship you'll ever have in your life … with yourself. Awareness enables you to notice when you are being hard on yourself and when you are being kind. Awareness gives you a private, safe inner space where you can tell yourself the truth without anyone else knowing.

This ongoing inside connection with yourself is the foundation for all your inner work, all your ability to find resources inside and out, as well as your ability to cry when you're sad, stop when you're done and feel good fast.

Outside yourself, awareness provides you the power to identify the people, places and things that are good for you – or not! For example, awareness helps you notice that every time you eat deep-fried foods you end up with a stomachache. Awareness helps you notice that every time you have lunch with a particular friend you end up feeling good about yourself. And awareness helps you notice that every day that you exercise or move your body in some aerobic way, you feel more alive and happy.

No matter how disastrous an outside event or overwhelming your inside reaction, awareness gives you a vantage point from which you can *plan* how to navigate even the most difficult situation. Awareness provides a constant, secure perch to stay connected to yourself – your deepest, truest self.

Awareness is Different from Thinking, Blaming and Judging

Some years ago, one of the participants in an Emotional Medicine course I was leading offered a clever distinction between awareness and what she called "thinkingness." Thinkingness contains all of your mental thoughts, labels, plans, strategies, etc. Awareness is bigger, more inclusive. Awareness gives you access to *all* of those aforementioned thinking abilities as well as to body sensations, emotions, and the subtle energies of Spirit – and it does so *without judgment or blame*.

As a matter of fact, one way to tell whether you're in "thinkingness" or awareness is to notice if you're caught up in blaming or judging yourself. While your awareness will notice any self-critical thoughts that may arise, it does not criticize. Awareness just *is*. Happily for us, deeply embedded in the "*is*ness" of awareness are the qualities of acceptance and openness.[1]

Awareness Enables You to Make Distinctions

Finally, awareness provides another essential skill for Emotional Medicine: *the ability to distinguish between your mind's thoughts and your body's emotional experience.* Using awareness to notice the various sensations, emotions, and thoughts arising in your experience, you can then learn to tell the difference between them. You'll be able to distinguish between painful thoughts thrashing you over and over and the brief, orderly movement of emotions through your body. Once you do this, you can safely ride any wave of emotion to completion. You'll never fear emotion again.

Making these kinds of distinctions is especially important because emotions often begin impacting you even before you know it. Since awareness helps you track the sometimes subtle emotional cues your body gives, you can manage all your responses with more mastery. Recent research at UCLA demonstrates that just being aware of and labeling (a thinking activity) your mad, sad, scared emotions helps the emotional centers in your brain calm down.[2] In this way your "thinkingness" can support your awareness, and vice versa.

It's good to remember this labeling strategy during those times you're aware of powerful emotions but aren't able to immediately cooperate with them. You can say to yourself, "Gosh, I'm mad (sad, scared) now, but I'll work that through later when it's safe and appropriate."

Once you're in an appropriate space to cooperate with any emotion, however, you'll want to avoid focusing too much on labeling. Because labeling is a left-brain, "thinkingness" activity, it can make you easy prey for habitual, dysfunctional thinking patterns ("stinking thinking"). Whenever you're safe and it's appropriate, you can cooperate with the natural flow of emotion so it can complete its brief, regulatory cycle and return you to feeling good.

Your Number Two Resource – Choice

Because awareness allows you to notice what you're sensing, feeling, thinking and intuiting moment by moment, it also presents the possibility of moving your attention in and around those experiences however you'd like. For example, if you're at a stuck place with a work or creative project, you can choose to take a bath and immerse yourself in a sense of effortless support, call a good friend for commiseration and compassion, focus your thinking on another project, or pray (literally or figuratively) for inspiration.

The bottom line is that *you make the decisions about what to focus your awareness on.* Make a note of this. You have the ability to *make choices* about taking effective action or stopping ineffective action inside and outside of yourself.[3] Here's an Action Tip to give you an experience of choosing where to focus your awareness. (You'll find a free audio download of an extended version of this tip at www. emotionalmedicine.com.)

ACTION TIP: CHOOSING FOCUS

Focus attention on your left hand. Notice how your hand is resting on the arm of your chair or alongside your body. Notice whether your hand feels comfortable or uncomfortable. No blame. Just awareness. Bring attention briefly to your right hand and then back to your left hand. Swing your awareness effortlessly back and forth between your two hands. Notice you can focus attention on both hands at once. Most importantly, notice that *you* are choosing where to focus awareness in your body. Slowly open and close both hands. Bring your hands together so they are close but not touching. Notice if you feel any heat between your hands. Notice that *you* are choosing where and how to move your hands and arms. Finally, be still. Be present with yourself to sense, feel, think and experience yourself in what may be a new way. Enjoy your ability to *choose to focus your awareness wherever you want to in your body as well as to make choices about how and where to actually move your body.*[4]

Although Emotional Medicine is a body awareness-based method, if moving your awareness around your body is problematic for you, you can still appreciate this "choice" resource by moving your attention around other aspects of your experience, i.e. images, thoughts and memories. For example, you can bring to mind images of favorite vacation spots, beloved people and pets. You can bring to mind contrasting ideas – say accepting or rejecting a new job. Similarly, you can also conjure up pleasant or unpleasant memories and move your awareness back and forth among all of the above.

What's important to understand is that *you* have the capability to choose where to place your attention and what body actions to initiate or resist. Feel the power in this. Thoughts, sensations and emotions all arise without permission. However, shifting your awareness among them and between them *is* under your control! Enjoy this freedom.

An Important Caveat

If you've been used to focusing your attention predominantly in your thoughts or your "thinkingness," even a simple experience of unplanned emotion may be unsettling. I had a client, Tina, a very experienced, cognitively oriented self-helper, who became very upset toward the end of our second session. Up until then she had been able to shift focus from her thoughts and drop down into body sensations. That day, however, when she was three or four minutes into focusing on some good feelings, a single tear rolled down her cheek.

Tina was so startled by this unfamiliar reaction she stopped the process. She said she didn't want to do this anymore. She didn't know what was happening. She felt out of control.

I explained that tears excrete stress hormones. So it was natural that as she was relaxing, her body might shed a tear or two in support of de-stressing. I explained that her body was programmed to seek well-being and healing at all times, whether she was consciously controlling that process or not. Once Tina understood this, she felt safe enough to ease again into awareness of processes other than thinking. The unplanned appearance of tears no longer represented just loss of cognitive control but an opportunity to surrender to her body's intention for healing.

Although Tina's response was atypical, I want to be sure you're not similarly surprised by the occasional experience of an unplanned tear or sigh. Tears happen! When they do, you can breathe a sigh of relief and rest in knowing that your body is doing you a stress-reducing favor.

Remember, even as a tear is running down your face, even as your hands are clenched in fists, even as your knees are knocking, even as you tremble with joy, awareness gives you the power to choose whether and when to cooperate with emotions trying to move through to complete their cycle. It's important to recognize that except for the occasional errant tear or sigh, you decide when, where, and how to take your Emotional Medicine.[5] As a matter of fact, you're already way more in charge of yourself than you may realize.

You're in Charge!

For example, you already know how to disregard hunger pains when you put off eating. You already know how to ignore thirst when you don't feel like drinking. You already know how to push past muscle pain when you're going for a long run or big work-out. You already know how to delay moving your bowels when you don't want to take the time for that. You can put off eating, exercise and sleeping even when your body is clamoring for food, movement or sleep. And of course, you've likely learned quite well how to suppress sad, mad and scared emotions when you don't want to feel them or when it's not appropriate to show them.

Although most of the above descriptions of taking charge depict actions that are not at all healthy when routine, I'd like to emphasize that you *already have a muscle of mastery and control* when it comes to bodymind experiences such as unplanned emotions. You discovered long ago that you're bigger than your sensations and your body urges. For the most part, at least in the short run, *you're the boss.*

The upside of being the boss is that you acquire skills that can make the switch Emotional Medicine requires much easier. Instead of resisting emotion, you'll need to switch to *resisting* resisting emotion. What say? What I mean here is that you can use your self-control resources to *resist your habit of ignoring your emotions.*

Instead of resisting by holding emotion down and back, you can be in charge of cooperating with emotions as they move up, around and through an emotional cycle. I suspect this is exactly what Zoe Bell did. As a stuntwoman, she had learned to control her fear so she could execute scary stunts. She likely chose to control her fear of experiencing emotion so she could ride the waves of anger, grief and fear needed to become an actor.

Now, I'm not suggesting you strong-arm your way through your fears. Not at all! What I *am* saying is that you don't have to be freaked out by the unfamiliarity of emotional expression, because you already have skills that can make this easier for you. For example, check now inside whether you don't feel a tad safer exploring Emotional Medicine knowing you can put the brakes on any emotional experience whenever you need to.

Furthermore, your existing "take charge" skills and the bodymind cooperating skills you'll need to develop to take Emotional Medicine are similar in two important ways. They both require you be *aware* of what is happening in your body and to *choose* the action you want to take vis-à-vis that experience – resist or cooperate. Notice that Tina, startled as she was by a tear, was able to choose to stop any more tears until she felt safe enough to continue.[6]

Another Caveat

The fact that you are in charge of where to focus your awareness and can stop yourself from cooperating with your body's physical or emotional needs, however, does not mean that you can stop your emotions from happening in the first place. For survival reasons, emotions have a "mind" (or rather a "bodymind") of their own.

Whenever a conscious choice to resist emotion becomes an unconscious or subconscious habit, your body will still be impacted by the physiological changes emotion evokes. While you can put the brakes on the obvious expression or conscious experience of emotions, you can't prevent the physiological changes emotions evoke from impacting your body. You've probably already noticed this. For example, you may have tried to brush off grief, anger, or fear and then suffered resulting stomach trouble, constipation, insomnia, or other symptoms. Transferring your ability to facilitate healthy emotional flow will enable you to alleviate or eliminate some of these syndromes that are strongly affected by suppressed emotion. What this means for Emotional Medicine is that you can always choose whether to co-operate, resist or delay *expressing* an emotional response even when it may already be altering your biochemistry.

Here's some more good news. Not only do the resources of awareness and choice make learning Emotional Medicine safer and easier, but you've got even more resources to support you in learning to feel good fast.

More Resources!

Now that you're aware of the benefits that awareness and choice provide for your Emotional Medicine journey, I'd like to bring your attention to additional resources I know you have. How do I know this about you when we've not yet met? First off, the very fact that you are reading this book tells me you have the resource of a self-helper. It tells me you seek information to change yourself and your life for the better. The fact of your reading this book tells me you are willing to invest some time and effort to make this happen.

The fact you are reading this book also tells me you have an irrepressible source of optimism deep within – that, at some level, you know your life matters. Somewhere inside you have hope for a happier life. Even if you're desperate, you're not giving up. And even if things are going reasonably well now, you're still a seeker. You're interested and inquisitive about your potential for transformation.

I also know that you are a survivor. I know this because no one gets to adulthood without some hard knocks. Whatever has happened, you've prevailed. Sure, you have your scars and wounds and some dysfunctional patterns, but you're still here, still seeking wholeness. Most likely, the worst is over. You'll never be as helpless and dependent on wounded caretakers again as you were as a child. You are now in charge of the people, places, and activities to which you are connected.

In addition to these generic resources gained by surviving to adulthood are the specific accomplishments you've accumulated, like learning to read, attaining some level of education, having some success in work, sports, creativity, relationships, spiritual practice. All these resources provide a foundation of safety and support as you continue your growth.

I'm sure Zoe Bell used the courage she'd honed to a sharp edge as a stuntwoman to face her fear of emotion. She already knew how to be brave when trying something new and scary. That courage supported her as she dove into the deep emotional waters required for acting.

Your Number Three Resource: You at Your Best![7]

You, like most of us, have likely had moments when you were exceptionally generous, brave, creative and positive. It doesn't matter how wounding your childhood or how strong the pull of your dysfunctional patterns, you've had moments when your biggest, best self came through. These are the moments when, against all odds, you made healthy choices, accomplished educational, professional and creative tasks, and behaved toward others in altruistic ways.

Although early psychoanalytic theory found an unconscious, dark motivation in all of human behavior including spirituality, another theory called Psychosynthesis[8] proposed that humans were also influenced by "superconscious" energies relating to what is noble, altruistic, and good about humans: their "higher" or best self.

Recently the field of positive psychology has suggested that in order to thrive and grow. it is just as important to look for what is positive about yourself as it is to uncover, understand and heal what is wounded. You are a complex, whole being – filled with light and dark, strength and weakness, joy and sorrow. You are always growing, always evolving, and always receiving subtle (or not-so-subtle) guidance from your biggest Self to help you find your way. The great thing about taking Emotional Medicine is that it is designed to help you get back to feeling like your best self – happy, confident, peaceful – quickly and easily.

Paul's Story

The importance of appreciating resources you already have was highlighted recently as I witnessed a new client, Paul, racked with anxiety while coping with a suicidal girlfriend. He cried several times as he described the current challenges he was facing. Although these tears helped him feel better immediately, I could see Paul was not yet connected with himself enough to explore the deeper issues this crisis evoked.

As I took his history, Paul described how, after 10 years of sobriety, he had recently resumed using heroin. After six months he knew he had to "kick" his habit again. Paul remembered how determined he was once he'd made the decision to get off opiates. Even though he didn't have funds for an upscale recovery experience, he didn't let that stop him. He found what he described as a "hellhole" detox program for homeless men and spent several miserable days detoxing.

While describing his determination, I could see Paul's jaw and shoulders relax as his chest expanded with pride and confidence. I asked if he could feel what I saw happening in his body. Once he focused his attention on his body, Paul became aware of an increasing sense of well-being.

I asked Paul if he would feel comfortable focusing on this natural pleasure in his body.[9] He agreed. I helped him stay present on feeling good with a guided bodymind meditation. Paul was amazed he could feel this relaxed. He said this was the first relief from anxiety he'd felt in months. Furthermore, he was surprised to realize he actually felt happy. Although I am sure Paul's initial tears primed the pump for his ensuing well-being, recalling and remembering his formidable resources enhanced his pleasure and happiness.

Here's an Action Tip to help you take stock of the already existing strengths you bring to practicing Emotional Medicine, and to experience some of the relief and support this brings.

ACTION TIP PART 1: WHAT'S KIND, STRONG, BRAVE AND POSITIVE ABOUT YOU

Take a sheet of paper or two and make four columns at the top – Kind, Strong, Brave, Positive (or pick your own four positive qualities). Set the timer for 10 minutes and *without thinking* write quickly about yourself in each of these columns. Write about triumphal experiences, courageous actions, survival skills from big and small events throughout your life. If you have difficulty with this, ask someone who loves and knows you really well to sit and help you fill out these columns. You can return the favor and help fill out his/her columns.

ACTION TIP PART 2: SELF-HOLDING

After you've recounted what is kind, strong, brave and positive about you, sit down in a quiet place where you can spend at least five minutes with yourself. Roll up your sleeves until you can embrace yourself lightly and comfortably with your hands touching the skin on your forearms or upper arms. It's important to have skin-to-skin contact with yourself. Do not strain. Be still and focus on the place where your hands and arms connect until you feel the warmth of your skin-on-skin self-connection. Be on the lookout for an experience of kindness, self-love, and self-appreciation as you rest in your embrace. Repeat as needed.

It is true: you are this kind, strong, brave and positive person. Fortunately, Emotional Medicine makes it easier to feel this is true. This is because Emotional Medicine helps you feel good inside. When you feel good inside, it's easier to feel good about yourself. Emotional Medicine puts well-being and self-love at your personal disposal 24/7. This is one of its most important benefits.

Giving Yourself Tender Loving Care

Ever since you were a baby, you've been accustomed to other people attending to you – helping you move from the discomfort of a cold, wet diaper, to the pleasure of a warm, dry one; from the pain of being hungry, to the bliss of being fed; from feeling scared and alone, to feeling safe and belonging in the arms of another. You have an instinctual and, when all goes well, learned pattern of turning to others to help you alleviate distress. This is normal.

However, no matter how safe and loving your relationship network may be, there are times when you need help but can't find it in others. There are times when your best friend, lover/spouse, therapist or pastor are not available for you. It's a fact of life: you don't always have someone there when you need them.

Even when you do have others physically around, they may not, for any number of reasons, be able to be there in the ways you need to feel safe and secure. It's often axiomatic in intimate relationships that when you're at your worst, your loved ones are also at their worst. Even though you weren't designed to be alone, unfortunately, too often you are.

Although it's not fair to need and be trained from such an early age to look to others for support since it's not always going to be forthcoming, the silver lining is that you can always be there for yourself. Awareness and choice give you this option. You can always offer your loving arms and compassionate awareness to yourself. Even when you're deep in despair, you can still use your awareness to make choices that lead to feeling good. Inside yourself is the only place you have 24/7 access to TLC. Being there for yourself is your ultimate safety net.

Sometimes this means that, regardless of how little self-tenderness is accessible inside you, you still need to take yourself by the hand to seek the right food, rest, water, sunlight, exercise, Emotional Medicine and companionship you need. Sometimes this means saying no to what doesn't work for you, even when an old pattern is beckoning beguilingly. And sometimes it means saying yes to what does, even when it's unfamiliar or new. Making healthy choices is the crux of living a life of happiness, confidence and peace.

However, the fact that you've got resources inside yourself doesn't mean you should stop seeking resources outside. You need others. Finding safety, love and support with others is more than a holdover from a long childhood of dependency; it is the bliss you were born for.

Your Number Four Resource: Other People

Human beings are pack animals. That means you are designed by instinct to seek contact with other people most of the time, especially when you're happy or scared. Unlike rabbits that scatter when frightened, you're programmed to move toward others for solace and safety when upset. And, as a human, you're also designed to celebrate good fortune with others. All things being equal, you are made to be close to others in good times or bad.

Our early human ancestors spent lots of time out of doors fending off animal predators or marauding intruders. During those very unsafe times, human families and communities would take turns standing guard so that everyone could feel safe.

If you recall any news coverage from the Northridge, California quake in 1996, survivors gathered in groups outside their homes to cook, cry, sing, console each other and create a sense of safety and connection even amidst the ruins of their communities. Similar "comings together" happened after the flooding in New Orleans, the tsunami in Thailand, the earthquake in Haiti, and the BP oil disaster. In those wrenching times, people turned to one another to share grief and anger, solace and support by just being together.

You may find it easier to feel your emotions, no matter how brief they are, if you know someone is standing guard – being with you to shelter and protect you when you are feeling vulnerable.

Anytime you feel lonely or would like support in taking your Emotional Medicine and feeling good fast, reach out to a friend or family member with whom you feel comfortable. Ask them to be with you. Feel their support and love. Take it in. You were made for this. You deserve this.

Just as I was writing these sentences, I got a call from a good friend, Anne, who had received some really good and really bad news that very day. Anne's offer for a lovely new condo was accepted; hours later, she got two bad lab results: one indicating she had osteoporosis and the other that there was a mysterious growth on one of her kidneys.

Anne said she needed to cry both happy and sad tears and knew she could do that with me. We took a few minutes together to be present for her emotions. We both came away from the encounter feeling more tenderly connected. When Anne hung up, she also felt strengthened in her commitment to take care of herself in whatever ways this health crisis required.[10]

If you can't think of anyone you'd feel this safe with, now might be a good time to consider finding a therapist, group counseling and/or 12-step program, or church, synagogue, or mosque where you could find support. If you're in a relationship where you don't feel safe being real and vulnerable, it may be time to consider some relationship counseling. You need to feel safe and loved with others just as much as you do within yourself.

Move Away from Judgments

When you seek support from others, it is important to find people who will not be judgmental of you, particularly when you're feeling sad, mad or scared. You need to find folks who can honor and be present for you while you are moving through emotional cycles.

If your early caretakers were abusive, however, you may have an unconscious/subconscious tendency to seek people who are not going to respond with love. Here's another place where awareness helps you recognize you're not getting what you need. Emotional Medicine can give you the inner strength and self-love to move away from such unsupportive people and situations.

If you don't feel compassion and safety when you are around others, move away – fast! Seek people you know will respond lovingly. If you have moments of feeling judged or not safe in ongoing relationships which are typically supportive, talk over what is happening. Perhaps the person is having a bad day, doesn't have the juice to be there for you, or needs some support themselves. That's OK. You can take turns, find someone else who is available or find tender care within yourself.

If a person is not willing to work things through with you, or not ready to open his/her heart, find your own safe space. Close a door literally or metaphorically and begin to restore your loving connection with yourself. It's important to have some actual physical place in which you can feel safe – your bedroom, office, or bathroom. Optimally this actual safe haven would be private enough for you to have a good cry, stomp or scream if you need to, followed by the self-holding exercise if appropriate.

In any case, keep seeking the compassion you need and don't settle for less – inside or out. Do not tolerate being judged. You and your feelings are too precious, too important, too healing to be mocked, derided, or dismissed by anyone – including you!

Finding a FGFF (Feel Good Fast Friend)

Consider finding a friend who would read this book along with you – an Emotional Medicine partner with whom you could practice cooperating with emotions and getting back to feeling good fast. You could take turns standing guard for one another while you begin to explore feeling some of your sad, mad, scared feelings and watch together as you discover how quickly they restore you to feeling good. Finding a FGFF makes it easier to stay on track with Emotional Medicine. You can help each other stay out of thoughts and support each other while you track sad, mad, scared feelings as they move briefly through your experience. You can make sure neither of you rush past the good feelings that always emerge when you've completed an emotional cycle. All of my close friends and I support each other in this way. We are FGFFs for each other.

If you have a therapist, you may want to take some of the ideas in this book to him or her to ask for help incorporating Emotional Medicine into your life. Therapy can be a very safe place to practice taking Emotional Medicine.

In the next chapter, you'll discover how to divert awareness away from the never-ending narratives keeping you trapped in negativity. You'll learn how to let go of your small mind's attempts to control everything. You'll discover the delights of dropping down into the ever-present, embodied moment of now.

THREE

Get Out of Your Head

There's a famous Zen parable about two priests walking along a country road in ancient Japan. They come to a small stream and are about to wade across when a lovely young woman walks up. She is beautifully dressed in the traditional long gown of the time. She is obviously distraught about how she is going to get to the other side. One of the priests offers to carry her across. She gratefully accepts. He lifts her into his arms, carries her safely above the water, and deposits her gently on the ground.

Meanwhile, the other priest is watching and glowering silently. After a brief exchange of pleasantries with the young woman, the two priests continue down the road. After an hour or so of silence, the glowering priest turns to his comrade and says: "How could you do that? What about your vows of celibacy?" The carrying priest turns to his companion and says: "I picked her up, carried her across and set her down an hour ago. You are still carrying her."

Being up in your head is like being the glowering priest – trapped in the past or worrying about the future rather than perceiving your whole body, emotion, mind and spirit experience in the present moment. Judging and catastrophizing keeps you carrying tombstones of resentment or chains of anxiety into your present and future, manufacturing more monuments to pain as you go.

Emotions in your body are more like the carrying priest: natural, effortless, and for the most part appropriate. *Embodied* emotions have a definite beginning, middle and end. Once you learn to cooperate with the simplicity of these emotions, letting them move naturally through you, they'll carry you more easily over the landscape of events and challenges you encounter in your life. They are designed to restore your resources and guide you to take action in the present moment.

Even when you're having an emotional response that seems out of proportion to the current life event that triggered it, your response is happening *now*. Even when you deem your response an inconvenience, that emotional wave is designed to deposit you on the shores of well-being in minutes.

Even bigger problems arise when you don't notice that you're actually having an emotional response. When you're caught in your head, you're riding a Ferris wheel of mind trips. Banners race across your mind: "Woulda', coulda', shoulda'" and "What if." Each thought may be triggering emotional reactions, any one of which could help you feel better fast, but round and round you go, stacking up unprocessed emotional reactions in your body as your mind turns.

Although your thoughts are caught in an illusory world of past regret or future worry, your real world body is manufacturing the same stress hormones *as if you were actually dealing with those imagined events now*. Unfortunately, your predicament is magnified because *you can't take skillful action in the past or the future as it lives in your head*. You can only take action – action that could heal your regrets or manage your worries – in the present moment as it lives in your embodied experience.

When you're up in your head, though, you barely notice what's going on around you right here, right now. It's as if you've got blinders on for everything except an anguished past or an anxious future. In the worst cases, being up in your head leaves your body numb, cold, and immobilized. You feel increasingly powerless as your thoughts get bleaker, your motivation flags and you soon start believing your situation is hopeless. And you don't even realize it's all a big, fat lie!

The reason hopeless thinking is a lie is that unless you're dead, there is *always* some action in the real world you can take to open fresh possibilities for yourself ... even if that action is to cry a tear, shake a fist, or tremble with fear. Those emotionally based actions clear the way for new possibilities to arise. Here's how Maya, who was trapped in hopelessness, did just that.

Maya's New Reality

Maya was a beautiful, frail 45-year-old woman who had almost used up a small inheritance while coping with chronic fatigue syndrome. She hadn't worked for over a year since her lover, Naomi (who she thought was going to be her life partner) had moved out. Maya had about six months of savings left. Even though her health was slowly improving, she didn't feel motivated to find a new job or start training for a new career, and she couldn't stop worrying about what would happen when her money ran out. Her worrying increased the stress toxins in her body, delayed her healing, and did nothing to help figure out her next step.

In our first session, I invited Maya to shift her focus from future worries to how she was feeling right now. She resisted and said she wouldn't know what to do with herself if she weren't thinking and worrying about her future. "How can I let go of that?" she asked frantically. "How can I live my life without the sense of control I get from my mind? I can't just chop off my head, you know."

"Of course you can't," I reassured Maya. "You need your fine mind for exactly those 'thinkingness' things it's good at: analyzing, organizing, and planning. However, the prerequisite for using mental powers in a way that will serve you is to be sure you are *feeling* strong and powerful. If you're not feeling good now, how about letting me help you generate some resilience inside yourself to cope with your situation?"

Maya was quiet for a moment, and then said, "Is that possible? Can I really feel good now even though my life is a mess?"

"Of course you can," I replied. "But there's a catch. You have to get out of your head. You have to be willing to stop, for a few moments anyway, obsessing about the future or stressing about the past."

Maya gave me a wary look. "OK," she replied, "but what do I do to stop thinking?"

"Well," I replied, "The good news is that it's much easier to get out of your head when you give yourself someplace to go. And I suggest you go to your sensations. What I mean by this is shifting your attention from thoughts to the simple *sensations* of your body's experience, right here, right now."

She agreed to try. Once Maya brought her attention to what was happening in her body, she realized she didn't feel good at all. Her jaw was clenched, her biceps were contracted. She felt a kind of dead weight in her heart and a slight current of anxiety in her limbs.

I asked Maya if she felt safe enough to keep her attention on the discomfort in her body. She agreed to continue. Very soon, Maya was startled to realize she was angry, furious, actually, at Naomi for leaving. She felt that Naomi abandoned her just like her mother had.

Maya's mother had not been a good one after Maya's father died. She often left a barely teenaged Maya to fend for herself for weeks at a time while she was off on international business trips with a new husband.

After some hesitation, Maya was able to allow her angry feelings for both Naomi and Mother to flow. She spoke out her anger to both of them and brought her fists down on the pillows next to her. I encouraged her to allow this anger to flow just until her body was done.

Maya was surprised by how quickly this anger moved and left her feeling hopeful for the first time in years. Along with this experience came a new reality. Instead of feeling desperate, Maya found a new sense of assurance that she would find a way out of her dilemma.

Maya's firsthand experience with shifting focus from uncomfortable thoughts to uncomfortable body sensations was a revelation. She was amazed at the power of her anger to get her to feel strong – fast. This experience of Emotional Medicine gave Maya a sense, a knowing that she would thrive again, even though she didn't yet know exactly what that would look like.

After a few weeks of practice with shifting attention from worry patterns to body sensations and emotional flow, Maya spontaneously got the idea that she would like to train as a dental hygienist. She was surprised to discover that she now felt motivated to explore options for this kind of instruction. Maya found an 18-month training program, arranged a loan and started her new life. In addition to opening up to a new life purpose, Maya's ability to get out of her head improved her health. Her chronic fatigue symptoms diminished as her vitality improved.

It's Axiomatic

Whenever you're obsessing or worrying about something, you're most likely holding back some emotion (consciously or subconsciously). It may help you to remember this simple axiom: If you're trapped in your head, there are emotions trapped in your body.[1] As night follows day, being up in your head is a tip-off that you need some nourishing flow of emotional energy.

Whenever you're feeling punk or piqued, ask yourself: "Am I sad, mad, or scared about something?" *You'll always know (as long as you're honest with yourself) whether or not you feel actually and for-real happy, confident and peaceful in your skin.*

As you saw with Maya, unacknowledged sad, mad, scared feelings dampen motivation and often lead to hopelessness. Even when you understand this, it's sometimes still difficult to acknowledge emotions. You've undoubtedly had experience trying to talk yourself out of reactions at the first hint of emotions. You say to yourself, "I shouldn't be mad about that," or "I'm not going to allow myself to get sad about that," or "There's no reason to be scared of that."

Unfortunately, attempts to reason away sad, mad, scared responses leave you *more* susceptible to head traps. You may not even be aware of how much time you're subconsciously trying to talk yourself out of your authentic responses; you've gotten so good at it. You miss emotional body cues and end up in your head before you know it.

Maya didn't realize that just below the surface of fretting and fatigue was a swamp of simmering anger. Up in her head, Maya didn't have access to the healing resources her survival-oriented emotions could offer. She couldn't see *any* way out.

Maya had been stuck in a grinding groove of anxiety, without knowing that her unacknowledged, unexperienced anger was fueling that anxiety, making it worse. Yes, she knew she wasn't happy about Naomi leaving her, but that unhappiness, too, was playing out in her head as a story of victimhood and the recurring thought, "How could she do this to me?"

Once Maya realized how much it would benefit her to get out of her head, even if she were down to her last dollar, she began to see emotional responses as the resources they were – delivery systems for clarity, confidence and action. Maya also realized that, even though the horrible story replaying in her head was true (it was terrible of her mom to leave her alone at 13, devastating for her life partner to walk out when she needed her most), her best bet for stopping this loop tape of victimization was to get out of that story, out of her head and back into her living body's resourcefulness.

Born Again

Once you learn to focus your awareness on what is actually happening for you right here, right now, in this very body, you become "quickened" to the movement of life within you. You then have access to the action-oriented power of your emotions. Dropping awareness into your body, now, enables you to become *incarnated,* or, as a spiritual teacher might put it, your spirit enters your flesh and you are whole.

It's a mistake to think you only incarnate once when your soul enters your body before birth. You actually need to incarnate and embody your spirit again and again. The pull to get lost in analysis, irony, worry or the graveyard of the past, is *the* dilemma of the 21st century. When you allow yourself to feel again, you can be born again, new into each moment. Rebirth is available for you in the present moment – as long as you're present for it!

The Gift of the Present Moment

Yesterday is history, tomorrow is a mystery and today is a gift; that's why they call it the present. – Eleanor Roosevelt

Unless you slow down and wake up, the present moment will be gone in a flash. What present moment? This one – this moment – right here, right now. *Clap!* And again: *Clap*! And this moment: *Clap!*

The present moment provides an oasis of relief in any desert of pain. It's a haven where you can rest your awareness as you navigate the droughts and deluges of life. It's also a launching pad for transformation and healing.

Once you decide to get out of your head, it will help you to have some other place to go, someplace safe and filled with possibility. The present moment is that place. Because your parents, your teachers, and your culture have most likely not taught you to nurture present moment bodymind awareness, you'll need practice and patience in getting there again and again. No blame.

Five thousand years ago, Buddha figured out that people needed to "get out of their heads" if they wanted to find inner peace. Buddha realized that letting go of your desires and aversions to specific outcomes and focusing awareness in the present moment was a way to end suffering. He taught it was possible to learn this by meditating: shifting your awareness from thinking about the past or future to what is happening *now*. Variations on this theme are called "mindfulness"[2] practice.

However, you don't have to become a Buddhist to benefit from present moment awareness practices. There is an increasing body of evidence that the use of mindfulness techniques (or what I prefer to call *bodymindfulness* techniques[3]) are of great benefit in reducing stress and supporting physical healing. Many hospitals are now including Mindfulness-Based Stress Reduction (MBSR) books and courses developed by Jon Kabat-Zinn as an adjunct to surgery and medication.

Interestingly, getting out of your head was also a priority for early Christianity. The Bible tells us that, two thousand years ago, Christ admonished, "Be not anxious about tomorrow, for tomorrow will be anxious for itself."

The Emotional Medicine practice of being present for your emotions as they are happening is a kissing cousin to awareness practices in Buddhism and Christianity. Crying when you're sad, stopping when you're done, feeling good fast helps you take any awareness practice into your life in a fresh way.

A Little Enlightenment – a Fringe Benefit

By the way, there is a possible fringe benefit in this business of being here now. When you bring your full attention and awareness to this present moment, NOW, you sometimes discover you stand at the portal of a *timeless* state. Time seems to stand still. You seem to have access to the past, present and future all at once. The delicious spaciousness of the present moment is way more accessible once you've learned to get out of your head.

Getting out of your head is not just a recipe for increasing confidence and personal power; it's also a formula for increasing your connection with the divine. Dropping down into the present moment requires you to wake up and become conscious and alive to your whole self, your whole situation, and ultimately the whole universe.

So are you ready to take the plunge and take some Emotional Medicine? You're likely more ready than when you started this book, probably even have your toe in the water. But if you're like most of us, you still don't feel comfortable enough to dive in. And you've got good reasons. Getting out of your head and feeling your emotions requires focusing on, being present with, and cooperating with your body. Yes, that very body you've skillfully learned to ignore, resist, and boss around.

In the next chapter you'll discover something that may blow your mind – or at least your preconceived notions. You'll learn that that your body is your best friend forever. Your body is a powerhouse of intelligence, guidance, and healing intention. It is always available to you 24/7. Furthermore, it's right under your nose!

FOUR

Make Friends with Your Body

The next step in learning to cry when you're sad, stop when you're done, and feel good fast is to make friends with your body. Yes, I mean befriending the body that craves chocolate and ice cream, eats and drinks too much, gets depressed and angry, has sexual feelings at all the wrong times for all the wrong people, gets sick and dies. This very body is your best friend for life.

No matter what is happening to you, your body is working as hard as it can on your behalf. When you get sick, whether due to infectious disease, genetic disorder, pollution, accident, or your own bad habits, your body is your number one line of defense. It brings every healing ability in its arsenal to your aid at every moment.

This built-in best friend doesn't judge you or withhold its services. It doesn't decide on some days to do everything it can to help you feel good and function well, and other days not. It doesn't punish you by refusing to handle whatever mess you've created when you don't eat or sleep enough or drink and drug too much or have sex with an inappropriate partner. Like an unconditionally loving friend, it digs in deeper to find ways of handling whatever you've done to make its job harder.

Your body has brilliant strategies to help you manage emotional distress and survive even the most devastating circumstances. And it's not just programmed for mere survival. Science has discovered that your body has something even more supportive in mind.

Your Body's Intention for Well-being

According to Dr. Antonio Damasio, our bodies are not only just focused on getting by or surviving, but also on "what we as thinking and affluent creatures identify as *wellness and well-being*."[1] This is good news. The goal or intention of your body is your well-being! And this bodily intention for your well-being is operating 24 hours a day, seven days a week from the moment you are born until the moment you die.

Some years ago Dr. Damasio and a group of neuroscientists at the University of Iowa devised an ingenious experiment to test the notion that our bodies are continually sending signals to guide us to choices that will enhance our well-being. They invited a bunch of gamblers to play a card game in which the decks had been rigged. Two red decks had been arranged so that participants who picked from them rarely won and most often lost big time. Two green decks were arranged for small losses and slow but steady wins. The scientists then wired the gamblers so that they could determine stress levels by measuring the sweat in their palms.[2]

It took most of the gamblers 40 draws before they began developing a "hunch" that the red decks were trouble. They didn't know why, but they began to prefer the green decks. By 80 cards, most of them had consciously figured out the game and could explain what was going on. But here is the fascinating thing: these gamblers' *bodies* started exhibiting stress responses to the red decks *after only 10 cards*. This is where their palms started sweating, signaling that the red decks represented danger. Also, at 10 cards, the gamblers started to draw less often from the red decks *though they had no conscious awareness they were doing this.*

These gamblers' bodies had figured out the game long before their conscious minds had, in a matter of minutes. Their bodies were sending signals in the language the body uses most, sensations. If those sweat sensations could have talked, they would have shouted: *Don't pick any more cards from the red deck!* The gamblers, however, weren't trained to notice what was happening in their bodies. They weren't aware they had a resource that could help them survive, even win the game, right in the palms of their hands.

What is this resource, this amazing "knowing" that your body contains? You may have had some experience when you "knew" something before you knew how or why. This is frequently referred to as "women's intuition," "gut instinct," or "a hunch." Scientists call this your "adaptive unconscious" or your body's "somatic marker" ability. Whatever it's called, these labels all point to the same thing: a built-in truth detector and wellness guide in your body which does *not require any conscious effort on your part.*

A woman, Jan, attending one of my workshops stood up with tears of gratitude streaming down her face when she heard me talk about this. She said, "This is blowing me away. I am relieved to hear that my body is actually my ally, my supporter, not my burden to bear. I feel like a weight has been lifted from me."

What would *your* life would be like if you, like Jan, knew you had an ally that existed for the sole purpose of supporting you, guiding you, delighting you as long as you lived? Wouldn't that be something? If you're like most of us, you've been looking for this kind of ongoing, unconditional support your whole life without ever finding it.

Oh, you might find it temporarily in the flush of new love or friendship, but that "in love" limerence is destined to disappear. Parents, friends and mates have their own wounds, survival strategies and needs to manage, as well as relating to yours. Relationships give you pleasure, partnership, and plenty of opportunities to grow, but they require you to attend to others' well-being as well as your own. No, I'm inviting you to consider that you actually do have an ally that is there just for you, only you, no strings attached.

If you have a strong relationship with God, Jesus or Mohammed, or take refuge in the Buddha, it may sound like I'm talking about a spiritual ally. We'll soon see that, in a surprising way, I am. For now, though, as important as spiritual connections are, I'm talking about an ally that you can touch and feel, an ally made of flesh and blood – your body.

Notice now how *you* respond to this news. Does the notion that your body has encoded in it an intention for your well-being seem possible, like a relief? Or does it seem impossible, that it may be true for someone else but not for you? The latter was certainly the case for Lyn. Lyn had no contact with any experience in her body which was soothing, comforting, supportive. Her body, she thought, was one big pain.

The Pain Magnet Syndrome: Pain Attracts Fear Attracts Pain Attracts Fear . . .

Lyn suffered from fibromyalgia, hormonal imbalances, severe environmental and food allergies, and back pain which surgery has been only partially successful in alleviating. Her body was sensitive to everything. She had to watch where she went and what she ate, and even had to ask her friends not to wear perfume in her presence.

When Lyn first came to see me, every ache, pain, twitch and tremble in her body triggered a panic response. She was responding not only to her exquisite bodily sensitivity, but also to her anxious thoughts about that sensitivity as well. Every bodily reaction would evoke fear which would evoke scenarios of doom which would evoke more bodily reactions which would evoke even bigger catastrophes which … well, you get the idea.

The pain in Lyn's body had become a big magnet, irresistibly drawing her awareness to it to the exclusion of anything else. Whatever her body was trying to accomplish on her behalf to heal her disease was disrupted time and again by fearful thoughts.

No blame here. I've been this sick; I know what this is like. When you don't feel well, it *is* easier to get stuck in thoughts which do not serve you. Someone can tell you your body is your ally and your eyes glaze over, until you actually experience that kind of support first hand. When you're up in your head, magnetized to pain and catastrophe, you aren't aware that you are only focusing on the pain, that your thoughts are in fact increasing your pain, that you are *missing* important healing signals from your ally, your body.

With Lyn, the first step was to help her separate the pain she was undergoing from her thoughts about that pain. She needed to experience pain as a body sensation rather than a doomsday scenario. That meant getting very interested in how deep, how sharp, how dull were her pains ... just at the level of body sensations. She also needed to consider that pain sometimes signals healing!

The Healing Cascade: When Pain Signals Healing

How come you, like most of us, get so upset when something new doesn't feel good in your body?[3] A simple answer is that you haven't been taught that your body's healing process *itself* often involves pain. You haven't been taught what doctors learn their first year in medical school: Whenever there has been a wound, the body rushes to the injury with a cascade of healing tools, such as inflammation and endorphins. Inflammation performs essential repair work for the body. It brings in needed medicine from the body's pharmacy to heal the wound. The pain of inflammation is a sign that the body is working to fix the problem. Endorphins bring in analgesic relief from the body's pharmacy to help ease the pain. Your body is trying to minimize your pain while it helps you heal.

But inflammation doesn't feel good! You consider it painful, bad, *"negatory"* – something to be avoided. You, and the pharmaceutical industry, want to get rid of inflammation as soon as you can. You reach for the anti-inflammatory pills, the aspirin, the cortisone. And while these exogenous (made outside the body) medications offer humane and often life-saving aid, they can also interfere with your body's plan for your recovery.

Doctors are now advising us to allow a low-grade fever to do its job of killing infection, and, similarly, to rest and allow a cold to run its course in order to avoid the misuse of antibiotics prevalent in the 80s and 90s. Lyn, like most of us, needed an antidote to her knee-jerk reaction to pain as something to be feared, mistrusted, and avoided. She also needed to learn to look for the relief her body was already offering.

As Lyn began to simply explore her uncomfortable body responses without going up to the panic stories in her head, she noticed that her discomfort was often so fleeting that it was gone before she could finish describing it. Granted, she would usually feel another uncomfortable sensation soon after, but Lyn discovered if she just waited a few moments, something would shift and release. She learned to keep guiding her attention back to the place where the pain wasn't present any more so she could notice the easing, and enjoy it.

Soon, Lyn started *actively looking for the ease* with which her body would let go of discomfort and move on to other sensations. She learned to relax and feel the ebb and flow of life energy in her body – expanding and contracting, painful and pleasurable, and always changing. With awareness of its intention for well-being as her touchstone, Lyn slowly began to make friends with her body.

Right after Lyn began to let her body lead, she stopped making her pain worse. She was able to see more clearly what was going on in her body and what was being fueled by her mind. She was able to tell the difference between pain that functioned as a fleeting, momentary adjustment in her hard-working body, and pain that was telling her she needed to change something, take action to support her well-being.

Cravings and Cramps: When Pain Signals Problems

As you've seen, pain sometimes means that normal, yet uncomfortable, body maintenance and repair is occurring. Pain can also mean, "*Help,* something is wrong and needs to be attended to right now!" It's always a good idea with pain signals to first rule out serious medical problems. Have the tests; check things out.

Once you've done that, if the pain persists, the next step is to look for the simplest solutions. If, for example, when you drink a glass of ice water your stomach cramps up (and you've diligently ruled out ulcers or other medical problems), your body may be trying to tell you in no uncertain terms: *Don't drink ice water anymore, I need room temperature water to maintain digestive comfort.* I am amazed at the number of abdominal pains encountered in my therapy office which disappear when a belt is loosened, or the back pains that melt away with a properly placed pillow.

Once you learn to be present with your pain as simple sensation, it is far easier to decipher the messages your body ally is sending and take the appropriate action. Unless, of course, you get rebellious and decide to ignore your body's warning signals altogether.

Truth. How many times have you experienced clear warning signals from your body ally: "Do not eat that, it will make you sick," "Do not even taste that drink, you'll fall off the wagon," "Go to bed now, you're tired," "Have a good cry now, you're sad," "Pound some pillows now, you're mad," and ignored those signals? I know you have. We all have.

If you're like me, you have weekly, if not daily, occurrences when you just decide to do whatever the heck you want to do, regardless of whether you have a strong inkling that it might not be good for you. You tell yourself, "No one's going to tell me what to do, including me!" You rationalize that you deserve it because you've worked so hard, deprived yourself in so many other ways, and you're stressed. Yes, that is all true. You are stressed and starved for pleasure, true pleasure.

Desperately Seeking Solutions

As a 21st-century human, you're bombarded with input so intense and rapid it would give your great-grandparents nervous fits in days, if not hours. These days this is referred to as TMI (too much information). While technology keeps finding more ways to keep you wired 24/7, your nerves haven't evolved along with it. Your nervous system still functions best at a slower, quieter pace. As you get more overloaded, you get more frazzled and start looking for relief. And of course you're looking for relief *fast!*

TV and other media are constantly titillating you to consume, imbibe, or ingest something that will help you feel good, *now*. When you need a break, and you're pressed for time, you're understandably impatient about how long it takes for your stressed body to unwind and find natural relief, especially because you know you can feel better instantly (albeit temporarily) by popping a pill, drinking a glass of wine, or eating sugar. And there's nothing wrong with an occasional quick fix, as long as it doesn't make you sick or addicted. (I'm no stranger to the quick fix. I've been known to turn to sugar or chocolate for an immediate hit of sweetness in a stressful moment.) But when you get in the habit of reaching outside yourself for gratification, you lose your ability to cultivate and appreciate the slower, subtly unfolding pleasure your body is waiting to offer. (And let me make it clear that "slower" could mean something as short as three to ten minutes, rather than the seconds we're accustomed to in this digital age.)

Warm and Fuzzy: When Pleasure Signals Support

As I mentioned earlier, even in the midst of your pain, your benevolent body is still sending tiny signals of pleasure. Although pain may signal *either* problems or healing, body-made pleasure *always* signals something positive for you. Pleasure is one of the ways your body trains you to seek out what's good for you! Of course, when your nerves are fried, or you're resisting the flow of sad, mad or scared energy, you may only get the faintest of pleasure signals, but those signals are not nothing. They are reminders that at some level your body is working on solutions to your pain and distress.

"Warm fuzzies" is a popular expression you may have heard to indicate the kind of soothing and comfort you receive from beloved pets, soft cozy clothes, and feeling safe and supported by friends and family. Your body lets you know it is there for you and help is on the way by this continual, subtle offering of "warm fuzzies" even during times of distress.

"I'm still here," your body says, as a warm ease spreads almost imperceptibly across your shoulders. "You're OK," it says with a tiny tingling in your hands and feet. "You can handle this," it says with a sense of strength in your legs. Remember, too, these subtle "OK" sensations during stress barely scratch the surface of the unmistakable pleasure and warm fuzzies you feel once you learn to cry when you're sad, and stop when you're done. In any case, warm fuzzies, like all body experiences, are fleeting. Blink and you'll miss them. Stay up in your thoughts and you may soon doubt they exist at all. In order to find warm fuzzies, you have to look for them!

Choosing True Pleasure

If pain and stress are like an icy wind or hot, searing gust demanding attention, pleasure and your body's intention for well-being are more like the gentle quiet of a high mountain forest, slowly infusing your awareness with an increasing sense of all-is-well-ness. Pleasure is often at its most elusive just when your body is shifting from pain to healing – when the worst is over and healing energy begins to spread through your body. Too often you're still *thinking* about the pain, so you don't notice the tide has turned; pain is receding and pleasure is coming in.

For example, if I invite you to drop your awareness into your body right now, you would probably notice what doesn't feel good, aches and pains. This doesn't mean something's wrong, it is just the way we humans typically operate. As a matter of fact, studies have shown that you have an easier time remembering what was painful about your childhood than what was pleasant. As a human, you are fascinated by pain, your own and others'. Getting as interested in pleasure as in pain requires an active choice on your part, as well as an effort to undo your early childhood training in this regard.

In Lyn's case, she had to reeducate herself to allow the pleasure of pleasure. This wasn't easy for her. Even as she became more comfortable being present with discomfort, Lyn still had a hard time finding and focusing on positive sensations in her body. She had guilt and shame associated with bodily pleasure.

Like most of us, as a child, Lyn had been very interested in pleasure. Her parents, however, punished her whenever she explored her body for these sensations. They didn't know that self-pleasuring at any age is a health booster, and good medicine in its own right.[4] Lyn's parents, in their quest to do the right thing by her, decided they couldn't allow her to masturbate because they had to teach her to be a good, respectable girl.

Little Lyn soon figured out that pleasure must be bad, because it could get her into such big trouble. In Lyn's childlike mind, this prohibition soon extended beyond masturbation to include almost all such experiences.

Now, as an adult, Lyn had to look inside her own heart and soul to make *her own, grown-up decision* about whether pleasure was bad or good. I'm happy to report that she decided to choose pleasure. Lyn decided that just as she was learning to relax into being present with her pain, she could also learn look for and enjoy pleasure. She was able to break the pain magnet syndrome by *actively* looking for what felt good in her body.

Once she learned this, Lyn increased her trust in her body and herself. She became adept at deciphering her body's signals. She was better able to make lifestyle choices which helped bring her nervous and hormonal systems back to balance: she was more careful with her diet, more regular with exercise, more willing to take time out at midday for a brief rest. Slowly but surely, Lyn mastered the ability to tune into her body's intention for well-being not only in the midst of pain and discomfort, but also in the midst of pleasure and comfort.

Lyn's has not been a miracle cure. She still has to cooperate with her highly sensitive organism and take really good care of herself. She can't cheat on her health regimen much, if at all. However, she is experiencing increasing periods of peace and pleasure. She feels more self-confidence, more integrity, more well-being than ever before. Lyn no longer feels like a lonely victim of ill health. She has an ally in her body, she knows it, AND she knows how to use it!

ACTION TIP: PART ONE

The next time you think you're happy, drop your awareness into your body to see what happy *feels* like. Scan your body from head to toe. Look for warm fuzzies. Look for *anything* that feels good. If you happen to notice a little pain here or ache there, pay it no mind for now, just keep bringing your attention back to something else that feels good. Make a note of the particular signals *your* body sends when you are happy. From now on, every time you feel happy, try to include your body in your awareness. Not only will this prolong your happiness, it will also make it easier to notice those faint hints of well-being even when you're not happy.

ACTION TIP: PART TWO

The next time you think you're unhappy, distressed or in pain, scan your body and look specifically for faint signals of well-being. Look in your hands and feet, fingers and toes. Look in your ears, your calves, your backbone. Even when you are in pain, even when you are not happy, your body is still sending you messages that it is your ally, that it is still there doing everything it can on your behalf. Let your body reassure you that you are not alone.

Body as Spiritual Ally

I said earlier that, in a strange way, your body is also your spiritual ally. Here's what I meant. As you've seen, science now knows that your body contains within it an intention and a design of support for you beyond mere survival. Your body *wants* well-being for you!

These words – idea, intention, well-being – all refer to intangibles. You can't touch an idea or an intention, but that doesn't mean it doesn't have power. Science can measure the *results* of an intention or an experience of well-being based on specific biochemical parameters such as change in stress hormone levels or change in blood pressure. But science can't measure an actual *intention* for well-being, just as science can't measure faith or belief in God. Your body's intention for your well-being is something like an energy, a force, something you deduce by its results ... something actually quite akin to spirit.

I like using the body as an ally in tuning into intangible intentions such as well-being because the results can be so immediate. I've always had a bit of an impatient streak, so *this* kind of quick fix has great appeal for me. You can feel the results of that soothing, supportive bodily intention for your well-being unbelievably quickly once you know how and where to look for it. Crying when you're sad and stopping when you're done not only opens the door of your inner medicine cabinet, but also unlocks profound states of peace and spiritual oneness. Wouldn't it be just like God to give you this gift?

I also enjoy considering how increasing body awareness and embracing your body as your ally are additional ways of praying or meditating, of being present with a power greater than yourself – God, Jesus, Mohammad, Buddha, Great Mystery – whatever best expresses it for you. After all, the Bible does say that we are made in the image and likeness of God, the quintessential spiritual force. Quantum physics has recently revealed that when you get right down through muscle and bone, tissue and cells, atoms, and quarks, your body is essentially energy ... waves of energy. These waves can appear to be (and can certainly feel) solid when you focus your attention on them. Some scientists are even saying that, beyond energy, the word "spirit" best describes what is arising there.

In the way that Spirit/goodness/God can be a subtle force in your life but requires you to tune into it for it to truly manifest, so it is with your body's intention for your well-being, and the good body-made medicine it continually offers.

If quantum physics has it right, you can literally help bring things into being with your awareness. The fact that your body is already programmed for your best interests gives you a leg up. The fact that your body has a medicine chest of remedies to restore self-confidence, happiness, and a sense of inner peace, provides you with real, tangible support.

Imagine what you can accomplish by bringing your attention to your inherent bodily intention and its medicine for well-being! When you choose to embrace your body as your ally you can tune into, even accentuate, its power whenever you need to, even when you're facing injury or disease ... even when you're dying.

Ally to Our Last Breath

A client, Stephan, was referred to me as he was facing the last stages of pancreatic cancer. His belly was protruding as if it was holding a bowling ball inside. His arms and legs looked like barren branches. His eyes, set deep in his already skull-like head, looked out at me with great yearning. He wasn't sure what we could do together to help him, but he knew he needed something.

As Stephan talked about his situation, he cried softly, weakly. His mind wanted to figure out why this dreadful thing was happening to him. I gently helped him bring his attention back to his experience in his *body* in the present moment. Almost instantly, he became more peaceful. As long as he stayed totally present with his experience in his dying body, he was soothed and eased. His body was sending him pain relief and spiritual solace to help ease his suffering.

When Stephan focused on his body and his experience in the moment, he could rest and relax into his dying. He came for one more session. The following week his family called to tell me he was gone and how grateful he was to have found this peace before he died.

As Stephan's experience demonstrates, one of the keys to enlisting your body as your ally is the ability to allow both pain and pleasure while accepting *whatever* is happening to you and *through* you. In *Going on Being*, a book I always keep close at hand, Buddhist psychiatrist Mark Epstein describes the power of taking refuge and "resting" in your awareness: "All of my pursuit of knowledge and understanding had to be centered in my heart. This meant that my emotional life could not be pushed away or ignored ... *If we can learn not to fear our feelings, we gain access to the real. We have the opportunity to reclaim our going on being.*"[5]

Acceptance of "what is" is a predominant principle in most forms of Buddhism. One form, Vipassana, teaches a method of observing and noting the thoughts, sensations and emotions which arise in awareness. The important thing in this practice is to notice and accept it all, an unending stream of material, and wait to see that it changes.

Embracing your body as your ally is a variation of this awareness theme. However, this is more of a *medicinal* practice, designed to help you get well. The active focusing of awareness on feeling good is one way that embracing your body as an ally differs from Buddhism. This is also where Emotional Medicine comes in.

When you specifically seek and focus on *pleasure* at the end of an emotional up-out-done cycle, or at any other time for that matter, you are acting as your own apothecary, your own emotional pharmacist, guiding your awareness in ways that have medicinal effects on your organism. Your body chemistry changes. You feel better. If you stay with it, with your body's intention for well-being, you'll soon restore your resources of calm, confidence, and vitality. In my cheekier moments, I sometimes also call this "medicinal Buddhism."

The Key to Making Friends with Your Body

The key to embracing your body as your ally is to work primarily with the *sensations* that arise. The reason for this is that bodily sensations are as close to your body's truth-telling talents as possible. Remember, your body is not neurotic. *You want to be as close as possible to whatever your body is trying to tell you, because your body is designed to lead you back to well-being.* Your body has no vested interest in staying sad, mad, scared or miserable. Your body is always looking for a way to take you back to optimal functioning, as soon as possible. And it's always talking to you in the only language it knows – sensation.

In the next chapter, you'll be learning all about this new language: the language of your body. You'll learn a new alphabet consisting entirely of body sensations. You'll see exactly what a sensation is and isn't. You'll learn how to distinguish sensations from thoughts and emotions. And you'll get a handy cheat sheet, a list of sensations you can copy and carry with you as you're learning to decode this new language.

We'll also take a closer look at sensations such as emptiness and nausea that seem to signal pain and misery but are actually the exact opposites: powerful portals to peace and transformation. Read on to discover how sensations strengthen your ability to drop into your body, open your inner medicine chest, find your unique emotional prescription, and experience well-being any time you choose.

FIVE

Learn the Language of Your Body

Marta was getting ready to meet Henry for the first time. They'd exchanged pictures and long email conversations about values and life after an online matchup. Henry had invited Marta to dinner at her favorite restaurant. Marta was impressed that he remembered her mentioning how much she liked the new Thai restaurant downtown.

Marta was humming as she put on her earrings and finished her eye makeup. Giving herself a final checkup in the mirror, she noticed a fluttery feeling in her stomach. *Gosh, I hope I'm not getting sick,* Marta thought as she stopped humming, put on her jacket and prepared to leave her apartment. As she looked into the rearview mirror to back out of her driveway, Marta realized this was her first date since the Leon disaster.

Driving to town, Marta continued thinking about Leon. That relationship was also initiated online, albeit through a different matchmaking service. Unfortunately, after two months of dating, Marta discovered Leon had lied about his marital status and employment. Marta was so upset she didn't date for six months. Meeting Henry was her attempt to get back into the dating world.

Henry isn't Leon, Marta said to herself. This service checks references thoroughly. *Relax,* Marta commanded herself to no avail as her grip on the steering wheel tightened. Her hands were cold. Marta began to think this date was a mistake. *Maybe these jitters are an omen things won't go well.*

By the time she got to the restaurant, Marta's face was ashen, her hands were shaking, and her heart was pounding. It took all her willpower to walk into the lobby. When she met Henry face to face, he took one look and asked whether she was feeling OK. Marta replied, "I think I'm going to be sick," and ran into the bathroom before she threw up on Henry's shoes.

Marta took her time in the ladies' room. She steadied herself at the sink and washed her hands with warm water until she stopped shaking and felt her heartbeat easing. When her stomach calmed enough to return to the lobby, Henry was waiting patiently. As Marta looked into Henry's open, forthright face, she began to relax. He seemed genuinely concerned. She said, "I think I need a cup of hot tea." Happily, the tea and Henry's kind demeanor helped to settle Marta's stomach.

Even more happily, Henry and Marta turned out to be a good match. A year or so later, they got married. The tale of Marta's taking one look at Henry and running off to the bathroom became a treasured part of their courtship tale.

Marta Misses Messages

What happened here? How did Marta go from happy and humming to ashen and shaking in the minutes it took her to dress, drive, and arrive for her date? The answers can be found by looking at the messages Marta missed from her body. Marta's body was talking to her in the only language it knows … sensation. Marta didn't know how to decipher this body language.

As Marta was dressing to meet Henry, her body was communicating with her – giving feedback about how she was feeling and what she needed, moment by moment. All human bodies do this "talking" from morning until night. (If you've ever gone to bed on an overindulged stomach, you're undoubtedly aware your body continues communicating with you throughout the night.)

If you don't know how to decode these messages, you could end up like Marta: switched from joy to misery before you know it. Learning the language of your body is an essential step in moving through emotional upset to feel good fast.

Sensations Are the Key

Marta's body was initially talking via happy humming sensations in her throat. However, soon after she felt sensations of fluttering in her stomach, she stopped humming. Marta misinterpreted these first fluttering communiqués of excitement as signals of potential trouble. Notice that Marta's first interpretation of those fluttering sensations was *to worry that something was wrong* – that she might be getting sick.

Worrying is a common response when you notice almost any body sensation – especially when you're not familiar with body language. Worrying also gets triggered when sensations don't feel good or are unfamiliar. Marta's initial worried interpretation that *something might be wrong* triggered a toppling domino chain of worries which in turn triggered another chain of unpleasant sensations.

Marta didn't know a cardinal rule of Emotional Medicine: *Any time worrisome or fearful thoughts come to mind, it's crucial to keep attention focused on bodily sensations rather than on thoughts.* That's because negative thoughts easily trigger negative body reactions. For Marta, each miserable Leon memory triggered a new slew of unpleasant sensations: increasing cold, clenched hands, tightening stomach, and the nausea often associated with fear. As those uncomfortable sensations increased, Marta's fearful thoughts increased.

Once caught in this fearful pattern, Marta's mind and body kept talking to each other, but all they were saying was, "I'm getting scared," and "I'm getting scared too" … until "Now, I'm really getting scared," became "I've got to get out of here before I throw up!"

Fortunately, Marta followed her instincts and ran to the bathroom. Undoubtedly, the running itself helped dissipate some of her fear. The soothing sensation of warm water on her hands helped stop the vicious cycle of fearful thoughts. (You can also accomplish this by just imagining your hands warming[1] – but that takes a little more practice.)

If Marta had known about Emotional Medicine, she could have also taken an additional moment or two in the bathroom to shake her hands vigorously and discharge some residual anger at Leon. She might have shed a tear or two about how much she was hurt, and even consciously allowed herself to experience some natural trembling about an unknown future with Henry.

The good news is that once you make a discipline out of identifying and checking sensations, you have the possibility to translate your body's language and find your way back to feeling good with Emotional Medicine. In order to check in with sensations, however, you have to distinguish them from thoughts, emotions, and states of mind.

How Sensations Differ from Emotions and Thoughts

Sensations always refer to some kind of physical presence, impression, movement or action taking place within, through, or on your body. *Sensations are the actual discrete body experiences beneath all of your labels.* Although sensations are not immune from mistaken identity, they're least likely to lead you down a path of misinterpretation. While it is possible to experience thoughts which are not inherently tied to body experience, you cannot experience sensations which are not tied to body experience. Sensations are, sine qua non, body experiences.

Sensations are processed in the oldest part of the brain, the reptilian brain. The reptilian brain hasn't evolved enough to be neurotic; it's very simple-minded. Sometimes, in learning the language of your body, it helps to be very simple-minded.

Thoughts, on the other hand, typically refer to an activity of mind.[2] Even people who are completely paralyzed, breathing with an iron lung and feeling nothing in their bodies, can have thoughts. One of the greatest theoretical physicists of our time, Stephen Hawking, has an advanced condition of neuromuscular dystrophy. He cannot breathe, speak, or function unaided. This has not stopped him from solving thorny space-time conundrums.

But what about emotions – they're body experiences, aren't they? Isn't feeling scared a sensation? Or sad? Or mad? Although emotions are an important part of body language, they're still one step removed from sensations. Each sad, mad, scared or glad emotion is made of a *cluster of sensations* in constant flux. The word "emotion" itself is derived from a Latin word which means *to move through or out*. One definition of *e-motion* is energy in motion. I'm going to amend that and say emotion is *sensation* in motion – and the sum is greater than the parts.

When distinct body sensations coalesce to become the flow of sensations you experience as sad, mad or scared, they impact you as a whole.[3] For example, the sensations comprising sadness often *build up* with heavy tightening of the chest and stomach, tensing of the shoulders, constriction in the throat, short choppy breaths, eyes brimming with tears, and move on to *discharging* as shoulders shake and shudder, throat erupts in sobs or sounds, chest and stomach heave, limbs jerk, and tears flow. These sensations move their way up and down (or through and out) your emotional experience. The combined effect has emotional power far beyond each discrete sensation.

However, one reason it is so important to stay in touch with the distinct sensations that unite to produce emotional impact is that sometimes vastly different emotions begin with or contain similar

sensations. Marta didn't understand that when her stomach flut-
tered, it could have been trying to tell her she was excited to meet
Henry. Or, it could have been telling her she was scared. Or her
body could have been trying to tell her she was *both* excited and
scared … and to proceed with caution, both inside herself (bypass-
ing her thoughts to focus on body sensations) and outside herself
(by taking it slow with Henry).

Let's take a look at how to tell the difference between excitement and fear when both contain similar sensations and are easily
confused. We'll also review other simple body language misinter-
pretations that can lead to not-so-simple problems in life.

Excitement often Mistaken for Fear and Vice Versa

In body language, excitement and fear both may involve sensations of increased heart rate and fluttering/sinking sensations in the
gut. It's possible to tell them apart, if you know how and where to
look. That place, surprisingly, is in your hands and feet.

If you're excited, your hands and feet are most likely warm. If
you're scared, your hands and feet will typically feel cold. At the
first sign of stomach flutters, Marta's hands (if she had checked) were
probably warm; moments earlier she had been relaxed and humming in happy anticipation of meeting a potentially great new
guy.

Here's another example. In sessions, I often see clients' happiness when describing some step they are about to take – new
job, hobby, or friend. Their faces are flush with excitement, eyes
sparkling. They seem joyous as they describe their news. When I
ask what they are feeling, they reply, "I'm scared." Now, of course
there may be a bit of fear mixed in, but the *predominant* energy is
excitement.

When I invited those clients to slow down and to tell me the
temperature of their hands and face, they would respond, "Warm!"
When I asked what was going on in their stomachs, they said,
"Butterflies!" Although having butterflies can go either way, they

typically signal excitement. It's almost as if the body is giving permission to go ahead and take the leap!

Imagine if Marta had known she could check her hands and feet to determine if she was scared or excited. She could have told herself, "Of course my stomach is fluttering. I'm happy and excited to meet Henry for the first time." She could have further circumvented a fear cavalcade if she had taken a moment to drop down and really *feel* her warm hands and feet. Experiencing their warmth and ease would have reassured her that she was OK.

Interestingly, while excitement is often mistaken for fear, fear is often mistaken for excitement. Research subjects who agreed to go out on blind dates, some of which included scary circumstances (such as hiking across a high, shaky bridge, or riding roller coasters), found their partners *far more attractive* than did those in run-of-the-mill situations (such as meeting in a coffee shop or bookstore).

Fear and excitement are similar experiences for our nervous systems. But they're not the same. They're easy to confuse if you're not used to focusing on sensations.

No matter what emotional experience you *think* you are having, looking for and identifying *all* your body sensations during any emotional experience will let you know what's really happening and put things in proportion. Although your attention will naturally be drawn to sensations of discomfort, it is rare that you won't be able to find some sensations that feel good, or at least OK.

Hunger/Fatigue Often Mistaken for Sadness – and Vice Versa

Sometimes sadness is accompanied by a *sinking or empty* sensation in your stomach which is mistakenly labeled as hunger. Conversely, when you have a sinking or empty stomach sensation because you *are* hungry, your mind might make up that you are sad. If you have food issues you know all too well how true this is.

A good habit to develop is to slow down before you make any assumptions about empty stomach feelings and have a little talk with yourself. Ask yourself if you are sad. Ask if you are hungry. Listen carefully. This takes practice, but if you keep at it you will soon be able to distinguish between these two and act accordingly.

The listlessness and weakness of fatigue is another experience easily misinterpreted as sadness, depression or hunger. Have you ever seen young children suddenly get cranky? Children, who otherwise are cooperative little tykes, often begin sobbing when tired or hungry and don't know it. Skillful parents know how to decipher what their children's bodies are really saying. You too can benefit from listening deeply to what your body is telling you.

Once you misinterpret hunger or fatigue as sadness or depression, this label, along with other activities of your inventive mind, can conjure up all kinds of reasons for sadness. No matter how great things are going, there is always something not quite perfect. Your mind gloms onto that and soon you're off in a loop of negativity (which, soon enough, generates uncomfortable body experiences of irritability, fatigue, etc.), when perhaps your body was only saying it needed a snack or a nap.

Angry Tears Often Mistaken for Sad Tears

Anger, especially for women, is often expressed through tears. Until recently, women have not had "permission" to express anger. It was deemed "unladylike." For generations, tears have been a more socially acceptable way for females to cope with the frustration of unexpressed anger. Women who expressed anger openly were considered shrews or harpies, and even today are sometimes considered unwomanly emasculators.

Both anger and sadness often begin with a tightening of chest and stomach, tensing of shoulders, constriction in the throat. You could easily confuse these if you didn't know to scan your body for other sensations.

An easy way to distinguish sad from mad is to check (once again) your hands! If your hands are compressed into fists, and/or your biceps are tight, that's a sign anger is present. Another place to look is in your mouth. If teeth are clenched and jaw is jutting, your body is trying to tell you – whether you like it or not, whether it's convenient or not – you're angry!

Any Tears Mistaken for Weakness

You, like many of us, may be embarrassed about your tears … thinking they make you look like a wimp, foolish or childish. This interpretation hinders both men and women from receiving the benefits of Emotional Medicine. Men in private life and women in public life are particularly susceptible to thinking they'll appear, or actually be, weak if they tear up.

This is unfortunate since tears are stress busters – wonders of well-being. Tears are needed more than ever as postmodern culture becomes increasingly complex and pressured. Instead of considering tears a sign of weakness, I suggest a new motto: "A tear a day keeps the doctor away!"

Happy Tears Mistaken for Sad Tears

Another common misinterpretation is thinking your tears automatically mean you're sad or upset about something. Sadness is only one reason tears flow. Tears often accompany happiness, joy, or the experience of being emotionally touched – having your heart tenderly opened.

Imagine the empowerment you'd miss if you mistake anger for sadness. Imagine the pleasure you'd pass up if you mistake an opening heart for unhappiness. Imagine the sweetness you'd overlook if you tear up during a touching moment and then wonder what you're sad about. Life is too short to miss precious moments because you can't decipher what your body (and soul) is trying to tell you.

Both happy and sad tears may begin with a sensation of your heart being squeezed or cracked open. Tears may flow. You can tell the difference, though: With sad tears, you'll typically feel an overall bodily heaviness or collapsing feeling. For happy tears, you'll feel a lightness and expansion.

Another way to distinguish happy from sad tears is to check out your situation. Is it a Hallmark moment or a Bravo TV drama? Try asking yourself, "What am I touched or moved about right now?"

Sensations in Situation

One crucial thing Marta didn't know about body language is that sensations need to be put in context of your *total experience*. Just as spoken language, tone of voice, the setting you're in and your social context help decipher the meaning of any particular communication in body language, you also have to gather data from your overall body experience to decipher the meaning of any sensation vocabulary.

For example, in spoken language, when you give a birthday gift and the recipient says with a big grin, "Oh, you shouldn't have," you don't feel troubled at all. You respond to the overall situation, tone of voice and facial expression which override the "scolding" words.

However, you'll likely interpret those same words differently if you forget an important client meeting and your boss, with narrowed eyes, clenched teeth and aggravated voice, says, "You shouldn't have done that!" In the first instance all's well, in the second all's not! In order to help you drop awareness down into your body to better hear its language, we first need to discuss a sensation that you might not even think is one: numbness.

Numbness: Sensation or Not?

You might think numbness is the absence of sensation – that it's what you experience when you don't feel anything. That is true, *but only in regard to emotion*, not sensation. When you feel emotionally numb, you are definitely *not* feeling sad, mad, scared or glad. You may feel blank or dead inside and think you're feeling nothing. But when you get right down to it, your numbness *itself* is a living body experience. If you look for the body experiences beneath emotional numbness you'll find heavy, dull, leaden numb *sensations*, whose dimensions you can quantify and measure as you would any other.

You'll discover, when you drop awareness down into the specific sensations of numbness, that the numb space is limited to only part of your body. It's like when your foot falls asleep. Your foot feels "dead" but the rest of you is alive. However, if you try to stand before your foot wakes up, your leg buckles beneath you. That's because you don't have your living, sensing foot sending signals about where the floor is and how you need to position yourself to stay balanced.

So it is when you are feeling numb emotionally. You don't have your living, moving emotions sending signals about how and where you need to stand in any current situation to stay balanced and thrive. You need to proceed carefully until you are able to experience your body talking to you again.

In my experience, however, the *moment* someone who has previously said, "I don't feel anything" or "I'm numb" begins looking and listening for bodily *sensations*, the body starts coming alive. This is very different from a numb foot where you wait helplessly for it to wake up.

Have you noticed that when your sleeping foot wakes up it often feels uncomfortable – tingly and weird? This is similar to when you reconnect with yourself after being emotionally numb. You may feel tingly and weird as you begin to feel your life force flowing once again through your body. This will pass. All sensations are fluid and temporary. Just as your awakened foot soon feels normal again, so your emotionally alive body will as well.

ACTION TIP: DE-NUMBING

If you feel numb, take a few moments to explore your numbness scientifically. By *scientifically,* I mean to observe without
judgment. As a sensation, numbness has dimension, location
and intensity like any other sensation brought into awareness.
Be sure you are warm enough. If you are cold, you may mistake
being chilled for being numb. Put on a sweater, or wrap up
in a blanket. Once you're comfortable temperature-wise, drop
your awareness down into your body. Look specifically for the
places that seem numb. As you find them, make careful calibra-
tions about how wide, deep, long and flat the numb areas seem.
Avoid blame and judgment about whatever you discover.

Next, actively scan your body for any other sensations
you can feel, pleasurable or unpleasurable. If you have trouble
finding any sensation other than numbness, take your pulse to
feel your heartbeat. Your pulse and heartbeats are sensations!
Other good places to look for sensations when you feel numb
are in your hands and feet.

Finally, move your awareness gently back and forth between any sensations you can feel and areas of numbness for
three to six minutes, or until you feel more present in your
body again.

If this de-numbing tip doesn't work, try drinking a cup
of hot tea, or taking a bath. Stay aware as you notice how and
where you feel the warm sensations of tea or bathwater affect
your body. Once again, try oscillating between sensations you
can feel and sensations of numbness.

When you actively scan your whole body to see what you are
sensing, you'll often unearth a panoply of living experience; some
things will feel good and some will not. You'll soon realize you are
not totally numb. Even when you think you are feeling absolutely

nothing, unless you're a corpse, you'll find some feeling somewhere in your body when you look.

For the purposes of Emotional Medicine, I've devised a cheat sheet to guide you through this new language of sensation. Think of this as your body language vocabulary. There are three categories of sensation that are important to remember: 1) sensations that feel good, 2) sensations that don't feel good, and 3) sensations that don't feel good but often herald healing or transformation.

Your Sensation Checklist (with Commentary)

1. Sensations that feel good: Warm, flowing, soft, gentle, pulsing, surging, muscular, vibrating, tingling, moist, wet, cool, dry, easeful, quiet, still, peaceful, calm, clear, rhythmic, vital, firm, heat (as in healing hands), loose, smooth, electric, easy breathing, energetic, full, satisfied, gurgling gut, hot (as in sexually aroused), expansive. (Add your favorites here.)

Since you, like many of us, may have a tendency to miss, neglect or ignore pleasurable sensations, you might want to copy this list and post it someplace where your eyes glance over it as you go about daily life. Posting this list may help you see the pleasure already cruising into your current bodily life.

Focusing on pleasurable sensations is one way in which my work is different from classical Buddhism or other meditation practices. Although the foundation for most meditation practice is acceptance of "what is," I am suggesting a new course here. I am saying, Hey, our culture is currently trapped in a trance of negativity; let's break out of this trance by focusing on pleasure – on sensations that feel good – whenever they arise.

I don't suggest focusing on pleasure so you can form a veneer over suppressed pain and despair, but rather invite you to keep in mind that you might be missing some good stuff. So, how about looking for and being open to experiencing positive sensations in your body, yourself, and in others at all times?[4] I'd like to promote a new bumper sticker: "I brake for pleasure!"

2. Sensations that don't feel good: Cold, clammy, tight, sharp, digging, confining, rough, prickly, painful, pressure, low energy, flat energy, rapid breathing, can't catch breath, gasping, frozen, hungry, stuffed, overfull, tight gut, jumpy, jittery, bursting, stagnant, hot (as in overheated), contracting. (Add your own dislikes here.)

Of course some sensations that don't feel good are messages that you need to get to urgent care NOW! You've probably heard descriptions of pains telling you you're about to have a heart attack: pressure in the chest, back, neck or stomach, pain radiating down the arm, shortness of breath, feeling cold, clammy and/or nauseous. When dealing with sensations that don't feel good, err on the side of caution. Check with your doctor about any sensation that is troubling to you.

As you begin to notice sensations that don't feel good, it's important to remember that much of normal body maintenance is experienced as uncomfortable. Whenever you start deciphering the message from any sensation that doesn't feel good, try not to add anything to it. You can relax into the knowledge that normal human experience doesn't always feel good. Sometimes sensations that don't feel good mean something really important is about to happen!

For a practitioner of Emotional Medicine, the most intriguing category is the next one: Sensations that don't feel good but often herald healing and transformation. These sensations are crucial because if you mislabel them and get caught in a whirlwind of worry, you may miss transformation, breakthrough or profound healing.

3. Sensations that don't feel good but often herald healing and transformation: trembling, shaking, itching, burning, vibrating, tingling, burping, stomach gurgling, tremulousness and emptiness.

While all of these sensations may signal healing, those especially important for personal transformation are: trembling/shaking, gurgling/burping, tremulousness and emptiness. These are your sensation allies.

Here's the scoop on trembling. Trembling is one of the most disastrously misunderstood sensations in the body language dictionary. What most don't know is that trembling is often your body's way of telling you it's *recovering* from fear or shock. Trembling (or mild shaking) helps your body discharge the built-up tension and stress that shock or fear engenders.

You'll get into trouble when trembling if you automatically think it means you're still scared. Here's an example: Let's say you've just had a scare. You get back to your car after dinner with a friend and discover that you can't find your wallet. Your heart starts racing; you check your purse, backpack. You race back toward the restaurant. As you open the door, you see the manager coming toward you with your wallet in his hand. *Whew.* You breathe a sigh of relief. As you head back to your car you notice that you are trembling. This is good – normal. It means your body is discharging remnants of fear.

If you don't know this, the trembling makes you think you must still be scared. This triggers the memory of what you've just gone through. Soon your heart is revving up again, your breath shortens. You and your body are now back reliving your scare.

Next time you're trembling, see if you can relax into it for a minute and consider that your nervous system is helping you recover. Once you slow down, you might also realize you're cold and need a sweater. Since low blood sugar also can show up as a trembling sensation, you might also decide you need to eat something.

Itching is another misinterpreted sensation. Physically, itching is often a sign that a wound is healing, that new skin is filling in gaps. Emotionally, it may be a sign that some new behavior or intuition is trying to work its way into awareness.

Often when I am about to get a new insight, or gain a new perspective, I'll experience an itching in the center of my forehead, right where the ancient traditions say our "third eye" is located. This third eye area is considered a power center for intuition and vast seeing. When it starts itching in a client session, I pay even closer attention.

Of course itching may also be a signal you've been eating too many sweets or foods your body doesn't like, or that you're allergic to a new cologne or laundry soap. Always rule out simple body solutions before assuming that any uncomfortable sensation represents a transformative process.

Although burning sensations can indicate a host of medical conditions (such as gastritis, cystitis or other body emergencies), burning sensations may also indicate that a healing or purification process is taking place. Many times I and others have noticed a burning in the heart area, just as we're about to experience a breakthrough in relationships or realizing self-love. This seems to be especially true during forgiveness work. Next time you feel a burning sensation, consider the possibility that something within you is being sanctified and transformed.

Burping is Good!

Gut gurgling and burping are vastly undervalued. I always listen for stomach gurgling and burping (mine and theirs!) during my work with people. Why? Because a gurgling viscera is a sign that healthy energy is flowing in the gut. The stomach is the seat of an enormous number of essential neuropeptide receptors that have a huge influence on well-being. When your stomach is in a knot, you can't receive the benefit of your "gut instinct" or "gut wisdom."

A bloated stomach is like a stagnant swamp, while a gurgling stomach is like a moving stream. Dr. Candace Pert has been dismayed that her seminal research about neuropeptide receptors and the "molecules of emotion" led to the development and overuse of antidepressants, many of which have hugely deleterious effects on the guts, and impede the healthy flow of those very "molecules of emotion."

Typically, what most do when they burp or their guts' gurgle is audible is apologize. You, too, may be embarrassed by the sounds of a healthy body. You don't want to seem rude and uncivilized. So, although I'm not fomenting rebellion against social niceties, the next time your stomach gurgles or you burp, take private pleasure in the notion that all is well.

I say "Burping is good" so often in sessions that a client made me a charming pillow with that saying emblazoned across the front (along with bubbles of burps rising up like cheerful balloons).

Tremulousness is another harbinger of transformation. It is different from post-fright trembling and shaking. Tremulousness is the quivering you might feel when you are opening to a whole new part of yourself – your power, your sexuality, or your self-love – which you haven't experienced in a long time. Just as a child's first steps are shaky during the transition from crawling to walking, you too might experience wobbly sensations as you open to parts of yourself long buried. Take a breath, relax and take joy in your new steps and even in the *temporary* unsteadiness that sometimes accompanies them.

Now for the pièce de résistance, the sensation signaling transformation above all others: emptiness! Unfortunately, whenever you experience emptiness your mind often automatically translates that into thoughts of loneliness and unfulfillment. That is not to say there aren't painful, true experiences of loneliness and unfulfillment that you may touch during your healing journey. But whenever you get to an experience of emptiness, the reality is often quite the opposite. Down in the embodied sensation of emptiness there is a wonder to behold.

Let's see what happened in a session with Zoe, a long-term client who was experiencing deep, disorienting grief about her lover precipitously ending their relationship. She sobbed and thrashed as emotional pain coursed through her. Soon Zoe came to a moment where she stopped sobbing. She got very quiet and said morosely, "I feel empty."

Now, although I was inwardly delighted, I contained my excitement so Zoe could make her own discovery. I gently encouraged Zoe to drop into the sensation of this emptiness. When she felt safe enough, I said, "Walk to the center of this experience. Feel what the emptiness is actually like, right now." There was silence. Soon Zoe reported that the emptiness felt, er – ah – er ... full. *Full!* We both laughed out loud.

I guided Zoe to luxuriate in this fullness. As she took her time feeling fullness in molecule and marrow, she felt happier and happier. She was amazed that she could feel so good in the shadow of this huge loss. I watched Zoe's confidence return. She now knew she could survive this disaster – and thrive. Zoe no longer feared the completeness of her emotional experience, even when it led to previously dreaded emptiness.

Full is so often what emptiness feels like when it is experienced in the body that it almost seems like a law of nature. Other clients have described being present with emptiness like this: "Well, gosh, it's changing now; it seems to be a peaceful feeling," and "I feel a comforting stillness and quiet."

When the sensation of emptiness appears in your embodied experience, you can rejoice. You are almost home to bliss and peace. An important caveat: The pivotal word here is "embodied." In order to move through emptiness to well-being, you have to be in your body, consciously able to feel and tolerate unfamiliar sensations.

In addition, Zoe had me by her side, helping and encouraging, metaphorically holding her hand. I could see Zoe was in her body, aware of her sensations, able to let her body lead. I knew this embodied emptiness was safe for her. I could invite Zoe to keep walking to the center of that emptiness without concern that she would get lost in thoughts about how scary emptiness is. In my own body, in my own experience, I was not scared or tense. I was transmitting safety and comfort. We were in it together.

So what can you do, dear reader, when you don't have me, or someone you trust, to be with you when *you* are facing unfamiliar sensations or scary emotions? The good news is that I've devised a process, VIVO,[5] to increase your ease and sense of safety while learning the language of your body. VIVO gives you a simple method for reducing stress any time.

Getting Down with Your Body: The VIVO Process

VIVO means "I live" in Spanish. The VIVO process is about being fully alive. An early intention for VIVO was to help recovering addicts learn to find peace and pleasure through other means than drugs. A year-long pilot research project at the Sanoviv Health Institute in Baja revealed that use of VIVO also showed a statistically significant ability to reduce pain.[6]

Some years ago, a woman named Clara found VIVO on my website. Clara was a reserve army nurse who had been deployed to a hospital across the country from her home at the beginning of the Iraq war. She was very stressed by her new situation, missed her family and said she was a nervous wreck. She had a responsible position at the army hospital and was called on to do lots of public speaking and public relations work. Clara used VIVO for 28 days and called me to report that not only did her emotional upset now last hours instead of days, but she had also lost a lifetime fear of public speaking!

Although initially designed to be used 28 days consecutively to build new habits, you can use VIVO any way you'd like. You can use it for body bonding and sensation learning, stress relief, studying for exams, public speaking, or as a way of preparing for sleep at the end of the day. Many clients and colleagues swear by VIVO to get a good night's sleep.

To try VIVO, you'll need about nine minutes and a minute timer. There are three separate three-minute sections to VIVO. Use a timer with a reasonably pleasant ring or buzz. First read through the entire process a couple times until you're sure you understand it and can remember what to do. (You can also download an audio clip from my website with me guiding the process if you'd like.)

Keep your **Sensation Checklist** handy for easy reference. Find a quiet place to sit or lie down, placing the timer nearby. Be sure your clothes are loose and comfortable. Finally, prepare to set a new goal *each* time you do the VIVO process.

Sample goals might be: "I am easily learning the language of my body." "I am comfortable being in my body now." "I am trusting my body is my ally." "I am relaxed and carefree as I drop into my body." Find words that mean something to you. Phrase your intended goal in the present tense. That means you'll need to begin your sentence with the words "I am." Now you're ready to go. Set the timer for three minutes, drop into your body, and enjoy!

VIVO

First, set your intention to feel safe.[7] Say silently or out loud: "I am safe and calm now" (or some variation of this). Next, drop your awareness down into your body. As you prepare to focus solely on body sensations, imagine for a moment you are an angel or extraterrestrial having your first experience in a human body. You have no preconceived notions about what anything means. You only notice that some sensations feel good, some bad and some neutral. Letting go of judgments about what things mean will enable you to explore body sensations with equanimity. Imagine all body sensations are arising in your awareness for the first time.

Next, direct your awareness to the qualities and dimensions of any sensations that *don't feel good* (numbness, clammy hands, tightening gut, increasing heart rate, etc.). Focus on these sensations for three minutes. Ask yourself how wide, deep, prevalent and/or intense these uncomfortable sensations are. Be specific and clinical as if you were writing a report on your observations.

After three minutes of this, scan your body for pleasurable sensations such as warmth, strength, pulsation, tingling, etc. Check your feet, legs, shoulders, ears for sensations that feel good. Now, shift your awareness back and forth between the sensations that feel good and the sensations that don't for another three minutes. Imagine you are on a carefree swing, arcing gracefully back and forth between sensations that do and don't feel good. Notice how your awareness can swing effortlessly between clammy hands and strong legs, a tight gut and solid feet. Notice, also, that you are big enough to include all aspects of your experience. At the end of three minutes, you'll discover your body has been easing up and relaxing, even if just slightly, as you've been swinging your awareness back and forth between sensations that feel bad and sensations that feel good.

Finally, focus only on the increasing (subtle or not-so-subtle) experience that something in your body is easing. Scan your body to find as many sensations as you can that feel good. Spend another three minutes focusing *just* on what feels pleasurable in your body. As you finish, scan your body and look for (subtle or not-so-subtle) sensations that signal that you are feeling safe. Notice how your breathing has become more regular, how your gut is looser, maybe even pleasantly warm. Notice how your hands are warm and tingly. Notice how you feel some warmth spreading across your shoulders, how your feet and legs feel strong. Even if you do not feel *completely* calm yet, notice that things are definitely easing up in your body. Keep focusing only on what is feeling better.

At the end of these nine minutes, ask yourself whether you'd like to take a little break from reading to give yourself time to enjoy feeling peaceful again. Of course, if you feel resourced enough, you may decide you want to continue reading.

Additional Information about VIVO

When I've led this process at workshops, people have all kinds of responses. Most find VIVO relaxing, soothing, reassuring. Some report pain vanishing or diminishing. Some have a hard time finding sensations that feel bad, some have a hard time finding sensations that feel good. Some have a hard time finding sensations at all.

If you had a hard time finding sensations that feel good, try to recall a time when you *did* feel good, when something good happened to you. Notice what happens in your body as you remember this. Look again for sensations that feel good. It is fine to take your time with this. Let your attention become ever more subtle. You may need to ratchet down your expectations. You're learning a whole new language.

Certain substances make it harder for VIVO to work its magic. If you are pumped on caffeine, wired on sugar, high on alcohol or stoned on marijuana or other drugs, the VIVO process probably just won't work. No blame. Give yourself a break. Try it another time.

What about Depression and Anxiety?

Are depression and anxiety sensations or emotions? The answer, for the purposes of Emotional Medicine, is no – they're states of mind. Depression and anxiety are accompanied by sensations, but they're not sensations or emotions in themselves.

The sensations comprising depression are (among others): heaviness, listlessness, numbness, frozenness and contraction. If you break an anxious state down into its discrete parts you'll find sensations of jitteriness, numbness, unsettledness and uneasiness, among others.

Depression and anxiety hang in the air like a weather inversion – thick, stultifying and *immobile*.[8] No matter what you try, they won't budge. The key to distinguishing between emotions like sadness and fear and states of mind like depression and anxiety is to see *whether they can move*. Do they ebb and flow, rise and fall? If those experiences don't change, if they're static, it's not emotion you're dealing with, it's a state of mind immobilization.

In the next chapter you'll learn more about this immobilization response and how to cooperate with nature's plan for unwinding any stuck energy. You'll also discover the 10 natural ways you can soothe and manage any anxiety and depression you experience.

SIX

Attend to Anxiety and Depression

Rachel arrived at my office in a state of anxiety. I hadn't seen Rachel, an accomplished administrator for a prestigious art foundation, in several years, since we'd used Emotional Medicine to work through a devastating relationship breakup and done healing work on myriad childhood abandonments. She said she didn't think she could use any Emotional Medicine just now because she wasn't feeling emotions – only anxiety and lovesickness.

Rachel was excited because she believed her new lover, Stella, was "the one." They were due to move in together in just a week. In light of this upcoming event, Rachel's anxiety and sporadic obsessive "tidying" disorder were rising to dysfunctional levels. Rachel was afraid that, once Stella saw how compulsive she could be about keeping things in order, she would end the relationship.

I knew that Rachel's "tidying" was one way she managed fears and feelings when memories of early abandonments were triggered by current life events. It was understandable that this potent new relationship might kick up some anxiety about being abandoned again. I figured that at some time we'd likely need to do more healing emotional work together. However, I also knew there were times the "tidying" was a nonissue for Rachel. I wondered if there might be something else contributing to Rachel's increased anxiety.

During our talk I noticed that Rachel, a tall, trim beauty, was looking especially slim. I commented on this and asked her how her diet had been lately. "Well," she said, "since Stella and I fell in love, I haven't had any appetite. I've barely been able to eat. I'm eating mainly yogurt and fruit."

"How much coffee and diet soda are you drinking?" I queried. "I drink a cup or two of coffee in the morning and then maybe one or two diet sodas throughout the day," Rachel replied.

Oy vey, I thought (reverting to an internalized Jewish mother voice picked up during my first marriage), no wonder Rachel's "tidying" is getting out of hand. Caffeine is poison for anyone with anxiety because it can mimic those very symptoms. Furthermore, the food Rachel was eating was not helping her nervous or endocrine system function smoothly. Her blood sugar levels couldn't normalize without additional protein and essential fatty acids. Like caffeine, low blood sugar can also masquerade as anxiety.

While Rachel obviously had life stress reasons igniting her "tidying" behavior, her anxiety was also fueled by the simple fact that she was hungry and over-caffeinated. Rachel wasn't eating enough to ground herself and calm her brain and the caffeine was jangling her nerves.

"Are you exercising regularly?" I asked as I continued my search for the reasons Rachel was having such a hard time. Rachel replied that everything had been so topsy-turvy since she met Stella that she had also let go of her regular exercise routine.

So, dear reader, there you have it. A normally stressful[1] life event, falling in love and moving in with a new partner, becomes a diagnosable disorder in part due to inadequate nutrition, caffeine overstimulation and lack of the mood management effects of regular aerobic exercise. (And, of course, in part also due to her history of childhood trauma.)

I asked Rachel if she wanted me to refer her out for a medication consultation. Rachel responded that she had come to me in part because she wanted to start with a non-medication approach. OK then: if she wanted to give a natural approach a try, I suggested she add more protein – particularly fish with its abundance of brain-soothing good fats (Omega-3s) – to her diet, as well as adding 30 minutes of daily aerobic exercise. I reassured her that she could stop this regimen at any time and we could set up a psychiatric consultation for medication. She was clear that she wanted to start by changing her diet and resuming her exercise program.

I ended our session with the VIVO process, to help Rachel feel settled and comfortable in her body once again. I reminded Rachel that she could use VIVO any time she was feeling edgy, to restore a sense of calm resourcefulness.

Rachel returned three weeks later. She told me that the combination of diet and exercise had diminished her anxiety and tidying behavior so much that she was no longer troubled by it. Stella and she had moved in and the relationship was going well. Rachel no longer felt undermined by low-grade anxiety about Stella abandoning her.

Some months later, Rachel brought Stella in for a couples' session to work through some of the typical control issues now surfacing in their relationship. While childhood abandonment provided the subtext for Rachel's responses, and Stella's concomitant over-responsible tendencies provided the subtext for her responses, we could explore all of this without the heightened stress of Rachel's extreme anxiety. As long as she stayed balanced in her eating and limited her caffeine, she could soothe her anxiety without medications or excessive tidying. (As of this writing, Rachel and Stella married, and last year Rachel gave birth to their baby.)

First Things First

If anxiety or depression is interfering with your ability to feel emotions, you, like Rachel, may not be ready to take any Emotional

Medicine just yet. Your first job is learning to soothe your anxiety or depression enough to feel emotionally alive and present in the here and now. Fortunately, there are many natural paths you can traverse to help you do this.

As always, if you feel you need medication, ask your doctor for an evaluation. Not everyone can shift things without medication as Rachel did. When symptoms are too debilitating, medication can sometimes help you remember what it's like to feel "normal" again. Once you've returned to a baseline of well-being, you can always ease back into non-medication approaches if you choose. Everything you learn here about non-medication approaches will also help you increase well-being even if you are already on medication.

Your two biggest natural anxiety-soothing/depression-diminishing aids are nutrition and exercise. As I was researching articles for this book, I was delighted to discover that there is now an emerging area of study called "nutritional neuroscience." The evidence is clear. Depression and anxiety are definitely impacted by what you eat and how much you move. The right balance of protein, essential fatty acids, minerals, carbohydrates and probiotics (apparently, the good bacteria that keep your gut happy also help keep *you* happy[2]) can make the difference between feeling anxious and miserable, or calm and confident. Research shows that eating fish or taking fish oil supplements works to treat depression without medication. Break out the sardines!

As for exercise, a 1999 research study at Duke University demonstrated that depressed adults who exercised regularly improved as much as those treated with the drug sertraline (commonly known as Zoloft).[3] Recent research by psychologists Jasper Smits and Michael Otto validates these results and shows that exercise affects brain chemistry in much the same way that antidepressant drugs do, by influencing the key neurotransmitters serotonin and norepinephrine. Smits and Otto point out that after just one 30-minute episode of vigorous exercise, people experience an immediate mood lift.[4] Make a note of this!

In addition, studies at the University of Georgia demonstrate that regular exercise switches on certain genes to *decrease* the body's stress response. Other research suggests that exercise also increases the production of a substance (BDNF, or brain-derived neurotrophic factor) which helps maintain and grow brain cells. Not only do you get an immediate mood boost from exercise, but simultaneously you are decreasing your stress levels while making yourself smarter! What's more, after several months of regular exercise, other great side effects kick in – you'll have increased cardiovascular health and be able to lose pounds and/or stabilize your weight.

These results have been so hopeful that Dr. Smits is surprised that more scientists aren't working in this area. (Perhaps the fact that there's no big money in free natural fixes has something to do with this.) Here's my checklist of natural mood managers and soothers for anxiety and depression.

Anxiety and Depression Non-Medication Checklist

1. **Check Nutrition:** Are you eating enough protein, essential fatty acids and carbohydrates in the right proportion for you? I have counseled way too many young, thin, vegetarian men and women as well as older, overweight, junk food-addicted men and women who were not getting adequate nutrition and ended up with severe mental problems. Food is a drug. Food is medicine. Healthy food is essential for happy, healthy living. If you are a vegetarian, it is especially important that you carefully address your nutritional needs. This takes more work, but I urge you to be as compassionate to yourself and your body as you are to the body of any animal you refuse to kill. If you are a senior citizen, it is also crucial that you get adequate nutrition to protect your aging body. This may take more effort than you feel like making. But remember: Your life depends on it.

    A. **Caffeine:** Are you drinking too much coffee, caffeinated tea or soda, or eating too much chocolate? If this resonates, switch to decaf. Try doing without chocolate (which has caffeine) unless the notion of giving it up is too anxiety-producing. If you can't give up chocolate, consume it with protein. (I'll often eat some nuts, smoked salmon, vegan rice protein drink, turkey dog or chicken breast.)

B. **Sugar Intake:**[5] Are you eating too much sugar, or eating it without balancing it with protein? Try eliminating or vastly reducing your sugar intake. If you can't give it up, eat protein with it.

C. **Alcohol and Drugs:** Are you drinking too much alcohol or taking too many recreational drugs? When you do this, your liver and pancreas are stressed. Things are *not OK* for them as they try to cope with toxic substances that interfere with healthy functioning. This often translates to your mind as some version of *"I'm* not OK." (A side note: check all prescription drugs to see if anxiety or depression is listed as a potential side effect. If so, consult with your doctor about changing prescriptions.)

D. **Food Allergies:** Eating foods your body doesn't like can create mental symptoms similar to anxiety and depression. Use your intuition to try and identify foods you suspect may be the culprits. *Hint:* these are typically foods you crave. Eliminate suspects one at a time from your diet for one week each. Notice results when you resume eating potential problem food. Keep a food/mood diary: write down everything you eat and then write down your subsequent moods. If this doesn't help and you still think food may be at play, get a formal workup with an allergist.

E. **Low Blood Sugar:** Low blood sugar masquerades as both anxiety and depression so often that I wish every doctor would check for this before prescribing medication. If you get lightheaded or really cranky or feel "down" when you go too long without eating, you may have low blood sugar. Remedy this with regular eating of protein/fat/carb meals. Always carry nuts or protein bars in your briefcase or purse. If that doesn't work, have your blood sugar checked professionally.

F. **High Blood Sugar:** Undiagnosed or poorly managed diabetes can also lead to symptoms which look like anxiety or depression. Diabetes can be a serious, life-threatening illness. If you suspect you have this issue, check with your doctor immediately.

2. **Check Exercise:** Are you moving enough? Are you getting enough aerobic exercise? Based on well-tested protocols, Drs. Smits and Otto recommend 30 minutes of moderate-intensity aerobic exercise five times per week, or 30 minutes of high-intensity exercise three times per week. No one knows whether more would be better or less would work just as well because that hasn't been studied. Be your own guinea pig. Figure out what works best for you. It seems that exercising is our normal condition and being sedentary is not.[6]

3. **Check Sleep:** Lack of adequate sleep may also give you symptoms of anxiety and depression. (Of course the converse is also true. Anxiety and depression can create sleep disorders but, for now, let's start with the simplest level of intervention.) Are you going to bed too late? Are you watching too much TV or working too late on your computer in the evenings before bed? Are you drinking alcohol or eating sugary things before bed? Sugar and alcohol can mess with your sleep. Turning off the TV and/or computer an hour before bed will give your nervous system time to unwind from electronic stimulation so you can get a good night's sleep.

4. **Check Sunlight:** Lack of adequate exposure to sunlight can create anxiety and depression. As a matter of fact, there is a medically

recognized diagnosis called SAD or Seasonal Affective Disorder. You need sunlight to function well and feel happy. While you can supplement with Vitamin D or specially manufactured light boxes, if you have access to natural light, get yourself out in it for at least 10 minutes a day.

5. Check Water Intake: Are you drinking enough water? Your body is 75 percent water. Brain tissue is 85 percent water. Staying hydrated helps your body perform *all* its jobs better. In his book, *Your Body's Many Cries for Water*, Dr. F. Batmanghelidj describes the benefits of drinking water as an aid in the treatment of stress, obesity, insomnia, asthma, back pain and more. If you only wait to drink water until your mouth is dry, you are waiting too long. When your mouth is dry, you're already in a state of extreme dehydration.

6. Check Time in Nature: Are you spending time in woods, mountains, deserts and beaches? Nature is an amazing mood manager. Whether this is because nature reflects the glory of God or Spirit, or because natural settings are filled with negative ions which have positive effects on humans, time in nature can restore *your* spirit. Find a greenbelt, park or hidden canyon near you and be in it.

7. Check Getting a Pet: Having the companionship of an animal can be an enormous aid in soothing anxiety and depression. Petting an animal has proved to lower blood pressure and decrease stress. If you can afford it, are not allergic and can take care of it, get a pet.

8. Check Homeopathy: I refer most of my clients for homeopathic treatment, because I find it a gentle, natural way of balancing body systems, as well as an effective method for soothing anxiety and depression. I highly recommend it for readers who want to find nonchemical solutions for bodymind distress. Check the web for information about this highly regarded 200-year-old natural healing method which is regularly utilized in Germany,[7] England, France, Brazil and India.

9. **Check Suppressed Emotion:** Finally, check for glimmers of emotion. If you can, drop awareness drop down into the sensations underpinning your depression and anxiety. Those sensations are fluid. They'll *naturally* begin to shift and change. Your body will be better able to lead you to and through whatever underlying emotion has been stuck. Once freed, those emotions can move and you can take some Emotional Medicine. Anger and fear often disguise themselves as anxiety, while sadness may surface as depression (and yes, certainly vice versa).

A caveat: Checking for suppressed emotion can be tricky. If you feel relieved reading that you may have suppressed emotion hiding beneath your anxiety or depression, *and you feel safe and settled enough in your skin to proceed, go ahead and feel into what's there. Speak out about it to yourself or someone who cares.* Find solace for any grief with loved ones. Try *skillful non-dumping* communication of any anger to involved parties. Arrange protection for any scared feelings. Remember, it can diminish your anxiety just to label underlying anger as anger, sadness as sadness, or fear as fear as you go about getting the support you need.

10. **Check Emotional Support:** Do you have emotionally supportive relationships? If yes, seek soothing from loved ones. If no, seek support from a professional counselor so you won't have to be alone when experiencing deep hurts.

Anxiety, Depression and the Immobilization Response

If you've gone through this checklist and essentially ruled out or remedied physiological causes, you may still find yourself subjected to anxiety or panic attacks. In addition to poor nutrition, lack of adequate exercise or other causes discussed above, the causes of both anxiety and depression may also include hereditary tendencies, traumatic events, a painful childhood, even social and political upheaval. Although the symptoms of anxiety and depression are often different, these two conditions are linked in important ways.

Recent research at the University of Minho in Portugal indicates that when you're depressed and/or anxious, your stress response system is *always* activated. Worrisome thoughts are keeping your body in a *constant state of vigilance*, preparing you for dangers which may never occur. This chronic experience of what they call "immobilized agitation" prevents you from riding normal waves of excitement/fear and peace/relaxation in daily life. Constant stress becomes the norm.

While it seems obvious that this kind of continual hyperalert state could easily lead to anxiety disorders, this research also indicates that chronic low-grade stress is one of the causal factors for depression as well. Any skills you develop to manage anxiety may help preclude ensuing depression.

If the phrase "worrisome thoughts that keep you in a constant state of vigilance" sounds familiar, that's because you already know how worrisome thoughts prevent you from accessing the feel-good-fast remedies Emotional Medicine offers. Here they are culprits again, capable of keeping you in a constant state of immobilized agitation.

However, what you may not know about this uncomfortable state of agitated immobilization is that it is a specifically human distortion of your mind's attempt to protect you from future trauma and/or a misinterpretation of your body's attempt to recover from past trauma.[8]

An anxious state which may be wreaking havoc on your life now was once a solution for survival. Remember, your human mind is more drawn to negative memories than positive ones because they have greater survival value. It's important to know which events lead to danger. When your mind goes over and over negative events, at least part of that relentless recycling originates in an attempt to protect you.

In a similar vein, agitated immobility is a distortion of one of the instinctual strategies your body uses to help you survive disaster. That strategy is called "freezing," also known as "playing dead." Understanding this instinctual freeze response, learning how to thaw out from any freezing (whether current or triggered by past incidents) and getting your life energy moving again gives you essential strategies for self-soothing.

Fight, Flight, Freeze and Flop: Nature's Gifts

Fight, Flight, Freeze and Flop are nature's gifts to improve your chances of surviving danger and avoiding a painful death. In any threatening situation, your instincts size up the scene long before your mind can formulate a plan and mobilize your entire bodymind to take the defensive gesture that will give you the best odds for survival and pain aversion.

This instantaneous assessment and marshalling of resources includes priming the muscles in your hands and legs to fight or flee; preparing to release massive quantities of hormones into your heart and body to inure you to pain and give you endurance and strength beyond normal limits; and the paradoxical ability to lie completely immobilized even as your body is poised for powerful action.

If you survive danger by fighting or fleeing, you are much less likely to develop an anxiety disorder. The reason is that the *actions* of running and/or fighting enable you to release the mobilized energy in your body. As a result, once you're safe, your body is spent, able to rest – and impacted by the feel-good hormones that follow intense exertion.

Distortion is more likely after you survive danger by freezing, feigning death or cooperating with a predator. This is because when you freeze or cooperate (in hopes that a predator will pass you by or not harm you), your survival depends on being *temporarily* physically immobilized and emotionally numb. The key word here is *temporary*.

In those cases, your instincts determine that running, fighting or *making any active defensive gesture or movement at all* would be too dangerous for the time being.[9] You have to appear, to the predator or any outside observer, perfectly still, compliant or dead.

Of course, inside your body, your nervous system is racing. Beneath an immobilized or compliant surface are a pounding heart, a clenching gut and tightening muscles ... outwardly invisible, inwardly intense micro-movements.

Even though you're frozen, those instincts to fight and flee are still there, waiting to move. Your emotions also await a safe moment so they can move. When you're frozen, your body is not the only part of you that is immobilized. *Your emotions are also temporarily numb.*

The most extreme form of a freeze response is a "flop" or complete collapse. In those moments, you don't have your sympathetic nervous system secretly pounding away. Rather your parasympathetic nervous system takes over as your organ systems start systematically shutting down. This is to prepare your body and spare you the agony of a violent death. In the case of such acute, *temporary* shutdown, if you don't receive immediate medical attention, you can die. This kind of frozen collapse explains why people can be "scared to death."

No Blame for Freezing, Feeling "Stuck" or "Dead" (You had no choice!)

Unfortunately, your advanced human mind has a hard time unwinding and recovering from these temporarily immobilized states. After surviving, you can still feel subtly frozen or dead for days, weeks, months, even years after a traumatic event without realizing that it is happening. If one of your ongoing complaints is that you feel "stuck" and your life is not moving in the direction you'd like, you may still be suffering from energy bound up in your nervous system from an earlier traumatic event.

Tragically, many victims who survive trauma by freezing blame *themselves* for not fighting or fleeing. Whenever the freeze response is used, it's because your brilliant body has sized up the situation and sees that freezing offers your best chance for survival. There is no volition in freezing, and there is no shame.

If you are one of those people still blaming yourself for freezing in response to danger, dear reader, see if you can feel a bit of relief just reading that you had no choice. Your freezing was a natural, instinctual response to aid your survival. And if you're reading this, it must have worked, because you survived! However, while there is no volition or shame in freezing or any habitual sense of numbness or stuckness, there is often ongoing panic and anxiety.

Panic and Anxiety – Particular Human Problems

You won't find many animals in the wild suffering from anxiety disorders.[10] When a rabbit narrowly escapes a fox's jaws, he clicks his heels and scampers off. Even if the rabbit initially froze to avoid detection, once the fox is gone, he will resume his rabbit life without complication. In a natural setting, all that matters to a brain without a highly developed cerebral cortex (and its propensity for worrisome thoughts) is being alive and safe now.

For humans, it's a different story. Panic and anxiety are a particular legacy of the advanced human brain. Even when the coast is finally clear, even when you've survived danger, you may not feel like clicking your heels and happily resuming your human life. You still have to deal with the tendency of your brain to replay an upsetting event over again and again, especially if you haven't been able to fully thaw out afterwards.

Long after a devastating experience, racing thoughts and heartbeats can be triggered by seemingly innocent sights, sounds, smells and images reminiscent of the original upset. Suddenly you find yourself anxious and you don't know why.

Although you may not have a clue about what is happening, your body is still reacting with instinctual intelligence to protect you from a subconsciously perceived threat (whether real or not), and/or trying to discharge the accumulated stress of an earlier trauma which has been triggered.

Unfortunately, you could stay frozen, stuck or anxious just because you didn't know the plan nature has devised to help you thaw and unwind any agitated immobilization left over from freezing. Rest assured, though: while your nervous system may still need some unwinding, it is always primed to do so. At the level of bodily sensations, frozen doesn't stay frozen, stuck doesn't stay stuck and dead doesn't stay dead.

Shake, Rattle and Roll[11]: Your Body's Plan for Unwinding

There are three instinctual actions your body takes to unwind stress when you've survived danger by freezing. These are:

1. Rolling your neck side to side to look for additional danger (the orienting response),
2. Trembling and shaking your muscles and limbs, and
3. Allowing some of the motions of fighting and/or running (at a minimum, with micro-movements in arms and legs) that your instincts wisely prevented you from making during danger.

Peter Levine, author of the seminal books *Waking the Tiger* and *In an Unspoken Voice,* and producer of the CD series *Healing Trauma,* describes how strong your nervous system's agenda is to complete these three instinctual actions, come heck or high water. He advises that no matter what kind of psychological and/or "talking it through" attention you give yourself after a scary event, if you don't cooperate with these innate *body* programs, some aspect of your nervous system may remain tied in a knot of thwarted instinct.

Of these three, the orienting response may be easiest to understand and cooperate with. Whenever you've survived danger, you still need to look around and take stock of your surroundings to be sure you're safe before you do anything else. If you're alone and you've survived, you'll probably do this automatically and naturally. However, if a well-meaning first responder tries to immobilize your head on a stretcher or some other way, this instinctive head rolling will be thwarted. This could set you up for ongoing neck pain.

As for shaking and shivering, the very action designed to help you discharge the pent-up energy mobilized for your aid may scare you into resisting if you don't know what's up. Post-danger shaking and trembling are *designed* to help your body release any remaining agitation. Unfortunately, these responses are often mistaken for the terror which has already left your system.

Shaking and trembling mean you've survived; they're cause for celebration. They are a natural aftermath to traumatic events. Now educated, you can say to yourself, "Oh good, I'm shaking and discharging stress. All is well!"

Similarly, when thawing, you may feel an urge to punch or kick something. You might also resist this if you don't realize it's another natural unwinding mechanism. You can cooperate with this urge by shaking your hands as if they were rattles, discharging the fighting energy your instincts prevented you from expressing. Punching a pillow, punching the air – these actions also help you let go of residual agitation in your body.

You may also feel some subtle activation in your legs and/or an urge to run. Another good thing! Your body is still working to release energy that was immobilized and is no longer needed. Go for a run or a brisk walk to support your body in unwinding that agitation, or at least take a moment and imagine doing so while you make small running-like movements with your legs.

Finally, the last aspect of unwinding after freezing involves feeling emotions again. It is very likely that you will feel like crying. Research shows that crying often indicates your body is shifting from an agitated, scared state to a relaxed and calm state. Crying is a sign you are coming back to yourself. You need not be embarrassed about this. It is a *natural completion* of post-trauma healing. It typically signals relief.

Of course, you may also feel anger or grief after surviving danger once you're back to safety. Again, totally normal! When you can feel your emotions and you're settled in your skin, it is safe to take Emotional Medicine. Find a safe place and/or person and allow mad, sad and scared feelings to complete their natural cycle.

Any or all of the above-mentioned shaking, rattling and rolling may emerge in obvious or subtle ways either immediately after you've survived danger or after it's long passed. As a matter of fact, just reading these last pages may have triggered a conscious or subconscious memory of your own panic and anxiety. You may already be experiencing some arousal in your sympathetic nervous system via an increase in your heartbeat, sweat in your palms, or anxious thoughts.

If so, fear not. I've developed three brief protocols which will help you feel safer in a matter of minutes. One is for orienting, the second for mild anxiety and the third for acute anxiety. It may help if you consider that any activation in your body now gives you an opportunity to learn how to thaw out and release residual stress later.

Remember, your body is not designed to keep replaying trauma over and over. It's designed to find you the quickest, safest, route back to well-being. There is a deep well of healing inside your brilliant body, your "bff" (best friend forever). If you are not experiencing an increase in distress now, what you are about to read can function as an inoculation for future anxious moments.

Below are three soothing protocols: **Orienting to Safety, Soothing Mild Anxiety** and **Calming Acute Anxiety**. Read through them all before you try anything. As always, if you don't feel comfortable trying them, don't do it. Listen to your own wisdom. Ultimately, you know best. If it seems overwhelming to try these processes by yourself, find a therapist trained in body-oriented trauma healing to help you unwind and restore resourcefulness.

The first step to soothing yourself is to assess your distress. Drop your attention into your body to gauge your distress level – none to mild, intermediate, or acute. Focus only on body sensations. (You may want to refer back to the last chapter for a list of these sensations.) Take a moment to check your heart rate, the condition of your palms, sensations in your stomach, and overall body temperature (i.e., are you warm, hot, cool or cold?). Depending on what you discover, choose the protocol(s) that seems most appropriate.

ACTION TIP: ORIENTING TO SAFETY – FOR ALL LEVELS OF DISTRESS

No matter what level your distress, it always helps to orient yourself to your current surroundings. Take a breath and consciously look around you. Roll your head from right to left. Look up and down; turn around to see what's behind you. Be specific in terms of the beauty, comfort and safety of your current setting. Spend three minutes being present with what is true about where you are right now. This will help your nervous system take in the information that you are safe in the present. Notice if you are too hot or cold and take action to remedy that. Notice if you are comfortable in your chair and take action to remedy that. Repeat as needed.

ACTION TIP: SOOTHING MILD ANXIETY

Use the VIVO process described in the last chapter.

ACTION TIP: CALMING ACUTE ANXIETY

If you feel *very* anxious and/or agitated, you may want to apply the following Calming Protocol. If this doesn't work, consult your doctor.

First, imagine again that you are an extraterrestrial having your first experience in a human body. As such, you have no preconceptions about what any experience of agitation, arousal or anxiety means. It's just an experience. Set your intention to be safe, and say silently or aloud, "I am safe and calm now" (or your own variation on that theme). Look around the room and orient yourself to your current, safe situation.

Next, locate sensations in your body that *only feel good.* (Good places to look are hands, feet, legs, arms and ears.) These might be very small and subtle. That's fine. It may help to tune into how comfortably the chair or sofa is holding your body. Sink into that support. Feel your feet resting easily on the solid floor. Rocking in a rocking chair or rocking back and forth while you hug yourself can also generate pleasurable sensations.

Make yourself a cup of herbal tea and focus on the soothing sensations in your throat and stomach as you drink the warm liquid. (No coffee or green or black tea, however, because caffeine can fool you into thinking you're anxious again.) If you are at home, consider taking a lavender or Epsom salts bath so you can focus on the warm, soothing pleasure spreading throughout your body. (If that's not possible, try imagining slipping into a nice warm bath.) As you do this, check your body again for pleasurable sensations. Look for the smallest hint of pleasure, ease or relaxation and cleave to it. This is your body trying to soothe you.

If you have trouble finding sensations that feel good, bring back a happy memory. Recall a time when you *did* feel good. Be specific and detailed about that memory: Where were you, what were you wearing, what was the season, who was with you? Focus on that memory until you feel even the tiniest pleasurable sensations arising in your body.

Focus *only* on anything that feels good in your body for three minutes. Notice the intensity, breadth, prevalence and temperature of the pleasurable sensations. After three minutes, while you are still focusing *only* on feel-good sensations, get up from your chair or bed and move around for another three minutes. Shake your hands and feet a few times. Make some sounds … sighs, growls, groans … *ahhhhhh.* Again, be sure you are warm or cool enough. Add a sweater or open a window if you need to regulate body and room temperature for comfort.

Finally, whatever you do, *stay out of your thoughts or sensations unless they are happy, pleasurable ones.* If your breathing has eased enough so you can focus on it comfortably, keep your attention on the exhale. Notice how your body settles and releases a bit every time you breathe out. Keep looking for and/or creating pleasurable sensations until you feel your body is signaling that your calming, parasympathetic nervous system is back on board. These sensations will feel something like warm, soft, flowing, tingly, strong and solid. Keep in mind the Calming Protocol may take longer than the nine-minute VIVO protocol. Stay with it!

Sooner or later, one or all of these techniques will work. You may even have some techniques of your own that you've used in the past. Bring them on. I promise, if you stay out of anxious thoughts up in your head and keep your awareness focused down in your body on whatever sensations feel good, you will calm down. This (panic) too shall pass.

Georgia Comes Back to Herself

Georgia, a 32-year-old insurance account representative, called for an emergency session after she discovered her boyfriend, Geoff, was having an affair with a coworker. When Georgia arrived at my office, her face was white, her eyes glassy. She wasn't crying; she wasn't even tearing up. It seemed all emotion had been drained out of her. When I asked how she was feeling, she said, "I'm worthless. Something must be wrong with me. No one will ever love me."

Georgia couldn't stop thinking bad things about herself. Her statements whirled wildly from one reason she was at fault to the next as she tried to make sense of this devastating loss. I didn't consider trying Emotional Medicine because I suspected she was numb and *didn't know it.*

Georgia was exhibiting all the signs of emotional shock. When she finally stopped talking for a moment, I gently asked what was happening in her body. Georgia replied, "I don't feel anything in my body. I'm numb. I can't stop thinking about Geoff and that other woman."

Even though Georgia *said* she couldn't feel anything, I could see that just directing attention to her body had slowed down her breathing and brought a bit more color to her face. This is typically what happens. As soon as you broaden your awareness to include body sensations, any agitation begins subtly to ease up.

Georgia, however, didn't notice the small easing signals I had noticed. She gave her body another quick once-over and returned to the story of her shocking news. I persisted, gently, and asked Georgia to look around the room and tell me what she saw. As she oriented to being in the room with me, I could see she was settling down even more. I invited Georgia to check if she now felt safe enough to focus back on the sensations in her body for a few minutes longer. I explained this would ultimately help her figure out what she needed to do to recover.

Georgia agreed. (A caveat: If Georgia hadn't felt safe focusing on her whole range of body sensations, I would have offered her the Calming Protocol to create some sense of soothing and safety before exploring any deeper pain about Geoff's betrayal.)

Once we were solidly focusing on body sensations, I asked Georgia to describe her numbness exactly: where in her body she felt it, how deep it went. After several moments describing it (predominantly in her torso), Georgia discovered, to her surprise, that numbness was not all she was feeling. She said that her hands and feet felt warm and even tingly.

I suggested Georgia focus her attention on the sensations in her hands and feet, in the same kind of detail she had given to the numbness. I then guided her to shift awareness back and forth between the numbness in her torso, and the tingly alive feeling in her hands and feet (the VIVO process). After several more minutes, I saw still more color coming back into her face. Georgia's breathing was deepening and her whole body was relaxing. As soon as she began to relax, she started trembling and shaking.

I encouraged Georgia to allow that trembling. "It's safe. It's just your body letting go of the stress of this news." After trembling came tears. Once frozen shock melted into warm shaking, Georgia was able to feel her emotions again. She soon realized she was sad and mad at Geoff. She sobbed deeply for a brief time, her shoulders shaking as the grief moved through her. I then invited Georgia to say out loud everything she wanted to say to Geoff, imagining she was looking him right in the eyes.

As Georgia began telling Geoff how she felt, she also felt a strong urge to punch something. I offered pillows. As Georgia punched, she became stronger, more vital, more herself. Her confidence was returning. Now that she was thawed out, Emotional Medicine could do its job!

After a few minutes, Georgia was startled by an insight that popped into her awareness without effort. She realized, she said, that anyone who would lie to her as Geoff did was not the kind of guy she wanted to be with, anyway. Georgia lit up as she realized this. She was radiant and filled with self-esteem.

Although Georgia still had a broken heart, she also now had confidence in hand (and sturdy, grounded feet) and was ready to take steps to continue living. Now, she felt conviction growing to find a relationship that honored her. Georgia created an affirmation to replace her negative self-talk. Her eyes sparkled as she stated, "I am worthy of true and honorable love." I invited Georgia to write this affirmation on different pieces of paper and spread them around her house, car, and office to subtly influence her subconscious programming.

What do you think would have happened if Georgia had tried exploring her worthless, self-hating story before she found enough safety and connection to her body to feel emotions again? Most likely she would have wandered through mental mind fields of myriad betrayals by men, beginning with an absentee father. She would have continued on past ancient monoliths of self-hate and ended up in a prison of ongoing insecurity and low self-esteem. Instead she stayed in her sensations until she thawed out and emotions could then restore her confidence.

This one experience helping Georgia soothe herself didn't take away all her pain. We discussed how Georgia would need to take great care in the days and months ahead to differentiate between the story of this betrayal and her body sensations in order to soothe herself. I encouraged Georgia not to linger in negative thoughts for more than the seconds it took to recognize them. This was important, I explained, because dwelling in the self-hating thoughts could unwittingly work her up into a renewed state of emotional shock.

I advised Georgia that as soon as she became aware she was thinking thoughts such as "No one will ever love me," she needed to drop awareness down into her body to see if she was sad, mad, scared or numb. She could apply the VIVO Protocol or the Calming Protocol when necessary until she felt embodied enough to allow Emotional Medicine to restore well-being. Whenever she felt resourced again, she could speak out her affirmation[12]: "I am worthy of true and honorable love."

It needs to be noted that when Georgia called me for an emergency session, she did so because *she didn't know whom else she could call.* Most of Georgia's girlfriends, family members and even close coworkers had been telling her for months that Geoff was no good. They all had harbored their own suspicions about his less-than-honorable character. Georgia knew she wouldn't feel safe taking her numbed, devastated self to anyone with any of these potential "I-told-you-so" reactions. She instinctively took herself to a place where she knew she was safe and could get the help she needed.

Before Georgia left that day, we discussed what she could do to find emotional support beyond my therapy office. I invited her to make a list of the people closest to her. From this group she could select a few with tender hearts and let them know she needed support, not judgments.

I suggested she start off by telling people that they were right about Geoff. He *wasn't* good for her. However, what she needed now was compassion as she moved through her shock, grief and anger. Georgia could also tell them that even though she had finally discovered what they had suspected all along, she still needed time to recover from the loss of the relationship, and her illusion of what that relationship was.

Distinguishing Anxiety from Fear

As you've seen with Georgia, it's important to get comfortable in your skin after any kind of emotional upset. You've seen, once again, how important it is to distinguish between sensations, thoughts and emotions. You've also learned how important it is to avoid recreating emotional wounds and anxiety reactions by getting out of your head and down into your wise, well-being-seeking body.

However, there is something else you'll need to know before you possess a full assortment of self-care strategies: how to tell the difference between an anxious response triggered by long-gone danger, and an appropriate fearful response triggered by danger now.

While anxiety and panic are distortions of a *past* freeze response, fear is a *present moment* truth-telling, life-saving guide for right now. For example, if you are about to get into an elevator alone with some guy who makes you feel anxious and afraid: *Don't get into that elevator.* Your brilliant body has sized up the situation, read the pheromone signals emanating from his body (indicating his own levels of fear or aggression), and decided he's dangerous.

Gavin de Becker, our nation's leading expert on personal security and safety and author of *The Gift of Fear,* describes countless incidents in which peoples' fear instincts were trying to warn and guide them to safety. In some of these situations, people listened to their fear, followed their instincts and saved themselves. In others, people *talked themselves out of their fear* and the dreadful results were that they, or someone they loved, died. These people couldn't make rational sense of their fear. Their minds couldn't surrender to a seemingly "irrational" caution.[13]

In one of these cases, a mother whose child was about to have a tonsillectomy had an ongoing fearful response to the anesthesiologist. She had met this anesthesiologist at the hospital several times before her son's surgery. She felt uneasy and suspicious of him – not a typical response pattern for her. She talked herself out of making a fuss by saying to herself, "Don't be silly. This prestigious hospital wouldn't hire someone who wasn't skilled and professional."

Tragically, this doctor overmedicated and accidentally killed her young son. Later, the mother discovered this doctor was an alcoholic who was on probation at the hospital. Her fear picked up something that her rational mind never could have deduced.

From now on, instead of trying to "man up" to avoid upsetting anyone, or gritting your teeth and going through with things that scare you, consider becoming fearless about saying, "I'm scared," or "I'm out of here!" When you experience anxiety or panic, look into your body and see if there is some message of caution or danger trying to get your attention, or whether there is just a need to shake, rattle and roll. It's essential to distinguish between these very different circumstances so you can take appropriate action.

In the next chapter you'll learn how multimodal awareness gives you the ability to make these important distinctions. You'll discover how it is possible to feel what you are feeling inside yourself, observe yourself having those feelings, and still maintain awareness of others around you!

SEVEN

Cultivate Multimodal Awareness

As a human being, you are blessed with many modes of aware-ness. That's because you're also blessed with many dimensions of experience: body, emotions, mind, spirit and relationships. Each of these dimensions has its own mode of awareness: sensing, feel-ing, thinking, mystical perceiving and relating. And, here's the really amazing part: while you're experiencing any or all of these dimensions you can also observe yourself having those very experi-ences. Because of your highly developed brain, you can be aware of being aware.

Of all the skills these myriad modes offer you, the three that are essential for Emotional Medicine are *feeling, observing*, and *relating:*

1. *Feeling* **that you need to cry and allowing your tears to come (or allowing any other emotion its embodied movement).**

2. *Observing* **how long any emotion needs to move through your body and noticing when it is done so you can stop and feel good fast.**

3. *Relating* safely and responsibly to yourself and others around you.

Although the concept of multimodal awareness may remind you of multitasking, they are different in an important way.

No Task Involved

Multitasking involves attending to more than one task at the same time, for example, talking to a friend while cooking or doing dishes, using the Internet while watching TV or texting while doing everything else (except, for heavens' sake, *not ever* while driving). In multimodal awareness there is no task involved. When you're employing multimodal awareness, you're not trying to achieve goals; you're just expanding the variety of ways you can be present for your experience. Although both multitasking and multimodal awareness involve focusing attention in several arenas simultaneously, in multimodal awareness there is nothing to finish.

Let's take a closer look at each of these modes – feeling, observing, and relating – to see how they differ from tasks. The *feeling* mode invites you to focus attention in your body to *feel* whether sad, mad, scared, glad energy is present and trying to move. This may mean feeling the most subtle of cues: eyes tearing, chest filling, fists clenching, teeth chattering. *Feeling* these body cues is not a task. It is awareness of an emotion (distinguished from a thought) rising and falling in your experience.

Observing involves witnessing what is happening to you emotionally – whether tears are flowing, fists pounding, or feet stomping. Just as importantly, *observing (along with feeling)* enables you to notice when emotion is subsiding. Both *feeling* and *observing* give you the crucial ability to notice when an emotion completes a cycle and deposits you at the shores of feeling good. This shift from the flow of sad, mad or scared energy, to the easing relaxation of glad energy, is often subtle. *Feeling* and *observing* help you stay present for that. Neither of these are tasks to cross off but rather modes of awareness to inhabit.

Finally, *relating* allows you to stay connected to others and your environment in a respectful way. *Relating* helps you recognize whether you need to find a private place to let emotion move freely without disturbing anyone. Or it helps you realize you're in a time crunch and thus need to settle temporarily for a grunt and/or a shaking of wrists. (I've done a lot of stomping while vacuuming when I needed some Emotional Medicine and had to get the house clean!)

Relating helps you ascertain whether someone is or is not available for emotional support or whether to attend to emotions later when you are safe at home with another friend, family member, teddy bear, or your own loving presence. *Relating* to others is, similarly, not a task, but a way of staying aware of others' needs in addition to your own.

Here's an Action Tip to plant the seed of multimodal awareness:

ACTION TIP

Write the words Feel, *Observe*, and *Relate* on a piece of paper, bolding the first letter of each word as I've done here. (Notice how they form the acronym "**FOR**.") Next, write the following sentence, making sure to note the bold, italic letters there as well: "**F**eeling, **O**bserving, and **R**elating **FOR**ward my ability to cry when I'm sad, stop when I'm done, safely and responsibly, so that I can *feel good fast*." Place this affirmation on your bathroom mirror, fridge, computer stand, car dashboard so you can support this multimodal intention while you're busy.

Being in Three Places at Once

The cornerstone of multimodal awareness involves being present for what you are *feeling* and how you are *relating to* others or the environment around you while at the same time *observing* yourself *feeling* and *relating* ... kind of like being in three places at once. How is that possible?

It's a paradox. And, like all paradoxes, the solution involves recognizing that different aspects of experience may operate simultaneously. A simple illustration is to think of the taste we call bittersweet. How can something be bitter and sweet at the same time? Because there are different receptors on your tongue for bitter and sweet tastes which function *concurrently but distinctly*. And the bittersweet experience is something more than just the improbable sum of two contradictory parts. It becomes a new experience in itself.

The ability to feel things and observe yourself feeling them is similar. Although you have, below the realm of awareness, different areas in your brain responsible for feeling, observing and relating (as well as for all the other modes of awareness), you can still cultivate conscious awareness of these different modes.

As a human, you've spent a lot of time having emotional responses to events without being *aware* that was what you were doing. This is partly due to the fact that emotional responses occur milliseconds before you are aware of them, and partly a response to being raised in a culture which has not valued emotion.[1]

Not being aware of what you are feeling is not such a big deal as long you are reasonably happy and all is well. However, once you're in physical, emotional or relational distress, you realize it would really help if you knew what you were feeling, could distinguish between what you're thinking and feeling, and still stay in relationship to those around you. Learning to distinguish between different types of experience requires the ability to be present for those experiences *and* observe yourself having them at the same time.

An Important Caveat: Observing Does Not Mean Separating

There's confusion, particularly in some spiritual circles, about what observing or witnessing your experience means. For some, "observer" awareness means *separating* yourself from feeling, and/ or resisting immersion in human experience. These "observers" make a spiritual choice to dwell primarily in a transcendent mode of awareness.

Transcendence typically involves leaving behind the travails of the flesh and focusing attention exclusively in awareness. Ramana Maharshi, the great Indian guru, was an example of this. He chose not to treat a tiny skin cancer which ultimately spread to his whole body. His disciples begged him to get treatment to save his life. He is reported to have answered, "Why are you so attached to this body? Let it go."

While Ramana Maharshi exemplifies a revered spiritual path of nonattachment and transcendent consciousness, his death dramatizes an extreme example of *separating* from body and emotional needs. When I speak of the observing mode, I do not mean separating from or transcending the blood, sweat and tears of your human experience. I mean you *stay connected to your body, your human self* even as you are aware and observing that you are distinct from that very body, that very self.

Multimodal awareness is a practice that combines your human tendency (and need) to be present in experience with your human capacity (and need) to be *distinct* from that very experience. In order to access Emotional Medicine remedies, you need to be fully immersed in any *feeling* experience (down to the most subtle movement of emotional energy through your body systems), while simultaneously *not* losing yourself in that experience. This takes practice!

I've configured a process to help you master this challenge. It's based on a classical Psychosynthesis exercise.[2] If you'd like, read this through first as a narrative, then go back and take your time to slow down and participate in each step.

Multimodal Muscle Building

Body: Begin by dropping your awareness into your body. Here's how to do this: Feel (or observe and then feel) in what specific ways your body feels supported by the chair or couch. Observe if you are warm or cold, then feel how warm, how cold. Be precise. Adjust the thermostat, open a window, take off a sweater or add a blanket. Make yourself as comfortable as possible.

Listen for sounds outside yourself in the room, adjacent rooms or outdoors. Let each sound deepen your ability to develop multi-modal awareness. Listen, also, for sounds inside yourself. Is your stomach gurgling? Can you hear your breathing? Observe the rhythm of your breathing. Feel how the breath enters your nose or mouth. Feel the rise and fall of your chest and shoulders. Look for aches and pains; look for good feelings. Differentiate between these. Move your awareness back and forth between pain and pleasure for a few moments. If you feel numb, check the dimensions of this numbness – how wide, how deep. Observe yourself moving aware-ness around in your body.

Look for any place that feels alive. If necessary, find your pulse and feel the beat of life within you. Move awareness back and forth between places of numbness and places of aliveness. As you con-nect with aliveness and numbness, observe that you can assess your overall body experience – do you feel predominantly comfortable, uncomfortable, neutral or 50/50? Notice as you do this that you *are* capable of experiencing your body sensations while simultaneously able to move awareness around in your body. In this way you are *distinct* but not separate from your body's experience. How could you move your awareness around unless it was distinct – something other than body sensation?

Emotions: Make a decision to place this overview of body sen-sation in the background of your awareness while tuning in to your emotional state. Breathe out slowly. Scan yourself for sad, mad, scared or glad emotions. Observe if there's emotional residue from encounters earlier in the day. Don't be surprised if an emotion arises that you didn't know was present. Allow it. Feel it. Observe its rise and fall. If you are emotionally numb, observe and feel the dimen-sions of the numbness. No blame. This is just numbness. (You can stop and attend to this now with VIVO or plan to do that later.)

If at any point you lose touch with your body experience, no problem. That's normal. Just drop back down into sensations (warm, cool, stiff, flowing) for a moment. Remember, strengthening multimodal awareness takes practice in the same way that developing any innate talent does.

Now, intentionally bring body sensations back to the foreground of awareness for a moment to check your jaw for tightness or relaxation. Observe whether your biceps are loose or tight. Notice the quality of energy in your solar plexus – contracted, open, pulsing? Feel sensations in your low back, left and right. (These are all places where you might be holding emotional energy.)

Sum up your predominant emotional state or "tone" at the moment by saying aloud or silently, "Right now I'm feeling _____ (use sad, mad, scared, glad or numb as emotion guides)." No blame. These are just emotions. Watch them roll in and out like waves. Notice whether these emotions need to move more fully to complete an emotional cycle. (Do this now or make a note to take some Emotional Medicine later.) If you feel neutral, peaceful or not stirred by anything, you can consider that a variation of glad. Notice that you are capable of being fully attuned to your emotional experience (with body sensations in the background) at the same time your awareness is *distinct* but not separate from your experience.

Mind: Allow your sense of your emotional "tone" or mood together with your sense of overall body experience to rest lightly in the background of awareness as you prepare to shift focus to your thoughts.

Scan your thoughts to appraise the quality of your thinking. You do this by checking whether your thoughts are focused on problem-solving analysis or whether they're involved with creative intuitive insights. Check if there are images accompanying your thoughts. Notice whether your thinking is narrowly focused on something specific or widely open to a variety of things. Observe whether your thoughts tend to be repetitive, obsessive, anxious or soothing.

Is there a story, an upset, an issue circling around in your thinking? No blame. Just notice. These are just thoughts; let them go by like clouds. Notice that your awareness is capable of observing your thoughts, while still keeping track of your background emotional state and body experience.

Spirit/Soul[3]: Place body, feelings and thoughts in the background while you notice your connection to Spirit. See whether you feel connected or disconnected to Spirit. Just notice without judgment. Perceiving the energy of your spiritual connection is a subtle practice. You may have your own unique markers for this. If you feel connected, notice where you feel this sense of spiritual coupling in your body. (Good places to look are your heart, top of your head, your spine, hands and gut.) See if the experience of spiritual presence is localized or rather an overall body impression.

Observe, now, that spiritual connection is different from awareness. Since awareness can notice whether you feel intimate or estranged from Spirit, it must be different from Spirit. Awareness observes what's happening for you in any moment in *all* dimensions of your being and (if you tune in to it) reports and gives you choices about where to focus your attention and energy.

Relationship: Put your observation of connection or disconnection with Spirit in the background of your awareness of thoughts, feelings and sensations as you prepare to shift focus to your situation vis-á-vis relationships.

Review your current relationships with friends, family, coworkers and your community at large. Are these relationships flourishing? Observe how your heart feels when you consider your important relationships. Is it open, closed, aching, hard? Does positive regard flow back and forth easily? No blame. Bring awareness back occasionally to check in with sensations, feelings, thoughts and spiritual connection while maintaining awareness of the quality of your relationships.

Notice that your multimodal awareness is able to immerse in relatedness with friends/family/community while still keeping subtle track of your background thoughts, emotional state, body experience and spiritual connection, all the time it remains *distinct* but not separate from all of them.

Finally, take a moment to feel fully present in emotions, mind, spirit and relationships as you observe yourself in these various experiences. Enjoy this fullness.

Seeds of Consciousness

Of course, while exercising multimodal awareness, you'll sometimes be more aware of one than another aspect of your experience. You'll need to dip back and forth between various modes to keep them current in consciousness. This is normal.

Just as a beautiful flower begins its life in the soil as a tiny seed or bulb, so can your multimodal awareness blossom when you give it attention and allow it to germinate and grow on its own, natural timetable. You cannot force multimodal awareness to grow, but you can help it. Once you attend to it and cultivate its growth, it will take root and thrive.

If you are the type of person who wants everything done yesterday, you may need to slow down so you can cooperate with this naturally evolving process. Even one moment of multimodal awareness or one minute of bodymindful practice is infinitely better than no awareness or bodymindfulness.[4]

You're probably already better at one or two of these multimodal awareness abilities than the others right now. For example, you might be better at knowing what you're *feeling* than how you are *relating* to what others are feeling. Likewise, you may be better at *observing* yourself than *observing* others – depending on your introversion or extraversion tendencies.[5]

In 1989, when I founded the San Diego Center for Bio-Psychosynthesis, a painful event spotlighted my need to strengthen my observing and relating abilities while in a leadership role. I was giving educational lectures around the United States and leading a training group in San Diego. As had been the practice in my earlier

Psychosynthesis training, I functioned not only as the leader of a group of trainees, but was also involved in collegial/friendship relationships with many of the same people. I was not initially aware of the many problems brewing because of these blurred boundaries.[6]

One day a member of my training group and friendship circle (I'll call her Angela) told me that another member, who was also a friend (I'll call her Bree), was talking with everyone else in the group about my deficiencies in leadership. I was dismayed. I couldn't understand why Bree hadn't brought her concerns to me directly. I felt especially betrayed because Bree and I had made a special pact to tell each other the truth in our relationship. I could feel fury rising within me and knew I needed to resist the impulse to dump this anger on her. I retreated to my office for some anger and grief medicine.

When I was finally settled enough to ask Bree why she hadn't come to me directly, Bree responded that she didn't believe I really wanted to hear negative feedback. I was shocked. This was not how I thought of myself. I *believed* in feedback! Although I was angry Bree had broken our agreement, I immediately began looking for ways I had unwittingly given her this impression. I also tried to discern how I had missed her cues of withholding, dissension and fear.

I underwent a painful self-inventory and realized that part of what she was saying was true. I *was* too easily caught up in adulation and agreement. There was a level on which I was defensive and only wanted to hear what I wanted.

As a result of this experience, I also realized that because I have a charismatic personality, I needed to pay particular attention to the ways people will defer to, comply with (or resist) me based on the strength of my personality. The fact that I prided myself on my ability to give direct feedback to others did not mean others would automatically return the favor. I had not seen the amount of fear Bree had about confronting me. While it was important for Bree to take responsibility for not communicating with me directly, I needed to take responsibility for not *observing* the disparity between her words and actions. I needed to take responsibility for not *relating* sensitively to her spoken and unspoken communications.

Fortunately, this was not the last big opportunity for me to develop my multimodal *relating* skills. There have been other important occasions in which I've honed my growing-edge ability to observe the needs, fears, and reactions of others in my personal life. I, like you, am a work in progress.

If awareness in *relating* skillfully to others is something you'd like to augment, nearly every moment of your everyday life offers terrific opportunities for developing multimodal *relating* skills. Marriages and other kinds of long-term authentic partnerships and friendships are perfect laboratories in which to practice. Invite those close to you to let you know when you are relating sensitively or insensitively to their experience. This goes for parenting, too. Ask your kids for feedback. Let them know you really mean it!

Take a moment now to review your own multimodal awareness abilities, if you'd like. Make a note of your strengths and weaknesses in *feeling*, *observing*, and *relating*. No blame. Be gentle with yourself. Below are two tips to help you strengthen areas you might like to develop.

ACTION TIP: FEELING AND OBSERVING SELF

Set your watch to ping three times a day. At each ping take a moment to notice what you are feeling inside. Then *observe* yourself feeling whatever you're feeling. Be sure to distinguish feeling from thinking. For now, focus primarily on feeling. Experience and observe what's happening in your body, working your way to check for sad, mad, scared, glad emotions. (As always, take Emotional Medicine or use VIVO when necessary.)

ACTION TIP: OBSERVING AND RELATING TO OTHERS

Take a moment in *every* interpersonal encounter to check out what seems to be happening in the relationship. Feel what your connection is like. Feel/sense what seems to be happening to anyone in relation with you. *Observe* whether others are moving toward or away from you, whether they seem happy, sad, fearful or agitated. If appropriate, get feedback. Ask how they feel about being with you and about the way you are being with them.

Ellie Becomes a Good-Enough Mother

Let's take a look at how one woman used *feeling*, *observing* and *relating* to break free from a family pattern of abusive parenting.

Ellie glanced at her watch as she poured steel-cut oats into boiling water to start breakfast. She checked on her two-year-old daughter, Nell, who was playing happily with blocks in a light-filled corner of the kitchen. Ellie felt her heart swell with love for this precious little being. *Nell is so important to me,* she thought. *I'm so glad I can occasionally work at home so I can be here with her. I don't want to miss her childhood.*

Even though Ellie was behind schedule editing a grant proposal, she sat down to play with Nell, letting out a deep exhale. She put the proposal out of her mind and got busy helping Nell build a big castle of blocks. Ellie observed the delight in Nell's eyes as they played together. She could also feel pleasure spread through her own body as she allowed herself to be a kid again. After 15 minutes, she was refreshed and relaxed as she returned to her laptop.

Ellie was a single mother as well as the director of a small environmental consulting firm she'd founded years before adopting Nell. Managing five employees at her firm had barely prepared her for the multimodal awareness skills she needed now as Nell's mother. She didn't realize how easy it was to fall into the parenting style of her parents, even as she swore she would be different.

Throughout the morning, Nell cheerfully interrupted Ellie, bringing various blocks for inspection. At one point Nell dropped a big block on the computer keyboard, wiping out a section Ellie hadn't saved yet. Ellie felt a burst of anger rising. She noticed her face was hot and her teeth were clenched. I'm angry, she observed. Ellie took a breath. This gave her a chance to also observe the innocent look on Nell's face as well as a tinge of fear in her eyes.

Ellie knew she snapped at Nell way too often. She had recently taken parenting classes to help become a less reactive parent. She didn't want her daughter to be afraid of her the way she'd been afraid of her hot-tempered father. *I am not going to dump this anger on Nell,* Ellie said to herself. She was committed to learning a different style of parenting than she had grown up with.

Then Ellie remembered something she'd learned in her parenting class. *Oh, yeah, Nell's just doing what toddlers do.* Ellie took another breath, let out a little grunt, and shook her hands a few times. Although this helped somewhat, she could still feel her stomach was tight.

To Nell she said, "That block makes a clang, doesn't it? Let's take it back to your play corner and hear the sound it makes when you drop it there." She led Nell to the corner where, for a few minutes, they both made a game of dropping blocks to see which ones made the loudest bangs. Ellie made a mental note to see how she felt after she dropped Nell off at the day care center later in the morning. If her stomach was still tight, she could release more of her anger in her parked car.

As Ellie prepared to return to her proposal, the smell of cooked oats told her it was time for breakfast. Almost simultaneously, another not-so-pleasant smell began drifting her way. *Uh oh, dirty diaper,* she thought, as she realized it was also time for a diaper change.

Ellie felt proud that she had not dumped her anger on Nell. She was learning new skills and becoming the parent she wished she'd had. Banging those blocks around was fun and seemed to undo most, if not all, of the knot in her stomach. After a diaper change, Ellie and Nell sat down happily to eat breakfast together.

Big Enough Brain

If you are a woman (especially a single mother) reading about Ellie's morning, you might have thought someone had a camera in part of *your* kitchen. You're used to flowing back and forth between different modes of awareness. This is because, as a woman, you are especially well-suited for multimodal awareness. Women's brains have a larger *corpus callosum*, the area that connects and carries information back and forth between the two hemispheres. This enables you to move with greater ease between feeling, observing and relating. While this makes multimodal awareness easier for you, some also say it makes women more subject to emotional overwhelm or "flooding." This is all the more reason women need to strengthen multimodal abilities and master torrents of emotion.

Having different brain capabilities doesn't let men off the hook, though. As a matter of fact, if you are a single dad reading Ellie's scenario, you might also have thought someone was spying on your own multimodal parenting. Although your masculine brain was originally designed for laser-like focusing, just being a single dad has already required you to develop similar bridges in your brain so you can be a good primary caretaker. In addition you, as a human being, have an inborn capacity for multimodal awareness.

Whether you're a man or woman, the fact that your brain is designed for multimodal awareness is good news for your ability to cry when you're sad and stop when you're done. The more you cultivate this skill, the easier it will be to engage in the internal dialogue that enables you to take your Emotional Medicine.

Multimodal awareness helps you ask yourself the kinds of questions that will lead you quickly back to feeling good. The first question is: "Do I need to cry (stomp, shake)?" This question involves distinguishing *feeling* from thinking. You need to be aware of how you *feel* at any given moment and of what sounds or movements would facilitate an emotional discharge.

Next is the question: "Is it safe for me and/or acceptable to others around me to cry here, now?" This question involves *observing* the situation you're in even as you are feeling the pressure of emotions wanting to move, as well as *relating* respectfully to anyone with you.

Assuming it's appropriate to allow emotions to move through their brief, embodied cycle, the next question you need to ask (while you are sobbing, pounding or shaking) is: "Am I (is my body) done yet?" This question involves *feeling* what is happening in your body and *observing* if the emotion is subsiding. Multimodal awareness enables you to distinguish your body's completion of an emotional cycle from your mind's tendency to go on and on with your story.

Finally, once the emotion has moved up and out and is done, the last question to ask yourself is, "What feels good in my body right now?" You need to feel and observe the sensations that are signaling you are beginning to feel better. This requires awareness of the sometimes subtle feelings of ease, warmth, flow and relaxation that are infusing your body with good feeling.

While cultivating multimodal awareness will enable you to ask yourself the right questions and access your Emotional Medicine cabinet, you won't be able to open the door of that cabinet if you don't align with your intention to feel your feelings, stop when you're done, and focus on feeling good.

At each of these points, you have patterns that can derail you. Very likely, your habitual mind will first try to talk you out of crying at all. If you're lucky enough to start crying, your habitual mind will then keep throwing your sad story in your face to keep you crying and make it harder to cooperate with your body once it's done. Lastly, once you do stop crying, your habitual mind will try to prevent you from really focusing on the good feelings spreading through your body. It will try to convince you that since you do feel a little better already, there's no point in dwelling in the good feelings. It will say you don't have time – you need to get on with your next activity.

In order to put all that resistance to feeling your emotions aside, it helps if you have someplace inside yourself to go that supports your intention to take your Emotional Medicine. Fortunately there is such a place you can turn to: your big "S" Self. In our next chapter, you'll discover what your big "S" Self is, as well as the power and freedom you gain when you align with it.

EIGHT

Align with Your Big "S" Self

Your big "S" Self is the keeper of your values, your intuition, your life's purpose. If your little "s" self gets you through daily life by managing the tasks of modern living mostly by rote, your big Self offers conscious choices to help you manage life's challenges and receive life's gifts. Even when your small self is all too easily co-opted by behavior handed down from generation to generation or by patterns created through childhood wounds, your big Self is there right now to guide you to actions in line with your values. If you have a lifelong pattern of avoiding embodied emotions and intend to change that way of being, it's your big Self that will help you make that change. Aligning with your big Self is crucial for taking your Emotional Medicine as well as tailoring your life to suit you in many other ways.

Some call the big "S" Self your "Higher" Self. Others call it soul, spirit, the voice of God within ... or just "Self" – the Ground of Being.[1] Whatever you call it, it's up to you whether you're ready to establish and maintain contact with it. Although your big Self has immense resources and wisdom, it has little interest in *forcing, insisting or demanding* that you live in accordance with its perspective. It takes the long view and waits through thick and thin for you to find and align with it.

Your big Self may whisper in dreams day or night, get your attention through coincidence and synchronicity, or even talk directly to you through its "still, small voice," but it's your decision whether you listen or follow its guidance. The deal is this: your big "S" Self is always there for you, even though you're not always there for it. Although healing runs rampant through the veins of *any* experience, if you don't look for this gold you won't find it.

Your Small "s" Self Has to Make the Effort

What's so confounding about big Self alignment is that it's your small self that has to make this effort. Your small self, with all the delights of your personality and darkness of your wounded patterns, has to make the decision to look within to connect with your big Self.

Fortunately, even though your small self[2] is typically the purveyor of habit and unconsciousness, it does have the intrinsic gifts of instinct, awareness and decision-making power permeating its existence. This means you can always *choose* to connect with your big Self.

You saw how this worked in the last chapter when Ellie felt anger rising about her toddler daughter, Nell, erasing her computer files. Ellie's small self, using multimodal awareness, observed her impulse to lash out at Nell. It's important to note here that Ellie's multimodal awareness first noticed this less than noble impulse. Ellie's small self had to be willing to see the unvarnished truth: She had an impulse propelling her toward behavior she would later regret.

As soon as Ellie became *aware* her anger was arising, her big Self offered perspective, enabling her to see she was on the brink of engaging in a family tradition of dumping anger. Even more importantly, Ellie's big Self was shining down new, consciously chosen values of skillful mothering like a steady beacon. Although the old pattern was exerting the magnetic pull of ingrained habit, Ellie's awareness and intention not to yell at her daughter but rather to stay connected to her new values helped her behave differently. Once she aligned with it, Ellie's big Self could then guide her to the actions of breathing, grunting (a way to release some anger energy), and gracefully diverting her daughter (and herself) to constructive, emotion-discharging play.

Fostering Big Self/Small Self Alignment

So how can you make it easier for your small self to connect and act in alignment with your big Self? Let us count the ways. They all begin with your intention to do so and require you to be conscious of as many levels of experience as possible. The good news is that you can set your intention at any time with a snap of your fingers. If you're ready, you could even do this right now. Here's a tip to help you.

ACTION TIP

Say out loud or write on a piece of paper some version of the following intentions:

- "I intend to strengthen my connection with my big 'S' Self today, tomorrow and always."
- "I intend to listen within for guidance from my big Self today, tomorrow and always."

Whenever you forget this intention, all you need to do to re-up your commitment is say it again. No blame! Forgetting and remembering are the hallmarks of any transformational process.

Another time-honored way of fortifying your little self/big Self bond is to sit quietly in meditation or prayer daily. Regular meditation actually changes your brain to be more conscious and less robotic. If you don't meditate regularly, now could be an excellent time to start.

More ways for reinforcing big Self connection include:

1. Taking time to reflect on yourself, your values, your life's purpose through journaling and/or conscious dialogue with friends and family on similar journeys.
2. Making an effort to remember and engage with your dreams.
3. Making art or involving yourself in expressive art projects.
4. Participating in any kind of integrative, somatic depth psychotherapy.
5. Studying any bodymind mastery endeavors such as martial arts, yoga, or other disciplined athletic pursuits.
6. Practicing Emotional Medicine!

Practicing Emotional Medicine Strengthens Big Self Bond

Learning to cry when you're sad and stop when you're done is a superb way to strengthen your little self/big Self bond. Your little self is always on the front lines, experiencing and absorbing the actual or metaphoric slights or blows life bestows. Even when you don't consciously notice that you've been wounded and need to cry (or stomp or shake), your body and psyche are struggling to handle these injuries. The practice of *observing* when your small self feels sad (mad or scared) and *asking within* whether you need to take some Emotional Medicine is as much an awareness/mindfulness practice as noticing your breath.

Looking within to see if tears are at hand, noticing whether it's safe to cry and observing when you're done crying, all require you be engaged in inner dialogue. And who do you think is there to answer those questions when you inquire within? Your big Self. At least, it's always trying to answer through the cacophony of habitual thoughts. Singling out your big Self's wise voice is a learning process. Don't feel inept if you don't hear distinct words. Often big Self guidance comes in the form of images, hunches, or gut feelings.

The good news is that just beginning any inner inquiry opens the door for big Self energy. And you've always got your body, your best friend forever (bff) as your ally. *Your body's experience provides a direct route to big Self wisdom.* When in doubt, ask your body. It will let you know what you need.

Once you make a practice of looking and listening within, you'll discover your big Self is continually offering subtle guidance for facilitating any emotional cycle. Your big Self notices whether your grief could flow more organically if you allowed yourself to make sounds while crying. It also notices whether slamming elbows on a mattress or a kicking a box would release your anger more easily. Your big Self is also aware whether just a tear or two or a grunt is sufficient to relieve stress and deliver emergency first aid if there's no time to take a full dose of Emotional Medicine.

Your big Self (in partnership with your small self's multimodal awareness) *observes* when your body is done even as some compelling story tries to reel you back in. Maintaining your Self-connection gives you resources to resist that narrative lure so you can stop crying when you're done and feel good ... sooner rather than later!

During emotional discharge, your big Self is working for you in yet another way: supporting responsible *relating* to others. Do you remember back in Chapter One when I described the emotional "refractory period"? That's the brief moment or two at the peak of any emotional upset when your *thinking mind* can't take in any new information. It's all caught in your little self's story that "I've been wronged."

During these "refractory" moments, it's not possible to reappraise your situation to take constructive action. However, even though you can't supplant victim thoughts with healing thoughts in those first gripping moments, *you still have the power to shift your attention from thoughts to sensations.* This is crucial. And while your small self is the one to initiate this shift, the moment you take that action you're in big Self territory.

No Matter What, You *Always* Have the Power to Shift Awareness from Thoughts to Sensations

This simple act of shifting focus from your little self's "world of hurt" to your bodily sensations reminds you that your Self is big enough to move awareness around. Even though you *momentarily* lose access to your core values, shifting focus gives you firsthand experience of being bigger than your rage and hurt. Once in touch with being bigger, you're much better able to resist inappropriate reactive behavior.

Shifting focus to sensations also puts you back in touch with your body, and its 24/7 commitment to healing. Consider shifting focus to sensations an amendment to that old adage of counting to 10 to tamp down anger. Go ahead and count if you'd like, but in this case count sensations.

Here's an example. Let's suppose you're so mad at someone that all your little self can think of is saying the cruelest words you know. At that moment, it feels as if every bit of your brain wants to hurl insults at your perceived perpetrator. Using your small self's multimodal awareness, you can drop into body sensations such as a hot flushed face, tight jaw, or a beating heart.

Delineating these sensations slows things down and gives you a place to rest while waiting for that refractory period to ease its grip on your thinking. It also provides that almost imperceptible easing that accompanies bringing awareness to your "bff" body. Focusing on sensations takes attention away from escalating angry thoughts and turns it toward your body's experience in the present moment.

Although focusing on bodily sensations doesn't eradicate angry thoughts, this shift enables you to reaffirm your big Self bond. Aligned with your Self (or at least aware that you are bigger than angry thoughts), you're better able to say, " I'm so mad right now, I can't think of anything but hurting you back. I want to say mean words or maybe even hit you, but I'm not gonna do that. I'm gonna get out of here until I calm down." (Shutting a door decisively behind you as you leave for a private place to take some Emotional Medicine often feels really good at this point!)

There's another intriguing aspect to coping responsibly with anger during a refractory period. Whenever you move awareness into body experience during a moment of anger, you may notice an urge to yell, bite, kick or punch. But even though your anger buildup may be quite intense, these bodily urges for release *do not actually require biting, kicking or punching a perceived perpetrator.* Thoughts of vigilante justice might insist upon unleashing rage on a real person, but for your simpleminded, non-neurotic body, a pillow or other nonliving substitute will do just fine. It's also important to remember that when circumstances are circumscribed, a tiny bit of grunting, teeth gnashing, or fist shaking is often enough to relieve tension.

Conversely, when a relationship upset leaves you feeling frozen and inarticulate, your big Self is still there to help you observe that reaction, and say to whomever is there, "I'm so numb right now I can't think straight. My blood has turned to ice. I am frozen. I need to stop relating to you until I feel safe again."

Your big "S" Self is there for you whenever you need it. The fact that it can walk in your shoes and yet remain distinct is what gives it dominion – and gives you the power to use emotions to heal your life. Let's take a look at how one woman used Emotional Medicine to strengthen her connection with her big "S" Self and stop settling for less than she deserved in relationships.

Isabel Falls in Love – with her Self

Isabel is a beautiful raven-haired Latina who looks at least ten years younger than her driver's license age of 49. She has a thriving career as an interior designer specializing in "staging" homes for real estate sales. Never married and tired of the singles scene, Isabel was ready to find her soul mate and settle down.

Most of the men Isabel found attractive were "charmers." Good at gab, these guys were smooth and sexy but not serious boyfriend material. Isabel had never experienced being cherished by a committed lover. While this was no fun, an even bigger dilemma was that Isabel would lose herself in these flings. Even though she could see these guys weren't right, and in spite of her intentions not to have sex until in a committed relationship, she'd end up in bed, opening heart and body prematurely and getting hurt.

Isabel was the fifth of eight children born to an overwhelmed mother and an absentee father. Normal childhood needs for love and attention went unfulfilled. Her typical self-talk was filled with judgments about how unlovable she was. Isabel's self-hating narrative would diminish only when some cute guy showed interest. She would gulp this attention like water at a desert oasis. This would quench her thirst until the days there would be no contact and no attention. Then Isabel would revert back to self-loathing.

In our initial work, Isabel learned how important it was to shift focus ASAP from self-loathing thoughts to the emotions roiling beneath. As each dating disaster restimulated memories of early abandonment and neglect, her grief and anger were profoundly wrenching.

After each dose of Emotional Medicine, Isabel had the pleasure of falling in love with herself. She would laugh with delight and say, "I *am* lovable." She could feel her big Self connection filling her with peace and confidence. Each time she felt this love coming from within her, for her, it strengthened her resolve not to settle for less than she deserved.

However, Isabel discovered that though she could experience her big Self effortlessly after taking Emotional Medicine in our sessions or by herself, when she was in the presence of a desirable man, she just couldn't maintain her alignment. As a result, Isabel knew that if she was serious about breaking this pattern, she'd need to make finding love inside herself as important as finding it outside.

Isabel decided to consider each dating encounter *primarily* an opportunity to stay connected with her Self rather than a chance to look for a boyfriend. She came up with three affirmations: "I want to be cherished in a committed relationship," "I can move through *any* emotional upset to feel self-love," "I am big enough to allow *all* aspects of my experience." She wrote these statements on sticky notes and placed them around her home, office and car.

Within weeks, Isabel had a date with a handsome artist, Rudi. Early in the evening Rudi announced he was not into committed relationships, he just wanted to have fun. At the end of the evening when he then stroked her face, looked into her eyes and told her how much he wanted to make love to her, Isabel clung to her affirmation like a prayer or mantra. "I want to be cherished in a committed relationship," she repeated silently over and over.

This was hard. Isabel was tempted and torn. She used multimodal awareness to feel the *powerful longing in her heart to be loved in a committed way* as well as noticing the *powerful longing in her genitals to have sex now*! Using every ounce of big Self-connection, Isabel resisted jumping into bed that night, but did make another date with Rudi.

Once Isabel got home, she took matters into her own hands. She allowed the burning anger about Rudi to move through her body, beating her fists on the big soft pillow next to her bed. She also acknowledged the burning sexual desire coursing through her body. Sure it needed attention, but it didn't need attention only from Rudi. Isabel could pleasure herself, or sublimate that energy into another creative outlet.

She grieved her losses, her loneliness, sobbing until she felt that reliable relief begin to spread throughout her bodymind. Isabel was soon filled with such a powerful experience of peace and love that it made Rudi seem insignificant.

She then had an "Aha" moment. She saw that although searching for her soul mate was natural and healthy, and something she would definitely continue, her longing for deep connection with a man was *also* a longing to be connected with her big Self, Spirit, God. Deep sobs of joy erupted from her heart. This was a connection she could achieve no matter what man was or wasn't in her life.

After that experience, Isabel knew what she had to do. She called Rudi to say thanks but no thanks. She was empowered, self-sufficient and self-confident. Isabel knew how to find self-love and a big Self connection that fortified her intention never again to settle for less than she deserved.

Making it Easy (or at least Easier!)

Have you ever noticed that when you feel good, it's easier to make healthy choices in line with big Self values? For example, it is much easier to be disciplined about food choices, avoid addictive substances, and maintain exercise, yoga and meditation programs after you've had a good night's sleep or on your first days back after vacation.

This is because a good night's sleep and the rest and relaxation of a vacation restore your resources and create well-being. You have less stress, more energy. You realize you can now think straight. Healthy choices come more effortlessly. You may even have more insight and compassion about how much of your self-damaging behavior has been the result of stressed quests for quick fixes to feel better.

When you're rejuvenated, it's as if the clouds part, the sun comes out, and you can see clearly who you are and what you need to do to live a happy life. If scientists were to check your blood levels at these happy times they would undoubtedly discover that your cortisol (stress hormones) levels were low, your dopamine (happy hormones) levels high, your serotonin (mood managers) levels balanced. In these times, it's easier to feel aligned with core values and big Self intentions.

Contrast that with times when you're stressed, fatigued, pained or facing chronic low-grade health issues. Of course you can still maintain healthy choices, but it's more of a white-knuckle experience. You continually have to summon your strong will to stay true to your intentions and maintain your integrity. You have a mental idea of who you are but you don't really feel connected to your self or your Self. You get by on sheer determination. There's nothing wrong with that in the short run.

Everyone has times when they're holding on to big Self connection by their fingernails. You saw how Isabel needed this kind of grit to not succumb to a fling when she wanted commitment, even though she was horny as heck. Although it was tough to resist Rudi's seductive charm, ultimately it was just a challenging few hours. For the long haul, however, it's too exhausting to get by on just this kind of will. You become an easy target for addictions, serious illness, illicit romance, even financial corruption.

This is where Emotional Medicine comes in. No matter what stress you're facing, in just a few minutes you can shift energy and restore your resources. You can generate an experience of feeling peaceful and restored and *voila!* – there you are connected to your big Self. Urgent issues fade into insignificance in the wake of completing an emotional cycle. Here too, clouds part, the sun shines, and you feel rejuvenated, connected and aligned with your Self.

Of course the flush of fulfillment fades as the stresses of life rise again and new sad, mad, scared feelings require attention. You'll need to take Emotional Medicine on a regular basis if you want to make it easier to strengthen your Self connection. But once you know any upset provides an opportunity to feel good fast as well as restore your connection with your big Self, you can rest easy. You can save white-knuckle will for those times when, for one reason or another, you're unable to take Emotional Medicine to restore the well-being which naturally strengthens your resolve.

Around now, you might be thinking that handling your troubles could be easier than you thought. You're right, but there's a small matter that needs to be addressed before proceeding further. That's the issue of your less-than-noble thoughts, impulses and actions.

It seems that God and/or the Universe has quite a sense of humor. Just as you learn about soaring to heights of big Self connection, you discover this doesn't eliminate your feet of clay. It's inevitable that the more connected and conscious you become, the more you'll discover aspects of yourself you didn't know were there, and even some you wish weren't there at all. In the next chapter you'll learn the essential role accepting your dark side plays in your ability to use Emotional Medicine for growth and healing.

NINE

Accept Your Shadow

So there you are reading along, feeling optimistic about connecting to your big Self and using multimodal awareness. Gradually, though, you're becoming aware of dark thoughts and feelings about yourself and others, thoughts that you don't like at all. You may have been reflecting on these or other "not nice" thoughts, feelings and actions and telling yourself, "This just isn't me! It can't possibly be."

If you're a human being, it *is* you. No blame! Having darker aspects lurking in the shadows of your psyche is a normal, inevitable part of life in a human bodymind.[1] As a matter of fact, these darker aspects are often called the "shadow" of humankind. In this chapter, you'll discover how important it is to acknowledge and accept your shadow. Furthermore, you'll learn how much Emotional Medicine helps with this.

Interestingly, your shadow represents not only negative aspects of your humanity, but also whatever aspects of you that have not been accepted or nurtured by your family or society. In this case, your shadow can contain anything in your life that has not been allowed expression. Examples of this could be strength, assertiveness and anger in women, and vulnerability, sensitivity and sadness in men.

While acknowledging and accepting your shadow is essential for growth, the process usually doesn't feel good. You, like most people, want to be accepted by others. You want to be a good person. You try to be thoughtful and generous to your loved ones and respectful, if not kind, to strangers. It's confounding that the better you get at seeing how "big" you are, the better you also get at seeing your cringeworthy petty, prejudiced, lascivious dark side, as well as hidden parts you've been afraid to express.

The Natural Interplay of Light and Dark

It's another paradox. The more you open to the light of awareness and Self-connection, the more you see your own darkness. "What goes up must come down" is not only a description of the laws of gravity; it's also an axiom for inner work. You may have already experienced this – being blasted open by increased healing, spiritual awareness, or transformative experience and then, soon afterward, finding yourself in the pits of despair or some black hole of reaction. Not to worry. This is the normal oscillation of expansion and contraction, light and dark in the Universe, in both inner and outer worlds.

Fortunately, although here on earth what goes down doesn't go back up of its own accord, in terms of inner work, this reversal often holds true. When you journey through dark times, it's like clearing dense undergrowth, making way for new life to poke through the crust of your experience.

Taking your Emotional Medicine will provide you with a good example of this. Allowing yourself to experience a few dark, painful minutes of sad, mad, scared emotions creates the space for good feelings to permeate your experience.

When you contract against brief emotional flow, you're unwittingly interfering with the natural rhythm of the Universe. Resisting emotional expression tips your inner scales toward darkness. Instead of a few minutes of anger release followed by lighthearted relief, your mind attempts to handle anger through ongoing scenarios of revenge.

Getting caught up in these mental shadow plays inhibits your ability to take healthy action in real life. Avoiding occasionally *feeling* a few minutes of murderous rage, wrenching grief or terrifying fear may leave you depressed, anxious and diminished for days.

After all, what is it that triggers these uncomfortable sad, mad, scared reactions that try to find their way simply and efficiently through your bodymind? Unmet needs! Aside from instinctual survival strategies, almost all emotional reaction is a result of being thwarted, i.e., not getting your needs met.

Unmet Needs Propel You into Shadows

Most social, behavioral and biological scientists agree that people ideally need some form of food, safety, sex, love, family, friends, work, play, independence, order, creativity and exercise to lead happy and fulfilled lives. When any of these needs aren't met and the ensuing emotional reactions are resisted, distortions arise, consciously and unconsciously.

Sibling rivalry and competition for the love and attention of either parent are considered archetypal human conflicts. They're called "archetypal" because, no matter where you go in the world, you find similar rivalries playing out. Forbidden and/or incestual sexual attraction and desire comprise other archetypal shadow conflicts.[2] In Western culture, one glance at ancient Greek mythology gives a quick tour of the seething unconscious conflicts existing below the surface of "everyday" awareness for humans.

Fortunately, we've come a long way, baby, from those earlier points in human history when a rageful, murderous thought toward someone was considered an actual command by the gods to murder them, or when sexual thoughts toward family members or other inappropriate persons were considered divine endorsement. This was way before people realized that they had a private interior life of thoughts, wishes and reactions, and way before most people realized they had vast reservoirs of multimodal awareness and big Self capacity.

Rivalry for Resources

If you have a brother or sister, you've likely had to cope with subconscious or unconscious competitive or guilty feelings about that sibling. Similarly, if you have parents (or parental-type care-takers), at some time or another you've probably been caught up in vying for one parent's attention and affection to the temporary exclusion of the other. These conflicts all involve normal childhood tendencies to want what you want (the attention and love you need) when you want it.

Unfortunately, even the most intact parents are not always skillful at helping you handle common competitive thoughts in which you wish your sibling (or excluded parent) would die or disappear. Because your parents often don't know that they, too, have had similar competitive thoughts toward their own siblings and parents, they respond unskillfully to your normal childhood behaviors.

Little John Wants his Parents for Himself

For example, six-year-old John is jealous of his little brother Robby, who is four, and sometimes tries to sock him. But John also loves his brother and gets very sad whenever Robby is unhappy. John has an unmet need to do something with the anger he can't express toward Robby.

John knows he gets into trouble with his parents whenever he socks Robby – and he also feels bad when Robby gets hurt. Both possible consequences prevent John from expressing the anger nat-urally arising in his experience as a sibling.

So John begins dreaming of Robby falling down and hurting himself, as his psyche puts on an unconscious shadow play to satisfy his need to express anger toward his little brother. Interestingly, what often happens is that John's anger takes on unexpected expres-sions, such as becoming overly protective of Robby or "rescuing" him from real or imagined danger. All of this, his anger at having to share his parents with Robby, his inability to express that anger in a healthy way, his guilty feelings about that anger, get pushed into the dark recesses of his psyche and become his shadow.

Enlightened Parenting Diminishes Shadows

Let's imagine for a moment how the above scenario would play out if John's parents knew his anger toward Robby was normal. Furthermore, let's give these parents knowledge of Emotional Medicine so they can help John manage his anger in a way that helps him feel good about himself.

In that case, whenever John's parents would see him socking or about to sock Robby, one of them could take him aside and explain: "Of course, you want to hit your brother. All children want to hit their brothers (or sisters) sometimes. That's normal. However, it's not OK to hit Robby. We'll get you a pillow and bat so you can hit pillows until you don't feel like hitting Robby any more." Of course John's parents would also occupy Robby with another caretaker, game, book or video, reassuring him they'll get back to him later.

As John and his parents head for another room, John can't quite believe he'll actually be allowed him to hit things, but he likes the idea. He's relieved to have his anger acknowledged as well as having a boundary set so he can't hurt Robby.

John's parents begin hitting pillows first. John joins in tentatively, glancing at his parents, who nod approvingly. Soon John is beating pillows with real fury, arching his little back, bringing arms overhead and down, allowing anger to move through the emotional cycle – up, out, done. Before long, John and his parents are beating pillows and laughing together.

These adept parents would also be watching to see when John's increasing happiness indicated he was done so they could direct his awareness to the joy he was experiencing. His parents could then ask him if there was anything he'd like to say to Robby, offering examples like, "Robby, please don't knock over my block tower anymore," or, "Robby, I'm sorry I called you a stinky butt and tried to hit you."

Finally, these parents would check on Robby to see what Emotional Medicine he might need. When both boys were in a state of reasonable calm these parents could facilitate a healing dialogue.

Using Emotional Medicine to help work through sibling anger and aggression would give John and Robby a better relationship and happier childhood. It would also provide them a beginning big Self boot camp. They could get a glimpse of their potential for multitasking awareness, noticing how sad, mad, scared and glad emotions moved through them. They could also discover what it was like to take action in line with core values – a beginning big "S" Self connection.

Becoming your *Own* Enlightened Parent

Imagine what your life would be like if you could be as enlightened toward yourself as John and Robby's parents were with them. What if you could be the good parent you never had, helping yourself move through shadow thoughts and impulses with creativity and compassion?

This is a choice you can still make. It's a choice many who had less than perfect parenting make, especially after spending countless years wishing mates or friends would take care in ways parents hadn't. It's tricky, though. Becoming your own enlightened parent requires that you take care of yourself – protecting, nurturing and guiding yourself in all the ways you always longed for. Letting go of the fantasy that one day you *will* find that perfect caretaker is a challenge. And, parenting yourself is a big job. Fortunately, you don't have be perfect, just "good enough."

Just as real parents of real children aren't always able to do the right thing, you won't always do the right thing for yourself. However, research shows that "good-enough" parents only meet children's needs perfectly about 30 percent of the time. The rest of the time is all about repairing ruptures and correcting mistakes. This is doable.

Your big Self bond is here to help. Since it is always there offering guidance when you're open to hear it, it can function as a kind of co-parent with you. Together you can provide a supportive inner narrative and transform each painful moment into a healing experience.

Furthermore, what if you, emboldened by your big Self connection, looked into each shadow moment for the possibility of transformation? What if, beneath your dark corners, you found not only archetypal conflicts and unexpressed emotions but spiritual qualities trying to be born?

Finding Light in Your Shadow

This is what Dr. Roberto Assagioli, founder of Psychosynthesis, proposed in the early 20th century. A true visionary, Dr. Assagioli suggested that at the core of each shadow aspect was not only an unmet need and unconscious conflict but also a spiritual *quality of being* trying to emerge. At the time Dr. Assagioli developed Psychosynthesis, prevailing psychoanalytic notions held that spirituality was only compensation for dark human drives of sex, death and aggression.

For Assagioli, this view did not reflect the true human condition. He believed spiritual qualities of big Self being (love, will, beauty, altruism) *were forces unto themselves,* actively impacting people by calling forth their best, most enlightened behavior. These spiritual forces, he postulated, were influencing humans at all times consciously and unconsciously, just like the shadow drives.

Let's take a look at what spiritual qualities might be hiding in your shadows, just waiting for you to turn on the light. Perhaps one of your shadow qualities is being envious. But take a deeper look … what arises as envy is often a cover for lack of appropriate self-care or self-appreciation. Whatever you are envious of – someone's success, money, beauty – consider that these are just symbols of a need for deeper fulfillment within you. Maybe it's not really another's success you're longing for but the appreciation, not really another's money but the security and financial freedom, not really another's beauty but the chance to value your own unique attractiveness.

Gossiping is another shadow activity which contains a core of spirit. Although almost everyone gossips at one time or another, critical tongue wagging about friends' or "frenemies'" imperfections is ultimately a barrier to nourishing relationships, even with fellow gossipers! When you tell tales about someone, you do feel temporarily closer to those sharing the gossip. You create a momentary "in-group" sense of belonging. However, you also have to live with the lingering insecurity as to what kind of gossiping may be going on behind *your* back.

The quality attempting to wend its way into your life via gossiping is, amazingly enough, a variation of love. Gossiping can hide both a longing for real love and connection with others as well as real love and concern about others' well-being.

What if you look beneath addiction, the scourge of so many lives? What unmet needs and soul qualities could possibly be trying to materialize in the agony of addiction? It's commonly understood that addiction often begins as an attempt to escape unpleasant emotions or experiences. While I agree, I also believe that addiction is the result of distorted needs for pleasure and spiritual union. Besides running from pain, addicts are, at some level, looking for bliss and are yearning to merge with something bigger than their small selves.

Feeling Better or Worse?

By now, you may be breathing a bit easier about having a shadow side. You may even feel inspired as you consider there's spiritual light for each of your dark corners. On the other hand, this information may feel like it's all just too much – piling on one more thing you've got to deal with. Ignoring or avoiding your dark side may beckon as a path of least resistance, especially if you're still struggling with shame about your shadow. If you're like many, though, it's not the "crime" of having a dark side but the "cover-up" that's the real problem.

Assuming you're not caught in a spiral of actually acting out your dark side,[3] your shame about such thoughts is far more destructive to your well-being than the fact that they exist. It's hard to know what life on planet Earth would be like if you, and everyone, were aware of the fact that *terrible thoughts and impulses arise in humans which they do not need to act out*. This kind of acceptance could go a long way to easing your pain in particular and human suffering in general.

Dr. Steve Hayes at the University of Nevada has conducted some fascinating research on the long-term beneficial effects of people learning toleration of their darkest thoughts.[4] Dr. Hayes studied addicts in recovery who were trained in either positive thinking (ignoring or avoiding negative thoughts), or basic awareness and mindfulness skills (allowing negative thoughts to move through awareness without resistance).

Although positive thinking training initially gave subjects an edge in avoiding relapse in the first month or two after completing detox, *those subjects who learned to be aware and accepting of negative thoughts as they moved briefly through awareness were better able to maintain their sobriety for months and years to come.*

This is hopeful news for all of us struggling with shadow sides. However, there is a wrinkle. While observing and tolerating dark thoughts seems to provide coping benefits, those benefits don't automatically stop you from judging yourself for having those dark thoughts. Judging tendencies, like the human dark side, are deeply embedded in your human design and require healing attention before you can fully accept your shadow.

Judgments Happen!

For your linear mind/left brain, judging is like breathing. That's what keeps it alive. The job of your linear mind is to differentiate, assess, analyze and judge things. Judgments give you important information about your values as well as guidance for the people, places, ideas, and activities that will serve you best. You couldn't live a happy, healthy life if your judging mind wasn't operating efficiently.

However, this also means you have to deal, day in and out, with judgments rising in awareness. It's very easy to cross over from judging what sandwich would be better to eat at lunch to judging how fat/dumpy/ugly the person making the sandwich looks. Once you're on that track, in another instant you're thinking about how fat/dumpy/ugly *you* look! Soon every aspect of yourself, your life, others' selves and lives becomes meat for the sharp scalpel of derogatory judgments. As you likely well know, this is no fun.

For one thing, judging yourself saps your vitality and confidence. It doesn't feel good. Second, every judgment derails an opportunity to understand and reveal your own humanity and true value to yourself and others.

You may not know it, but getting caught up in judging others is also not beneficial for you. Sure, judging brings an initial feeling of shadowy superiority. But for your psyche, every judgment hurled at someone else *is received internally as a judgment about some aspect of your self.* Since judging others ultimately diminishes your inner experience of being worthy, judging others hurts *you.* Make a note of this.

Fortunately, although you have no choice about whatever self/other judgments arise, you do have a choice about whether to indulge in them or use them for transformation. You can always make the choice not to dwell in judgment. You do this by committing to letting judgments go. You notice judgments arising. You take a breath, then look beneath them for unexpressed emotion or unmet needs. And then, you let them go.

Here is a two-part Action Tip to help you do this. Both parts of this tip can be used equally effectively for dropping judgments about yourself or others. To apply this process to another person, just place his or her name and attributes in each category.

ACTION TIP PART I

Make a list of three things you don't like or find difficult to accept in yourself. Write those on the left side of a sheet of paper under the heading "Shadow Side/Self-Judgments." Divide the paper into quarters with three vertical lines down the paper so that you have added three more columns, for a total of four columns. On the top of the second column make a heading called "Unmet Needs." On the top of the third column, write "Underlying Unexpressed Sad, Mad, Scared Emotion." At the top of the fourth column, write "Spiritual Qualities Trying to Emerge."

Take a breath and look inside yourself. Contemplate what shadow impulses, unmet needs and unexpressed emotions are hiding beneath aspects you find objectionable. Leave the Spiritual Qualities column for later.

You may have some immediate insights, or you may need to take your time with this. Keep looking until you uncover needs and archetypal human conflicts. Look specifically for sad, mad, scared emotions. Be gentle with yourself. You may touch some tender places during this process. Allow any grief, anger or fear to move and lead you back to peace.

After you've filled in the first three columns, look specifically for spiritual qualities trying to emerge. Consider such qualities as responsibility, creativity, sensitivity, generosity, kindness. Take your time. This may take days, months or even years before you fully perceive what spiritual forces are trying to work through your life.

ACTION TIP PART II

Once you've developed a deeper understanding of your own shadow aspects (or even if you haven't yet), prepare to add the following sentence to your self-talk repertoire: *Of course you feel that way.* Every time you're aware of berating yourself for some shadow thought, impulse or mistake, replace your blaming self-talk with that new sentence, or a variation such as, *Of course you have those thoughts. Of course you want to do that. We're not going to act on that because it would bring us more pain, but given what you've been through, this is completely understandable.*

If you've already taken action you regret, say to yourself, *Let's find a way to make amends. Let's see what we can learn from this. Let's make this mistake worth something.*

If you're trying to mitigate blame and judgment of another, say to yourself, *I wish they hadn't done that because it brought so much pain, but given what they've been through in their life, I can understand how this happened. I can see their pain. I'm going to check if there's anything he/she could do to make amends to me, and (if appropriate) ask for that.*

Note here that replacing your shaming or blaming inner talk with an accepting voice does not mean you condone acting out shadow impulses, or whitewashing shadow actions. You always continue to set boundaries for behavior in line with your big Self values. You similarly set boundaries for others concerning what behavior you will or will not tolerate. Substituting understanding for judgment means you bring to yourself the compassionate voice and guidance of a skillful parent as well as your big Self's wisdom in your darkest hours.

It's important to note that your big Self connection can help you refrain from acting on shadow impulses. It is always beckoning you toward actions you can be proud of. Your big Self is also there to guide you to make appropriate amends when it's too late for restraint and some dark deed is already done. Remember, though, as crucial as restraint and responsible action are for your growth, it's just as crucial to keep working to accept and forgive yourself for your shadow thoughts and actions.

Accepting your shadow actually makes it *less* likely that you will act on any dark thoughts or feelings. Accepting your shadow means you begin to open your heart to yourself. When you do this, the soft energy of compassion begins to quell the urgency inherent in impulsive action. Acceptance also gives you the opportunity to find and work with the sad, mad, scared emotions hiding in your shadows – to bring real relief.

In the next chapter, you'll learn step by step how to let your body lead you to that real relief. You'll learn how to assess what energy is predominant in your body and how that reliably guides you to work through any emotional cycle in the most efficient way. You'll discover why you don't have to figure everything out once you let your body lead you to the deeper wisdom within. You'll also learn how to master the biggest challenge most people face in letting the body lead: letting go of control!

TEN

Let Your Body Lead

From 1960 to 1968, Gerda Boyesen was clinical director of several psychiatric hospitals in Norway. In that part of the world it was (and still is) common for psychologists to be trained in and offer exercise and massage as an essential adjunct to psychological treatment. To her great interest, Gerda noticed that when patients experienced physical release in their bodies such as shivering, crying and sweating, they made more progress in their psychological healing. They got better faster!

From her observations, Gerda, a licensed physiotherapist, went on to develop a theory that emotions in the body move through a predictable cycle of buildup, discharge and release. (See diagram, which I have abridged to include a focus on the good feelings at the end of a cycle.) She called this the "Biodynamic Emotional Cycle." She believed that when emotions were free to move with tears flowing, feet stomping and limbs shaking, they helped the body discharge the physiological buildup accompanying those emotions as well as restore a sense of bodily well-being.

Gerda also noticed that bodily emotional release was usually accompanied by rumbling in her patients' stomachs. She began listening carefully not just to their words, but also to the noises emanating from their guts.

Soon Gerda was listening to stomach noises with a stethoscope while she developed massage techniques to facilitate the kind of healthy gut gurgles indicating that her patients' stomachs were re-laxing and de-stressing. Years before neuroscience discovered the importance of what is now known to be our "second brain" – our guts – she observed that the stomach and alimentary canal not only digested food, but also helped the body digest stress and normalize emotional functioning.

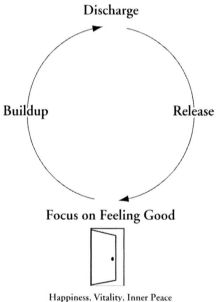

Emotional Cycle*

Discharge

Buildup

Release

Focus on Feeling Good

Happiness, Vitality, Inner Peace

* This diagram has been abridged from Gerda Boyesen's
Biodynamic Emotional Cycle

While you probably haven't noticed how merrily your guts gurgle when you are relaxed or happy, you have most likely noticed that when you are tense and stressed, your stomach is tight. You may have pain or a feeling of stagnation in your stomach or bowels. You may even get constipated. As a moving, burbling brook is a likely source of healthy water and a stagnant swamp is a source of decay, so it is with your bodily emotions.

Decades after Gerda's discoveries, affective neuroscience is beginning to detail the active changes emotions cause in all your body systems, from your clenching jaw, through your pounding heart and hard-breathing lungs, to your quivering gut. When anger arises, blood rushes to large muscles, particularly your arms and legs, to give you the resources to fight and kick. When fear appears, your nervous system goes on high alert for "freezing" while, simultaneously, your leg muscles get ready to run. When grief descends, your eyes fill with tears that are ready to eliminate the stress accompanying any loss and signal to others that you need comfort.

The Purpose of Tears

According to biochemist Dr. William Frey of the Dry Eye and Tear Research Center in Minnesota, tears are designed to remove stress hormones and toxins from the body for *both* men and women.[1] Tears have a part to play in keeping you healthy. You may not know why you are crying when your eyes fill up, but rest assured, your body knows that you need some detox, stress reduction, and/or hormonal balancing.

I have found that tears, whether from sadness or joy, open and soften the heart. Crying tends to increase vulnerability and openness, preconditions for fulfilling relationships with others. I call tears "the oil of the heart."

Gerda Boyesen believed that emotional release provided by tears profoundly affects the regulation of fluid levels in your tissues. Fluid levels in tissues play an important role in the experience of well-being. When you retain water in your body, you don't feel comfortable at all (think of yourself or someone with PMS).

Dr. Arthur Janov, author of *The Primal Scream* and the originator of Primal Therapy, proposes that the act of crying *itself* is curative.[1] He provocatively states, "The amount of tranquilizers necessary in adult life will depend, by and large, on the amount of crying *not done*. The optimistic part of all this is that the amount of crying needing to be done is *finite*, so that after you cry for a certain amount of time you feel good again, because you have done something that the body needed to do."[2] Dr. Janov believes that part of the purpose of tears is to wash pain away.

Even in the face of all this good news about tears, you probably still carry some residual shame about crying as about many body-fluid excretions ... sweat, urine, semen and vaginal juices. You've been taught to hide most evidence of your body's efforts at Emotional Medicine, fluid regulation, procreation, waste management and sexual arousal. Unfortunately, in a technologically advanced society such as ours, our models for functioning are silent, tidy machines, rather than messy bodies with minds, sounds and excretions of their own.

I continually receive emails and calls from people (OK, from women primarily) telling me that ever since they have heard about Emotional Medicine or just simply read the title of this book, they stop and relax into their tears whenever they feel them. They say they now give themselves permission to cry when they are sad, or at least allow their eyes to water and leak a tear or two without being inundated with shame. All report feeling more whole, happy and alive when allowing tears to be a natural part of their lives.

My own discovery – that a few minutes of brief, body-based emotional release followed by a few more minutes of focus on the subsequent relief results in profound well-being – provides a prescription for managing core emotions and the physiological effects they evoke. The challenge, however, is that a prescription of Emotional Medicine requires *letting your body lead you through the process of emotional release*. And letting your body lead means letting go of your ego – or at least letting go of its desire to dominate.

Cooperating with Your Body

Alexander Lowen, M.D., the founder of Bioenergetic Therapy, described his own struggle to let his body lead in the following way: "The surrender to the body and its feelings may strike one as a defeat, which it is for the ego that seeks to dominate. But only in defeat can we gain freedom from the rat race of modern life to sense the passion and the joy that freedom offers."[3]

Although I would alter Lowen's words to emphasize cooperation rather than surrender, it's true that cooperating with your body and its feelings may register as a defeat for your ego. This is because cooperating with your body means your ego is no longer the sole boss of you.

Mark Epstein describes the fear of being overwhelmed by feelings as fear of loss of (what I've described as your small "s") self. "The self that we are afraid of losing is a false self. If we can learn not to fear our feelings, we gain access to the real."[4]

Letting your body lead means listening carefully to what your body is trying to tell you because you know it has crucial information for real well-being. Being in partnership with your body means that, whenever safe and appropriate, you let it lead you to do its bidding. You cry when your body signals sadness, you stop when your body signals it's done, you then luxuriate in the pleasure that follows. Similarly, you sleep when tired, eat when hungry, drink when thirsty, stop when full, move when muscles request, and reach out for others when your heart aches with loneliness.

Letting your body lead means you honor the fact that your body knows best how long you need to cry, stomp, shake in discharge, or pulse with pleasure. You honor the kinds of postures, gestures, positions or movements your body offers because you know it helps emotion move through its cycle of up-out-done elegantly and efficiently.

When you let your body lead, you drop down from analytical ego dominance into whole-being partnership. You do this because you recognize that through your body you can access wisdom be-yond your wildest dreams that will lead to your healing. You also do this because you know that in a healthy partnership, each part-ner has times of leading and times of following.

Letting Your Body Lead Does Not Mean Letting Your Body Rule!

Letting your body lead is not about switching one boss for another so that your body or your emotions become the tyrant. When you let your body lead, you, in multimodal awareness with your big Self alignment, are still there. You're the one who chooses when and where to let your body lead. You are still there observing, even as you surrender to rhythms and reasons in your body that you might not initially understand.

Although it may sound strange, it's possible to simply ask your body what it needs, either out loud or silently. You then imagine your body responding as if it had a voice. You ask inside specifically what would help any emotion complete its cycle. That's it! You just ask and see what you get. You might get a sense, a word, an image. The first response is usually the most trustworthy.

Aligned with your big "S" Self and using multimodal aware-ness, you've got a built-in buffer for the "out-of-control" worries your ego associates with emotional flow. Multimodal awareness ac-tually gives you aspects of that needed "in-charge" feeling, even as you're letting your body lead. You have your crying and sobbing, you have your *awareness* of crying and sobbing, <u>and</u> the knowledge you can shift focus at any moment.

The Decision to Feel

The first step to letting your body lead you through your nat-ural emotional cycles, interestingly enough, involves your mind. You'll need to ponder whether you are *willing* to let your body lead. That's right – letting your body lead means deciding to let go of being in charge, for the time being. You let go of your "I just won't think about it" avoidance behaviors, your "I can rise above it" stoic behaviors and your "I'll just have a drink/ joint/cookie and feel better" addictive behaviors long enough for your body to show you what emotion is present and how it wants to move through. You don't need to be willing to feel every emotion every time, but you do need to be willing to start.

A caveat: While you can get big rewards from big emotional releases (in safe places) including wailing, kicking and shaking, you don't always have to go for the big gestures. Sometimes the tiniest homeopathic dose will be enough to support your body in releasing stress and restoring sufficient resources to keep functioning. However, in all cases you need to choose to welcome your emotions into your awareness. You need to choose again and again to slow, soften, open and listen to what your body is trying to tell you, and what it needs *you* to do to restore balance. Your commitment to letting your body lead is your guiding light.

You will need a strong commitment. Your social conditioning and your mind's attempt to boss your body will want you to push emotional pain under the rug, often before you are aware this is happening. You'll need to be exquisitely clear about how important emotional experience is for your health and well-being.

ACTION TIP

Complete the following sentences:

I have been **unwilling** to feel my emotions before now because
_____.

What has changed, or is changing, about that now is _____
_____.

I've been **afraid** to feel my emotions before now because _____
_____.

What has changed, or is changing, about that now is _____
_____.

I understand, or I'm beginning to understand, that my emotions are important for my well-being because _____
_____.

I am **willing** to pay more attention to my emotions now because _____.
It is important for me to experience my emotions in my body
because _____.
I am ready, or almost ready, to make a commitment to let my
body lead me through emotional release, big or small, because
_____.

You may find it helpful to check in on the commitments you
have made in these sentences in a week, a month, or a year.

Once you've made the decision to feel, here's another tool to
help you: the "Let Your Body Lead" Checklist. Below are some
things you might ask yourself to promote a positive experience as
you follow sadness through an emotional cycle.

"Let Your Body Lead" Checklist

1. Check body signals for sadness

Although your body's natural signal for sadness is tears, you may have pushed them down so often that it is now trying to get your attention in other subtle or not-so-subtle ways. You may feel any or all of the following: itching or tearing eyes, a welling of fluid around your nose, sniffling, sighing, a tightening or lump in your throat, swallowing, a swelling pressure in your chest, feeling as if your heart might burst, or an increase in your heart rate or your body temperature. You also might be surprised to hear yourself inadvertently moaning, groaning or sighing as sounds spontaneously emanate from your throat.

Sometimes sadness disguises itself in symptoms like wheezing or diarrhea. If you suspect that is the case, be sure to check with your doctor to rule out diagnoses such as asthma, CPD (Chronic Pulmonary Disorder), IBS (Irritable Bowel Syndrome), etc. However, if you are already receiving appropriate care for these conditions, you may discover that taking Emotional Medicine can lessen symptoms and speed your recovery.

My own long-absent childhood asthma returned in a mild form after my mother died in 2003. I took it as a message to do more grieving and look more carefully for signals of sadness. When I took my Emotional Medicine for sadness more regularly, my wheezing disappeared.

Caution: For women, sad sensations may be signaling mad (and vice versa for men)

If you are a woman, body signals associated with sadness may also signal anger. Since the Industrial Revolution, many women have been taught it is not ladylike or appropriate to be angry. You are culturally more likely to handle emotional upset, be it sadness or anger, with tears. Furthermore, neurological studies indicate that women's limbic systems (the part of the brain dealing with emotions) are eight times more active than men's when both are asked to recall painful memories.[6] Women also have higher levels of the hormone prolactin (responsible for milk production) which promotes greater tear stimulation. And of course, as a woman, you know or may remember how much easier you could be brought to tears during the hormonal fluctuation of your menstrual cycle.

On the other hand, if you are a man, you might have a hard time catching your body's sad signals. You've probably been taught that it is not manly or appropriate for you to cry. Sadness might appear for you first as anger. Scientists now know that men have less volume in the corpus callosum (the part of your brain that bridges thinking and feeling). As a result, it is much harder to figure out your own or another's emotional responses (and you can tell the women in your life this is a scientific fact!). Finally, as a man, your brain chemistry and male hormones predispose you to anger rather than sadness.[7]

2. Check inner safety and strength

Check your general well-being. Are you exhausted, hungry, depleted? If yes, take care of these needs first. If you try to take some sadness medicine when you're pooped out, you're already overriding important requests for rest, food, relaxation. Your body won't be able to function well and you're likely to feel worse when you're done. Timing is everything. You'll have plenty of opportunities to cry later.

3. Check if you need someone to be with you

Do you need a shoulder to cry on, a hand to hold or a compassionate ear to hear you? Or would your emotions flow more easily if you were by yourself? If you don't want to be alone, put your sadness on hold temporarily until you arrange support from a friend, family member or counselor.

4. Check for conducive environment

Look around to see if you can comfortably make the gestures, motions and noises your body may want to make. See if there are some pillows nearby you can pound or embrace (or use to muffle sound). Is there a tennis racket nearby in case anger arises? Is there a blanket nearby to hide under or cover yourself with if you get cold? Are there some favorite stuffed animals available for comfort?

5. Check with others nearby to be sure they are OK with your emotional expression

Make sure anyone with you is going to be supportive while you take some Emotional Medicine. It they are not, don't do it. Wait until you are alone or with a person who is comfortable with emotional expression and understands its healing value.

6. Check to see what actions, sounds, postures will support emotional flow

You may *sense* you need to curl up in a ball. You may *picture* wrapping yourself up in a blanket. You may *hear* inner guidance to lie flat on the floor or bed to feel the firm support of those surfaces as you let your grief "flatten" you.

Ask your body whether it would help to make sounds. See if you are holding back a whimper. Perhaps you need to sob. If you're concerned about the noise, find a pillow to put against your mouth and wail away. As you allow your emotion to flow, use your multimodal awareness to check in with your body, asking, "Is what I'm doing with my posture, voice, gesture helping move this sadness through its cycle?" Make whatever adjustments seem to be called for. Experiment with different postures and gestures.

7. Check if recalling painful details will facilitate emotional flow

Finally, your story may come in handy! If the sadness you sense in your body isn't flowing, focus on why you're sad. Yes, I'm actually encouraging you to think, ever so briefly and specifically, about the painful details of your situation. These details will remind you of the reasons your sadness got triggered in the first place. When you're not used to having emotion move through your body, you sometimes need to prime the pump with the painful details to get the flow going.

However, *this is practically the only time this is true.* It is very important to use your story ONLY to facilitate emotional discharge in your body. Take great care not to get caught up in your head. Keep focused on how recalling the details increases the flow of emotion through the emotional cycle – up, out and done.

Here's an Action Tip to help.

ACTION TIP: SPEAKING OUT THE DETAILS

Say out loud or write the following statements:

I am sad that _____

_____. Again, I am sad that

_____

_____.

As you repeat the sentence "I am sad that _____," get very specific about what happened that hurt you. Every detail you speak out can stir the sadness to move through your body. Feel what happens in your body as you say these sentences. Allow yourself to cooperate with the sadness as it rises and builds.

---

8. Check if your initial emotion has morphed into a different emotion

If you started to let your body lead you through sadness, you may soon observe your fists clenching, your gestures becoming more emphatic and angry. This is normal. Sadness and anger are flip sides of the same coin of emotional upset. If you are sad about losing someone or feeling hurt, you will often also feel angry about that loss or hurt. For example, even when someone dies through no fault of their own, you may feel terrible sadness followed by anger that they are gone.

9. Check if you're getting overwhelmed or numb

Anytime you start to feel overwhelmed by the intensity of your sadness (or any emotional flow), *stop* and reassess your situation. Perhaps focusing on the details of your upset has trapped you in your head. Shifting awareness to your body sensations is often enough to alleviate overwhelm and enable your sadness to complete its emotional cycle. If that doesn't work, stop and shift your focus to something you know will help you settle down.

On some rare occasions you may find yourself going numb in the middle of an emotional cycle. This is another signal to stop. Emotional Medicine only works if you are alive and present in your body and sensations. It's important to get back into your body before proceeding. Use VIVO or apply the de-numbing protocol. Try a bath or walk. If this is a common occurrence around a particular emotion or issue, you may need to seek professional help in restoring natural emotional flow.

When clients are on the brink of big emotional release, I'll often ask them to check inside to see if they really want to cooperate with the emotions that are pushing for discharge or, instead, smooth out any distress with VIVO. I let them make the choice. Give yourself this same option and make sure taking Emotional Medicine is your free choice at all times.

10. Check if it's time to go for it

There are times, in the safety of your therapist's, pastor's, or holistic practitioner's office (or with an experienced FGFF – Feel Good Fast Friend), when you are feeling strong and supported enough to stay with a particularly intense emotion. In these cases you can keep moving into the red-hot center of sadness, anger or fear. This is strong medicine that needs to be taken with great care, and usually with a professional prescription and presence.

With trained guidance, you might find yourself experiencing the unfathomable pain and profound healing of early childhood emotion. Even though letting your body lead will decrease the amount of time you'll feel this pain, it can be scary stuff if you're not used to it. You might feel that you will die. Of course you won't, and the pain goes away faster than you could imagine. However, unless you're comfortable riding big waves of emotional energy, don't try this at home.

11. Check if it's time for just a tiny dose

As stated earlier, while you can get big rewards from big emotional releases such as wailing, kicking and shaking, you don't always have to go for the big gestures. Sometimes the tiniest dose of emotion (one tear, one fist shake, one trembling moment) will be enough to support your body in releasing stress and restoring sufficient resources for you to keep functioning.

12. Check *continually* to see when your body is done

While you are crying or otherwise releasing, continually ask inside, "Body, are you done yet?" Keep looking for sensations signaling that sadness has completed its cycle. These may be subtle, but they always involve some sense of easing, lightening, relaxing. You may sense a warm flow of energy along your shoulders, an easing and expanding of your breath, a loosening of your stomach or gut. *It's important to notice when the easing begins, because that is the sign that your body is winding down and then done.*

Stopping when your body is naturally done is so important that I've devoted the next chapter to help you learn the fine points. For now, you can rest in knowing that your body will definitely let you know when emotion is subsiding and that you can use your multimodal awareness to watch for those signals.

While you're checking in during emotional flow, don't hold back, but *don't push yourself either.* It is important to let go of any preconceived ideas about how emotional release should look, how somebody else does it, or what your small mind thinks would be best. Your body is a brilliant guide. It knows just how much emotional expression is needed at any moment. Typically, your own defenses will stop you from going farther with any emotion than you are capable of handling.

In all cases of letting your body lead, you begin by welcoming emotion into your awareness. You'll need to decide again and again to slow, soften, open and listen to what your body is telling you about what you are feeling, and how it needs you to cooperate with it to restore balance. Even when it's not appropriate or you're not ready to take Emotional Medicine, it's still important to know what your body is trying to tell you. Knowing what emotions are rising within you gives you the power to decide when, with whom and what you want to do. This is especially true with anger.

The Gifts and Challenges of Anger

Dr. Gabor Maté, the author of *When the Body Says No: Understanding the Stress-Disease Connection* describes anger as one of seven essential tools for healing *any* physical disease. He cites numerous studies of cancer patients indicating that the "most consistently identified risk factor is the inability to express emotion, particularly the feelings associated with anger."[8] However, he accurately describes the conundrum anger presents science, since recent research also revealed that heart attacks can follow outbursts of rage (especially after long periods of simmering hostility). There is a strong correlation between hostility, high blood pressure and coronary disease.

While this conflicting research might be a maze to science, from an Emotional Medicine point of view, it is not a puzzle at all. *Harboring hostility is the hallmark of being in your head,* nursing grievances without getting any relief from a brief, safe, body-led anger release. Blind rage dumped on another person is most certainly driven by a mind trap of victimhood rather than a body-led experience of healing emotion. This is because letting your body lead requires multimodal awareness and big Self alignment, both of which mitigate unconscious anger dumping.

When you, aware and aligned, create a safe and responsible space to cooperate with your anger as it briefly moves through your body, you'll discover that, just as with sadness, you are only minutes away from feeling good.

Back in 1986, when I was making friends with my anger during a course of neo-Reichian therapy, I taped to my bathroom mirror the following sentence: *Anger is a direct route to vitality, clarity and love.* As I write this book 25 years later, this statement still holds true for myself and my clients.

Someone who is labeled an "angry person" or "hostile person" usually does *not* express or experience his or her anger. An "angry person" is typically one whose angry mood stays on simmer for days, weeks, months or a lifetime. You have probably noticed that you can sense the tension when you are near someone who has anger that needs to move.

If you've been trying to experience your anger on your own and nothing seems to help, you might want to consider professional help. Find a body-oriented therapist to help you. It is always important to be sure you feel safe, resourced and ready to welcome your anger before you proceed.

Body Signals for Anger

Your body may naturally signal that anger needs to move by any or all of the following signals: an increase in your heart rate and respiration; an increase in body temperature (witness the expression "the heat of anger"); a tightening of your jaw, teeth, stomach and biceps; a clenching of your fists; a sense of wanting to strike out, slam a door, break something; an urge to shout or yell; a sense of tears coming to your eyes; and an urge to stomp or kick.

As an adult, you may only have a recollection of some of the body's natural anger signals from your childhood. As a woman, even now, some of these sensations might be quite unfamiliar. You may experience embodied anger only when you are at your wits' end, premenstrual, or very hungry. You need to be patient with yourself as you look beneath your composed exterior for the fleeting sense of a clenched jaw, tightened biceps or fingers unconsciously forming a fist.

I often see my women clients pounding their fists for emphasis, without any awareness of what they are doing, when describing how they felt about being mistreated. When I invite them to awareness and ask if they would like to hear what that pounding fist might talk about, they often shrink. We may have to do many sessions in preparation for anger.

As a man, you are probably quite familiar with some of these anger signals but have learned to suppress them to keep yourself and/or others out of harm's way. For all of us, men and women, there is an underlying concern with the "danger" associated with anger in terms of hurting others or getting hurt yourself.

A good way to alleviate any fear of anger is to make a promise to yourself that you will not dump it on another person. This is a hard rule to follow, because with a strong pattern of suppression and/or repression you are probably just as surprised as anyone if you hear yourself say things in an angry tone, or observe yourself acting in an angry way. However, even if you "lose it" temporarily and catch yourself (thanks to your multimodal awareness) dumping anger, you can stop and immediately say, "I'm really angry. I feel like saying and doing more angry things to you now but I'm not going to do that. I need to go and take care of this in another room."

The exception to this no-dumping rule is when you and a partner (romantic, friendship or business) know and trust each other so well that you can both ask *permission* to blow your top for a few minutes when you get upset with each other. This works best if the permitted anger release is time-limited. If each party takes a turn, an impasse can often dissolve.

While it rarely works to try to resolve upsets during an un-planned discharge of anger, it is also almost never helpful to try and work things through when either party is in a state of increasing *buildup* of anger. The rising tension of emotional buildup clouds your clarity. Your body is out of balance and so is your neurochemistry. Things often look very different after an emotional release. I'm sure you've had the experience of regretting something you've said when your perspective was skewed by hormonal imbalance, hunger or fatigue.

Caution: For Both Men and Women, Fear May be Disguised as Anger

Whenever you're feeling mad, it is always a good idea to check deeper within to see if this is a cover for fear. Fear is such a vulnerable feeling; many of us learn early on that it seems more powerful to get angry than scared. (Plus, getting angry is sometimes an instinctual defensive strategy to disarm a predator.)

Let Your Body Lead You through Anger

Once you have removed yourself from the intensity of any relational upset, checked to be sure you're not really more scared than angry, and made sure you're in a safe and appropriate place to discharge anger, you can let your body tell you what it needs to move through your anger. Here again, your "story" comes in handy in fueling the movement up and around the emotional cycle. In this case, imagine speaking out loud to the person or situation that has triggered your anger. (And, yes, it's OK to get angry at God.) Begin saying some sentences out loud: "I am so angry that _____," "I am furious that you _____," and "How could you_____?" Be specific. Now is the time to say all the angry things you wanted to when you wisely held back from dumping. Have at it. Set the timer, though. Check in with yourself in three minutes to be sure you are not caught in a never-ending story.

As you are expressing your anger, check with your body to be sure that you are getting the job done. I have noticed there are times when I want to hit things with an old tennis racket, others when I want to stomp and kick pillows, and still others when I want to use my elbows. I have even been known to smash and break old dishes (purchased for this purpose at the thrift store for my clients and myself), pulverizing them into satisfying little bits. Stomping and crushing cardboard boxes can also be very therapeutic. Pushing away pillows propped against a couch or wall, or held by a supportive friend, can help restore boundaries that have been violated.

Although it is true that feeling emotions sometimes feels awful, it can also feel really good. This is especially true of anger. When you are cooperating with natural, body-led anger, you feel enormously alive and invigorated. All that kicking and pounding is like aerobic exercise, with similar benefits.

Interestingly, when holding back anger becomes a pattern, the body's natural signals often get submerged by suppression. In those cases, anger signals may sometimes be disguised as anxiety, high blood pressure, colitis, etc. While I always encourage you to get a thorough medical evaluation of any distressing symptoms, I also suggest you consider whether suppressed emotion may be contributing to your physical and emotional discomfort. Here's an example from my own life of how anger (and grief) were disguised as anxiety.

Penelope's Story: I'm not Anxious, I'm Angry!

Once, when I was lecturing out of town at a conference, I went to dinner with a small group of other presenters. At our table was a very well-known speaker with expertise in a field tangential to Emotional Medicine. I'll call him Tom. We each took turns talking about our work; he spoke first and I was next. I was aware of being animated and excited as I spoke. The others at the table were obviously involved and enjoying my enthusiasm, except for Tom.

Every time I looked in his direction, all I could see was a flat disinterest. He rarely looked at me and seemed more interested in what was happening around us in the dining area. I knew our work had overlapping areas and I had been quite interested in what, if any, his response would be. When he spoke, I had asked him several questions to draw him out further about his work. I was quite disappointed in what I experienced as a lack of interest from Tom. I couldn't even tell if he were listening to me or reviewing the next day's presentation in his mind.

If this had been a one-on-one conversation with Tom, I would have certainly stopped what I was saying and asked him if he was OK. (Perhaps he had a gas pain or indigestion.) In this format, there was no opportunity to gracefully check in to see what was going on with him. I watched him carefully as others were speaking. I could see that whenever the men were speaking, he leaned into the conversation and seemed to listen with active interest. When any of the women spoke, his attention waned. In one instance he even began a cross conversation with a man sitting next to him while one woman finally took her turn speaking to the whole group.

After the dinner, my husband, Arturo (who had accompanied me on this trip), came to pick me up after spending the evening with an old friend. After we got into the car and exchanged greetings, Arturo began driving us to our hotel. I was uncharacteristically quiet.

I was up in my head mulling over Tom's response to me and the other women in the group. Using multimodal awareness, I noticed my thinking was going round and round in unhappy circles about my lack of self-worth: Maybe I wasn't as smart as Tom was … Maybe I didn't know as much as Tom did … Maybe my ideas were wrong.

Arturo noticed how quiet I was and asked how my presentation had gone. I told him I was having a bit of a hard time. Would he mind if I moved through some energy and explored what was happening for me? He was fine with that. He pulled over to the side of the road so he wouldn't be distracted while driving.

I immediately shifted awareness to my body. I was surprised to discover that I was anxious. My heart was beating faster than usual. I had a metallic taste in my mouth. I felt uneasy and apprehensive. I checked inside to be sure I felt safe and resourced enough to explore my body's response. After getting an inner green light, I prepared to proceed with Emotional Medicine.

Interestingly, though, as soon as I dropped my awareness into my body, some of my feelings of apprehension dissolved. I knew that whatever was up with me, I was most likely just minutes away from feeling better. I knew I'd soon be connected to myself again in a confident, peaceful way. Since Arturo also knew that I'd be able to restore a sense of well-being quickly, he could relax and just be a compassionate presence.

I started by reciting some sentences out loud, starting with "I am scared" and continuing with my first insecure thoughts. After a few sentences, though, I realized what I really felt was anger. I then switched to sentences beginning with "I am angry that _____!" A flood of energy moved through my body. I was angry that Tom was rude to me and the other women. I was angry that, all too often, many men monopolize conversations and do not honor women's contributions. I was angry for the numerous times I had been professionally and personally disregarded because I was a woman. I was angry with my father, benign influence though he was, for not being interested in me in a deeply personal way. I was angry he didn't really take the time to get to know me. I punched the car seat with my fist, and shook my hands in anger.

I soon found myself crying. I was grieving for the loss of a fulfilling relationship with my father and all the other men I had idealized but who didn't value me back. I was crying for myself and for the pain most women have faced in this male-dominated culture. I grieved the lack of a true partnership with Tom, with my dad, with so many of the men I loved and respected. We had all missed out. I alternated between anger and grief for another few minutes, checking in with my body and continually asking, "Are you done yet?" Although these were profound issues, it didn't take long for my emotions to complete their cycle; it was just minutes until my anger and grief subsided.

Once on my way to feeling restored and calm, I turned my attention to Arturo. Although Arturo knows I feel blessed to be married to him and that I don't consider him to be a disregarding, dominating male, I wanted to express again my gratitude to him: for his presence, for the partnership we shared and for the way he supported, valued and respected me.

Notice, dear reader, that this past (his)tory of men dominating and disregarding women didn't change during the minutes I was moving through my anger and grief with Arturo's support and compassion.[9] The fact of Tom's lack of support of me and the other women at the table had not changed, either. However, *I* had changed! I no longer felt anxious, downtrodden, victimized. Instead, I felt strong. I was no longer shrunken, slumped or diminished by my own internalized anger. I was myself again – ready to walk my talk and be true to what I knew.

I was then able to tell Arturo about all the great people I had met and about how well my presentation had gone, as well as to inquire about the details of *his* evening. In a few minutes we were laughing and loving, filled with the pleasure of being alive and happy together.

Let Your Body Lead You through Fear

The obvious ways that your body signals fear are through an increased heart rate, a tightening of your gut, a sour or metallic taste in your mouth, cold hands and feet, an overall drop in body temperature, shaking and chills. You may experience a buckling of your knees or an urge to run away. Anxiety, apprehension or feeling jittery may also signal fear, though as mentioned, anxiety can often cover anger. Not-so-obvious ways the body signals fear are nausea, diarrhea, vomiting, and urinary or bowel incontinence. (As always, if you have any of these physical symptoms, check with your doctor to rule out illness.)

Once you are feeling safe and resourced enough to be present with fear, proceed as you would with sad and mad emotions. Begin some sentences with "I feel scared that _____." Watch what happens in your body. Be specific. You may begin to tremble and shake, which you'll remember is a signal your nervous system is discharging fear energy. Welcome the shaking. It is part of your healing. In all cases, it is important to stay out of your head. You might want to put a blanket around you to support the warming and releasing.

Notice if your legs and arms feel like moving. If they do, and it is possible, cooperate with them. Pace and walk; allow a visualization of running, or go for a brief run. Notice if your hands and feet feel as if they'd like you to shake them. Look for any urges to push away. Keep asking your body what you need to do to support the movement of fear through an emotional cycle.

Set the timer. If, at any time, you are becoming more scared rather than less and feeling overwhelmed, stop the process. Do some VIVO to smooth out your nervous system. Three minutes is a long time to actively feel fear in your body. You may be finished way sooner. Stop when you are done and notice how and where in your body you are feeling better.

Once fear begins to move, it may very well change to anger or sadness. In that case, proceed with saying out loud, "I am mad that _____" or "I am sad that _____" and let your body complete an emotional cycle with anger or grief.

What if you feel both anger and grief? How do you know which one to focus on first? My rule of thumb is to first evaluate which emotion feels predominant in your body. The fact that one emotion seems predominant is your body's way of telling you what is up and what is most important. If you are feeling 60 percent anger and

40 percent sadness, go with the anger. In the case of a 50/50 split between emotions, flip a coin. Either one will be fine.

Whenever you are feeling a mix of emotions, you may find yourself going back and forth between them briefly. You may cry, you may pound, or you may sob, stomp, or even laugh. No problem. Just keep letting your body lead and hang on for the ride. Stay connected to your big "S" Self through your multimodal awareness to be sure you are not getting derailed in a head trip. Look carefully for the emotional energy in your body to subside in way less time than you thought possible.

As you start playing with Emotional Medicine in yourself and your relationships, you will most likely discover that you need to teach people who love you that you don't need them to fix you or do anything while you are feeling your emotions because the emotions themselves are the medicine! Let your loved ones know that all you need is for them to *be* with you. When family and friends observe that you really do know how to take care of yourself, and they really don't have to do anything, they will be relieved. Once they see there is a finish line – that you will stop when you are done – and that, in just a few minutes, your energy is joyous and alive again, they will welcome your emotions and be grateful for the gifts you bring.

Stopping when you are done is an essential part of your Emotional Medicine remedy kit. It requires you to employ your multimodal awareness. Stopping when you are done also enables you to deepen your trust in your body and let it lead. In our next chapter you will learn how to do just that.

ELEVEN

Stop When You're Done

E ve was in a panic when she called me for a session. She was barely able to eat, sleep or concentrate since Chris, her boy-friend of seven years, ended their relationship a few days earlier. She hadn't been able to work at her job as a coordinator for a success-ful local theater's children's drama program, and knew she needed help. Eve was committed to a natural food, alternative-health life-style and wanted to avoid taking antidepressants or anti-anxiety drugs if at all possible.

Fortunately, I had a cancellation that very evening and was able to see Eve within hours of her call. When she arrived, Eve told me the devastating facts of her current situation. Six months before this breakup, her father had died unexpectedly. Suicide was sus-pected. Eve had been very close to her father and estranged from her mother since her parents divorced when she was a teen. Her father, depressed and an active alcoholic, had neglected to make legally binding the changes he enacted to his will after the divorce. At this point Eve's mother stood to inherit his considerable estate. Eve was currently embroiled in a lawsuit against her.

Chris first told Eve he wanted to break up with her just a week before her father died. In light of Eve's tragedy, he agreed to postpone the separation for a few months until she regained some equilibrium.

Three months had passed and now Chris said he needed to end the relationship immediately.

Eve told me that Chris had been so kind and loving to her since her father died, she kept hoping he would change his mind about leaving. Now that he was finally gone, Eve felt that she was coming unglued. The loss of her father, his failure to provide for her financially, the betrayal by her mother and Chris's departure seemed more than she could bear.

Eve described how, since her parents' divorce, she had been unable to cry without becoming hysterical and unable to catch her breath. She'd been crying continuously (or so it seemed) since Chris moved out and had to keep breathing into a paper bag to restore proper respiration. When not crying or hysterical, she was consumed by anxiety.

I asked Eve if she wanted to learn how to let her body lead her through this crisis. She did. I explained that continual focus on the terrible facts of her situation was overwhelming her nervous system.[1] If she wanted to get some relief, Eve would need to shift her attention to what her body required in the present moment to restore well-being. I reassured her that her body was constantly sending her cues and clues about what it needed and that I would help her decipher those messages.

I advised Eve not to move into any crying or grieving unless she felt safe to do so. We started with the VIVO process to help settle her nerves. Once Eve calmed a bit, she wanted to talk about the breakup. I asked her to check whether her body was ready for that now, or if she would prefer just to spend more time chilling out. I could see that her body was moving into an R&R (Rest & Recuperation) mode and I mentioned this. Eve, however, wanted to tell me what had happened. I suggested that while she was talking, she keep her focus primarily on what was happening in her body rather than on the story she was telling.

Soon Eve was crying. "This is so unfair," she said. She couldn't believe how many ways she had been violated. "How could he leave me?" she wailed. After a few minutes of sobbing, Eve sighed. Her face seemed more relaxed. I asked her to focus on her body. I said, "Perhaps your body is really done for now." I was surprised by what happened next.

Eve got angry. No, she didn't want to stop crying. She wasn't done; she hadn't finished telling me her story. There was no stopping her. Eve cried until she was hysterical (about five more minutes) and then asked me to get a paper bag to help her catch her breath. When she could breathe again, I asked her if she felt that "losing control" was doing justice to the enormity of the injustice in her life. I wondered aloud whether she thought if she didn't grieve every ache and agony every time she cried that she wasn't really honoring her pain. Perhaps her hysteria was a makeshift memorial to her wounds?

Eve got very quiet. She had never thought about it that way. She could see how much stress was created by getting hysterical. She felt weak and exhausted, miserable even, and really did want to find another way. As we explored other approaches for witnessing her pain, Eve had a brainstorm. Perhaps she could use her art and drama training to create a ritual to officially commemorate her losses. Eve could then use her tears "medicinally," to help restore resources and cope with her challenging life.

In her next session, Eve reported that the rituals had really helped. She was now ready to slow down, cry, and let her body tell her when it was done. She could now tell the difference between her mind being done with telling a story and her body being done with moving through an emotion. Eve began to understand that when she pushed herself to hysteria, she was *unwittingly perpetuating injustice against herself*. She also saw that whenever she didn't take care of herself, she was unconsciously perpetuating the family pattern of neglect and betrayal.

Eve began to use her big "S" Self-awareness to see and listen to what her body was telling her. Slowly and gently, she learned how to stop when her body was done with sad, mad, scared feelings. She began to sleep better, regained an appetite and the ability to concentrate. Eve now had some remedies to take with her to face whatever life presented.

Because Eve now knew how to decipher and honor her body signals and now had the will to stop when she was done, she no longer feared her sad, mad and scared feelings. She discovered it was possible to use Emotional Medicine to restore confidence and clarity. Unfortunately, Eve's mother prevailed in the lawsuit. By the time the court case was over, however, Eve had found the strength to take care of herself and navigate her own course. She was no longer a victim.

What Does it Mean to be Done?

What were the signals Eve learned to decipher to help her stop when she was done? I'll get to that in a minute. The first thing you need to know, though, is that for the purposes of Emotional Medicine, "done" means specifically that your *body* is done. In most cases, when you get emotional your muscles are activated, your breathing and heart rate alter, your gut contracts and you experience a myriad of body changes – subtle and not so subtle. Your metabolism is primed with a buildup of energy in case you need to fight, flee or disengage. This happens even when the "predator" you are facing is a departing boyfriend, an irritated coworker, an unpaid bill, or an important business presentation.

If you're like most of us, you've probably noticed that once you get upset about something, it's not so easy to stop. Sometimes you just can't seem to shake off the sadness, irritability or anxiety. You might feel bad for days. That's one of the reasons you may have tried not to get upset at all. However, now that you know how important it is to allow your sad, mad, scared emotions to manifest, it is even more imperative to know how to stop when your body is done.

The changes that occur in your body during emotional buildup are meant to be *short-term*. When an emotional event is over, your body is ready to relax and return to normal. In the case of crying, "done" means your body is done with tears, sobbing and chest-heaving action. According to Gerda Boyesen's Biodynamic Theory, as emotions move through you, the energy in your body shifts: from moving upwards toward expression to moving downwards towards R&R.

One of the ways I describe the rest and recuperation phase of Emotional Medicine is to equate it with going to the beach. For most of us, the beach represents R&R. At the beach you can laze about, snooze, and let yourself recover from the hectic pace of your life. So it is after emotional discharge: Your body lets you know in various ways it is done – done with preparing for action and expression; done with hormonal and nervous-system buildup; and ready for the beach.

Body Cues and Clues

What is one of the first things you do when you finally get your blanket spread out at the beach ... after you slather on your sun-screen ... smoosh the sand around under your body just so ... place your cool drink conveniently next to you ... and finally rest your weary head on a soft towel? Why, very often you sigh – a long, deep sigh. This is a cue telling you you're *done* for now. It's OK to let go. You're done working, planning, efforting, done with getting *to* the beach. Sighing says that, for now, you're all about R&R.

Sighing is also one of the main clues your body uses to let you know it is done with sad, mad, scared feelings after you've experienced them for a few minutes. Interestingly, when you are sad but stuck in buildup and resistance to crying, sighing is a signal that you need to cry. On the other side of the cycle, after crying, sighing is a clue that you are *done*. In most cases, sighing signals it's time for a change in what you're doing.

Other signals that your body is done with emotional expression include breathing and muscular changes. You start to breathe with less effort. Each breath is deeper, slower and more effortless. You may notice that your muscles are less tense and more relaxed and that you have an overall, increased sense of release and relaxation.

Temperature changes are also important clues that you are done with an emotion. Your hands and feet may change from cold to warm. Your face may shift from hot and flushed to cool and dry. You may experience radiating warmth across your shoulders or down your spine. Whatever changes happen, when you are done your body shifts from tension, discharge and discomfort to release, relaxation and comfort.

There is one cue that your body is done that isn't *initially* comfortable, but which, when you stay with it, you'll soon find so. That cue is a feeling of fatigue, of being deeply spent. If you're like most of us, it's sometimes hard to allow yourself to feel just how tired you really are. You've probably already experienced resistance to feeling your own fatigue, fighting it with coffee or caffeinated sodas. Being fully present to fatigue may trigger a blip of fear, especially if you don't know that once you *feel* the fatigue, it starts to change.

After just a few moments of feeling even the most aching weariness, you'll be amazed how it smoothes out into relaxation. I believe that first experience of fatigue is so uncomfortable because those initial sensations contain all the tightness your muscles, joints, blood vessels and cells have been holding prior to your emotional discharge. Once you allow yourself to feel tired, tension releases and everything eases. Bringing awareness to *anything* invites expansion and release. Awareness itself is medicine!

Another cue that you are done with an emotion may surprise you: You may find yourself laughing. As tears and sobbing subside, there is often a moment when you laugh spontaneously. Suddenly your divine tragedy becomes a divine comedy. You laugh and gain a sense of perspective and proportion. You effortlessly experience what it means not to take yourself so seriously – for a moment, anyway. This crack in the gloom may give you just a brief glimpse of light.

A caveat: This spontaneous lightening up is vastly different from any efforts you make to "look on the bright side." When unexpected laughter signals that you are done with crying, it is an effortless gift, a harbinger of the pleasure and peace that await when you allow yourself to flow with the natural rhythms of life: sad, mad, scared, and *glad*.

Gut gurgling is another guarantee that your body is in recovery mode. It is not usually the first clue that you are done because typically it doesn't appear until *after* you've already eased into R&R. Sometimes, when you have completed an emotional cycle and are in recovery mode, but your mind still wants to dart back to your painful story because you're not sure you're really done, your gut will gurgle and burble. When this happens with clients, I often smile and say, "Busted." Your habitual mind may be pulled back to your sad story, but your body is telling you it really *is* done – it is already back at the beach.

The switch from active emotional expression to R&R is often very subtle. When your body shifts from tears moving up and out to tears moving down and done, it doesn't shift all at once. As there comes a specific moment in the rhythm of the ocean when the tide turns, so it is with your emotional tides. Even though an ocean-ographer can tell you exactly the minute the tide turns, it doesn't suddenly go out or come in as one big whoosh. The tide current changes direction subtly. You often can't tell, when you start walking along the beach, whether the tide is going in or coming out. But, as you continue walking, you notice either that the waves are coming closer to your toes or moving away and providing an expanse of sand. You tune into the tides and can soon tell in which direction the ocean is moving.

The moment of being done with an emotion may be similarly subtle, but once you start looking for when you are done *you will be the first to know*. You will be the first to notice that the intensity of your sobbing is subsiding; that your tears are no longer gushing, but slowing to a trickle; that your chest is no longer heaving, but gently rising and falling; and that your stomach is not so tight. Your body may also have its own idiosyncratic ways of letting you know it is done and ready for R&R. As you practice focusing on your body signals, you will discover its unique language.

Even when an ocean or emotional tide has turned from flowing to ebbing, there may be a rogue wave or two that comes crashing back to previous levels. When this happens at the beach, you hustle towards dry sand to get away. When this happens emotionally, though, it is OK to let another wavelet of feeling move through your experience. Cry again, briefly, but stay aware of the changing undercurrent, the pull towards completion. Check in with your body for the predominant energy. Usually you will see that it is basically done. You can then let that extra wave carry you back to the beach for your R&R. (A caveat: When you are experiencing a horrific loss, you may find yourself going through a few sets of emotion – buildup, discharge, and release – with just a little respite between waves, 10 to 20 minutes at most. But be VERY cautious to discern that these emotional waves are truly your body leading you into deeper discharge and not your sly, habitual mind pulling you back into a never-ending story of misery.)

Am I Done Yet?

Back in my divorce crisis of 1983, when I first discovered there was an end point to any episode of emotional upset, I had a devil of a time putting my insight into practice. I was so distraught about the end of my marriage that every time I got sad or mad, I would get caught in my story and go round and round. Before I knew it I'd be dragged through tsunamis of emotion triggered by continuing to focus on my loss. My old unconscious pattern of dwelling in misery would take over and I would be tumbled by those seemingly unending waves of grief. Of course, once I became *aware* that this was happening, that I was restimulating grief with my thoughts, I would check in with my body and let it lead me to peace. But, I wondered what I could do to loosen the grip that familiar pattern had on my behavior? I knew I needed something to keep me conscious and focused in my body.

Consciousness seekers and meditators have historically employed a word, image or "mantra" (the Sanskrit word for an inner prayer) to focus awareness and as a touchstone. Rosaries, prayer beads or mantras such as "Be still and know that I am God" are all techniques humans have devised to support and develop awareness. I knew I needed something like that to help me stay conscious, out of my head, and in my body.

I finally decided that whenever I was in the midst of a powerful movement of emotion, I would continually ask myself, *"Am I done yet?"* Even when I used my sad story to help me feel more deeply my mad, sad, scared energy, I would keep this mantra in the back of my awareness as a guide. As I was sobbing or stomping, I would ask myself, *"Am I done yet?"* When a powerful set of emotional waves had subsided but another seemed to be rising, I would also ask, *"Am I done yet?"* before allowing myself to get caught up again. This mantra, *"Am I done yet?"* helped me stay conscious and develop new behaviors. Now, as I write this book, following my body's cues and letting my body lead is reflexive and effortless. I no longer need to specifically ask myself if I am done. Mostly, I just cry when I am sad and stop when I am done.

What Science Says About the Duration of Emotion

Current research about the duration of emotion is all over the place. From Dr. Paul Ekman's early report that "the great majority of expressions of felt emotions last between one-half to four seconds, and those that are shorter or longer are mock or other kinds of false expressions"[2] to Dutch scientist Nico Frijda's description of a Turkish immigrant's feeling of joy at passing his driving instructor's examination, which lasted almost 11 hours,[3] the evidence so far is contradictory.

From my decades of observation as a clinician, I believe these discrepancies could be accounted for by studying the difference in how long an emotion lasts when you let your body lead you through the experience versus how long an emotion lasts when you let your story lead you. You have probably done enough of your own personal research to know that when you are up in your head, focused in your stories, you can keep yourself upset for hours or even days by continually restimulating yourself and recharging your physiology, for better or worse.

This is vastly different from tracking the fresh movement of an emotion through your physiology and keeping your attention focused on your body. I have not found any research yet that explores *this* essential distinction, though a Belgian scientist, Bernard Rime, has found in at least one study that the amount of time you spend thinking about or mulling over an emotion (ruminating) does increase its intensity.[4]

I am also encouraged that scientists including Kevin Ochsner and James Gross are recommending that future research focus on measuring the difference emotion generates in experience, behavior, and physiology as well as changes in brain activity.[5] I believe they will discover what I have observed for years: most emotion courses through the body in a very short time – perhaps not the four seconds that Ekman reports,[6] but an average of about three minutes.

Set Your Timer

Several years after I repeatedly observed the short duration of most emotions in the body, I started suggesting clients set their timers whenever they were embarking on the journey of feeling them. Initially, this was a kind of a joke, a way of defusing the fear of emotions many have. "Set your timer," I would say when a client was on the brink of an emotion but afraid to let go and feel it. "Three minutes and you'll feel better. Try it."

Of course, no one has ever actually set a timer, but the notion is another touchstone for learning to stop when emotions are done. If you keep an inner timer in mind, you will most likely notice that your emotions, too, are done in just a few minutes. Keep the image of a timer in your imagination and the mantra *"Am I done yet?"* in your awareness and you will be well-supported in not crying one more tear than necessary.

Not One More Tear than Necessary

Finally, the last support that may help you stop when you are done is to make a decision not to cry one more tear than necessary.

If you've already made the decision to let your body lead, this will seem easy by comparison. Deciding to let your body lead involves the important challenges of letting go of ego control and surrendering to wisdom that at first feels unfamiliar. However, deciding not to cry one more tear than necessary is a decision where you get to take charge. Resolving not to cry one more tear than necessary is a decision you make when you are ready to masterfully shift your focus from hurting to healing.

ACTION TIP

Fill in the blanks in the following sentences:
I am ready to shift my focus from hurting to healing because

_____.
It is time for me to shift my focus from hurting to healing because _____

_____.
It is important for me to shift my focus from hurting to healing because _____

_____.
When I shift my focus from hurting to healing I will benefit in the following ways: _____

_____

_____.

Being ready to shift from focusing on your pain to focusing single-mindedly on your healing often takes some time. This may involve shifting a generations-long pattern of hurting. The women in your family may have been very good at hurting. At least in Western culture, women have a long-standing association with pain. If you are a woman, the Old Testament tells you it is your punishment to suffer the pains of childbirth. Interestingly, since the Bible was written by men, they didn't mention the ecstasy that usually accompanies giving birth (assuming you're not overmedicated) when you finally see and hold your baby. Perhaps women thought it wise to keep it to themselves! Menstrual cycles have also kept many women tied to monthly experiences of cramping and discomfort.

For you to break out of a long-standing personal or cultural pattern of cleaving to pain requires readiness and will. And, as always, transformation requires no blame! If you are not ready yet, be gentle with yourself. Just the fact of your reading this book and entering the territory of Emotional Medicine will rearrange your molecules.

Why is it Important to Stop When You're Done?

When your body is ready for R&R and you push past that for another round of emotional discharge, you create more stress for your body and yourself. You are then working at cross purposes to your natural rhythms and body wisdom. Your body misses an important chance to recoup and restore resources. You keep yourself in a chronic state of tension. How do you finally stop crying once you've pushed past your body's natural marker? You probably cry until you are exhausted. There is little Emotional Medicine to be found once you're exhausted. You'll miss the peace and bliss that usually await the end of every natural emotional cycle.

Once you learn to stop when you're done, you open your inner medicine chest of feel-good remedies. However, in order to take those remedies at full potency, you need to ensure you are able to enjoy, and even indulge, pleasure. While this may seem like a no-brainer (of course everyone knows how to enjoy pleasure), you will be surprised to discover how much you have been unwittingly holding back from enjoying the full benefit of Emotional Medicine. In the next chapter, you'll learn exactly what it means to enjoy pleasure, and how it can open your heart and soul to a deeper experience of spirit.

TWELVE

Focus On Feeling Good

The fact that you'll find some variation of happy, confident and peaceful feelings at the end of every emotional cycle is a gift from God/Nature/Spirit. Just as gravity keeps you tethered to earth, you can count on emotions to deposit you at the threshold of good feelings.[1] However, in order to use Emotional Medicine to feel good fast you have to be willing to focus on the good feelings that complete every emotional cycle – for at least three minutes. Does that sound doable?

Although this may sound like a no-brainer, you might be one of the many people for whom this is difficult. I know, because I'm one of them. This is the hardest part of the Emotional Medicine method for me. *Crying?* Easy. *Stopping when done?* Learnable. *Focusing on feeling good?* Now that's a challenge.

This can be tricky partly because once you learn to stop emoting when you're body's done, you'll feel somewhat relieved and stronger immediately. It's so easy to just move on to the next item, activity, or appointment on your to-do list. However, if you don't take a minimum of three minutes to sit with, be with, focus on and luxuriate in those good feelings, you will not experience the amazing shift in state of mind and being that Emotional Medicine fosters. Even worse, you may get caught back up in your sad, infuriating, scary story.

This happens because your human mind has an innate tendency to remember negative experiences more than positive ones. Scientific speculation is that negative experiences held more survival value when early humans faced a host of natural dangers. The problem now is that, even as emotion drops you at the doorway to pleasure, your mind may still keep trying to protect you by regurgitating negativity.

So there you are at the end of an emotional cycle: you've cried, you've stopped, you feel a bit better already, but your mind is still likely to throw up the painful problems that triggered your upset unless you focus fiercely on feeling good.

Fortunately, you get to choose where to focus your attention. Multimodal awareness and Self-alignment give you the skills to do this. Fortunately, too, although your mind is programmed to use pain as a survival guide, your body is programmed to seek and utilize pleasure for optimum functioning. Focusing on pleasure lays down new pathways in your mind as well as supporting a joyous shift in your human experience.

Sally Gets Glad

The other day I was giving a session to Sally, a brilliant 70-year-old retired editor scraping by on Social Security. Sally was having a terrible time focusing on a serious and personal legal matter. She was unable to organize timelines, data, and the myriad details of her case. What she needed, she said, was clarity.

Although Sally couldn't manage the piles of papers on her dining room table, paradoxically, her mind was capable of absorbing complex psychological and metaphysical concepts quickly. Sally had done a lot of transformational work over the years, trying various therapies and spiritual practices. Currently she spent several hours in mantra meditation daily. Sally often got impatient with folks (including me) who could not keep up with her intellectually.

In earlier sessions we had evaluated and changed her diet, adding more protein to support brain function and overall health, ruled out any age-related syndromes or medication side effects (there were none), and assessed her current living situation: noisy, uncooperative neighbors as well as her 88-year-old, miserly father living, *in her same building*, very comfortably on a trust fund swindled from an inheritance set up for Sally by her grandmother. In this particular session, we began to explore how focusing on feeling good could help her regain mental acuity.

Sally acknowledged that although she was quite furious at her father ("that old dingbat"), she didn't want to do any anger release work. She'd done "primal scream" therapy in the 80s, she said, and didn't want to go down that road again. I explained that Emotional Medicine was different – brief and body-led. I suggested that the daily insult of watching her father fritter away her trust fund was likely triggering ongoing anger. The energy it took to suppress that anger response could leave her so depleted she wouldn't be able to concentrate on anything else.

Sally had read some of the chapters of this book and decided she'd give it a try. In preparation for anger release, I invited Sally to bring awareness to her body. It wasn't until I was guiding her to focus on body sensations that I discovered Sally wasn't interested in either acknowledging or feeling pleasure.

Although *I* could see that she was clearly getting more relaxed and happy as she dropped into body sensations, the best Sally could come up with was vague absence of pain and a neutral sense of "there-ness." As I tried guiding her to enjoy her clearly visible relaxation, she said, "I'm not really interested in focusing on pleasure. That's a waste of time."

I explained that Emotional Medicine couldn't deliver clarity if she wouldn't slow down and feel the pleasure, relaxation and good feelings waiting at the end of any emotional release. Taking some time to slow down and be present for the healing taking place in her bodymind would support both body and brain in rebalancing. She would end up feeling relaxed *and* alert!

This perked up Sally's motivation. She decided to explore those "there-ness" sensations to see what pleasure they might contain. Sally was first able to identify a "kind of tingling" in her spine. She had felt this before, she said, during her daily meditation. As she followed the tingling sensation with her awareness, she experienced new sensations of openness, floating and flow. As Sally became increasingly comfortable, she simultaneously became ready to address the anger she was carrying toward her father.[2]

Sally described how furious it made her to watch her father throw money at the local scoundrels who were exploiting him. As she was telling me this story (a variation on previous visits), Sally felt the fury in her body. With encouragement, Sally was able to bring her fists down on some pillows while imagining speaking out her anger to her father. Several minutes later, she said, amazed, "I can't believe it, it's working. I really feel better." She was laughing and smiling.

"Now," I said, "this is the tricky part. Bring your attention to focus only on what's 'feeling better.' Stay in your body." I then invited Sally to name the specific sensations that comprised "feeling better." Her breathing eased. Her color was alive and healthy.

After a minute of focusing on feeling good, angry thoughts popped up in Sally's mind again. "I can't believe he's such a jerk," she said. Although I could see her body was still pulsing with positive energy, her mind was recycling old patterns. She still needed a few more minutes of pleasure focus before her mind would settle into a groove of happy talk.

"What is predominant in your experience now," I asked, *"feeling* better or *thinking* anger?" "Feeling better," Sally replied. "Then focus on the predominant energy," I said. "Let those angry thoughts go by like clouds. Let your body lead." Sally sighed a deliciously relaxing sigh. I guided her to focus on the floating, tingling, more positive feelings. "I get it now," she said.

Soon Sally's eyes twinkled. She said, "I'm amazed. I feel like my old self. I feel clear-headed. I guess I'll have to practice this!"

Clarity restored, Sally devised a plan to hire two friends who loved organizing to come and help out. I encouraged Sally to practice discharging anger whenever triggered, and, most importantly, to look for and focus on the pleasure that ensued.

"If you want to," I continued, "you could also look for pleasurable sensations any old time of the day or night." In doing this, she would be opening new bodymind grooves for feeling good. I invited Sally to consider she no longer needed to tolerate feeling bad for longer than the minutes it would take to shift her biochemistry. Doing this, I explained, would take focus and commitment to keep at it – to shift her basic orientation from pain to pleasure.

Dear reader, although this chapter describes the importance of a specific focus on good feelings at the end of an emotional cycle, it's just as important to consider the value of shifting *your* basic life orientation from pain to pleasure.

Shifting your inner home base from pain to pleasure means you become impatient whenever you don't feel some variation of happy, confident or peaceful. I'm suggesting you consider feeling good your default state – the place you plan and expect to come home to.

Although this reorientation is complicated partly because of your innate brain programming, it also involves a gob of cultural/religious/societal fear. For at least 5,000 years, history has not been kind to pleasure-seekers. It's only recently that pleasure has regained a good reputation.

Culture Clash

For millennia, churches, schools and cultures have demonized pleasure out of ignorance of the essential role it plays in healthy living. Many holy men, leaders and teachers did not know natural pleasure provides a direct route to physical health and productive citizenship, as well as a pathway to spiritual experience.

Pleasure has been equated with sex and temptation for so long in our Western religious history that it's no wonder many still shy away. At one time, experiencing pleasure was even grounds for death. Even the word "pleasure" itself may bring a blush of sexual shame.

Beyond Sex

Not that there's anything wrong with sex. Sex is good for your mood, your heart and your immune system. As a matter of fact, Dr. Mehmet Oz, author of *You: The Owner's Manual*[3] and a regular guest on Oprah's TV show (and now headlining his own show) recommends everyone have at least four orgasms a week to maintain good health.

It's important, though, to distinguish the natural day-in, day-out pleasure available by virtue of being alive in a feeling body from arousing sexual pleasure that's heading toward orgasm. You need to feel free to seek nonsexual pleasure, talk about it freely and indulge it without shame.

Sometimes even nonsexual pleasure can feel downright sexy, juicy and erotic. When pleasurable, tingly feeling arise in your body, you may also feel those same tingly feelings in your genitals. This is healthy. You can allow these feelings to be present without fear. Enjoy them for their own sake. Keep them to yourself and smile sweetly.

Born to Be Good

While the early religious canon was bent on scaring people away from pleasure, early psychological theory was geared toward analyzing dysfunction and pain. Fortunately, as Western theology now turns to embracing sexuality and pleasure, there is a tandem movement in the social sciences toward "positive psychology." Positive psychology is focused on bringing attention to affirmative human characteristics and the innate resilience of the human psyche and spirit. That means focusing on and enjoying pleasure!

Dacher Keltner describes the key to happiness in his timely book, *Born to Be Good*,[4] as an ability "to let these [positive] emotions arise, to see them fully in oneself and in others, and to train the eye and mind in that practice." Keltner considers this a meditation practice and so do I. Focusing on pleasure is a spiritual practice and a healing practice.

Even though almost everyone's childhood wounds are problematic, new brain research indicates that your brain is resilient. Under certain circumstances it can regenerate new cells and establish new connections. Neuroscientists call this "neuroplasticity." In simple terms, your brain has the potential to keep learning and growing through every stage of life.

If you've been carrying crippling beliefs from childhood, e.g., pleasure is selfish, dangerous, and sinful, there is now great hope for healing. Finally culture, religion, and science are all conspiring to help you bust out of any dungeon of self-denial. You do not need to suffer any more.

You were born to enjoy pleasure. You were born to seek it. Your innate human drive to feel good is so strong it will not be denied. Ultimately, pleasure can't be beaten, frightened or proselytized out of you. Pleasure plays an integral role in all of the healthy, creative, spiritual, fulfilling aspects of your life on planet Earth. Finally you are free, in the words of my favorite poet, Mary Oliver, to "let the soft animal of your body love what it loves."[5] Let's take a look at all the good that pleasure brings.

Pleasure Helps You Be a Better Person

Riane Eisler, in her seminal book *Sacred Pleasure*, describes how most of us "have been taught to associate pleasure with such terms as *hedonism* and *narcissism,* with self-centeredness and selfishness."[6]

She describes how the requirement for feeling pleasure – *an ability to be aware of feelings in your body in the present moment* – actually leads to an increase of empathy and connection with others. In this way, feeling pleasure is actually an antidote for selfishness and cruelty.

See if you don't breathe a bit easier knowing that every bit of pleasure you learn to enjoy will make you a better person: healthier, happier, and more generous to others. You've probably heard the saying, "If mama ain't happy, ain't nobody happy." Good mothers everywhere know this to be true. You, mother or not, need to take time to replenish yourself, to fill up your tank so you have enough gas to get through your busy day. And don't forget that once you're an adult, you're always on call to be your *own* good mother.

Pleasure is Good for You

The jury is in on this one. Psychologists Carl Charnetski and Francis Brennan describe numerous scientific studies in their book, *Feeling Good is Good for You,* which prove pleasure decreases stress and pain, improves immune function, and improves your mood.[7] And of course, it's free … such a deal!

You feel pleasure because of the release of certain chemicals in your body called endorphins. Endorphins are substances your body produces which are the endogenous (body-made) counterpart to the opium produced by poppies (*end*ogenous plus m*orphin*e equals *endorphin.*) When your body makes endorphins, they are typically beneficial to your health with no side effects, no withdrawal.

You've probably heard of or had experience with endorphins in relation to an "exercise or runner's high": the experience of well-being following a moderate run or aerobic workout. You may not know, though, that whenever you do *anything* that feels good – stroking your pet, listening to your favorite music, watching clouds go by – your body is also exuding endorphins. Endorphins are there to help you recover from stress and they are there to help you deepen pleasure. Whenever you are feeling good, there's an endorphin around somewhere.

For endorphins and pleasure, however, balance is the key. Have you ever heard someone describe something as "too much of a good thing"? The same holds true when it comes to endorphins. Too many endorphins and you end up feeling depressed and sluggish. Too few and you end up feeling irritable and unhappy.

Pleasure Brings New Possibilities

Another benefit pleasure brings is supporting you to explore new possibilities. In their book *The Pleasure Connection*, Deva and James Beck describe how "endorphins give us the biochemical (including mental and emotional) *motivations we need to perceive, reflect, and adapt with flexible responses to our changing environment.*"[8] (Italics mine.)

Yes, yes, I say. This is exactly what I have seen with Emotional Medicine. When you focus on a few minutes of pleasure after a brief cry, pillow-pound or tremble, you'll typically end up feeling open to new possibilities as well as motivated to handle whatever challenges you currently face.

Check out whether you now feel more ready focus on pleasure. See if you feel it's possible, no matter what your baggage, to get ready, get set, and *go for it*. If so, it's time to make a new decision.

Getting Ready: Making a New Decision

In all cases, whether your embodied, pleasure-puppy behaviors were suppressed by a pleasure-crushing culture or smashed by personal approbation from wounded caretakers, getting ready to resurrect pleasure requires you make a new, grown-up decision.

Even though you have wounds, habits and beliefs that have previously locked you into a life sentence of suffering, you *always* have the power to make a new choice for yourself. Old patterns only have permanent power when you are not aware of them and when you live your life by their default settings: garbage in, garbage out.

Here's an Action Tip to help you make a new default setting to welcome and allow pleasure.

ACTION TIP

Try saying the following words out loud. "I welcome (choose, embrace, allow) pleasure." Write your new decision on several pieces of paper and place them where your eyes will fall upon them often during the course of the day. (Make up your own sentence, if you'd like.) If you want to be more private, you can write your new decision on a piece of colored paper. Hide that sentence away. Place unobtrusive bits of that same colored paper (with nothing written on it) around your home, office and car. Research indicates just seeing that tiny bit of colored paper will anchor your affirmation in memory. No one else needs to know what you are doing. Let this new decision be your mantra, prayer and intention for the next weeks and months ... or for the rest of your life.

Your next step to enjoy pleasure involves setting yourself up with the support you'll need to allow post-emotion pleasure to flow and grow.

Getting Set: Time, Space and Big "S" Support

Plan, in advance, to set aside at *least three minutes* to focus on your body's pleasurable response the next time you cry when you're sad and stop when you're done. Scope out some comfortable spaces at home. (Your safely parked car can also work fine.)

Your plan can include either being alone or accompanied by a tender person or your FGFF. Even though every aspect of Emotional Medicine is designed to use solo, you can increase the potency of this medicine while in the presence of another caring person.

Human beings are herd animals. You may be able to open more deeply into pleasure when a caring person is nearby. Still, it's important you learn to take your Emotional Medicine, at least sometimes, by yourself. That's because there will always be times you desperately feel the need for someone to help you and he or she, for whatever reason, *will not be available*. As a matter of fact, it is almost axiomatic that when you are at your worst and most stressed, your intimates, similarly, will likely be at their worst and most stressed. Your big "S" Self, on the other hand, is always there for you, ready to provide a haven of awareness and support.

Slow Down – Profound, Life-Altering Pleasure Ahead!

As mentioned, you may feel so much better whenever you do cry and stop that you automatically race ahead to the next item on your list. Of course, sometimes it's right to grab a quick gulp of relief and then go on. Life often moves very fast. However, while it *is* always great to feel even a little bit better, the moments at the end of an emotional cycle provide a remarkable opportunity for self-healing.

What's happening biologically in these pivotal moments is that your body is shifting from a state of emotional arousal to a state of release and relaxation. Your biochemistry is changing. Your body is trying to reestablish a state of balance and well-being.

Do you know what you would miss if you rushed past this pleasure to solve your next problem? For one thing, natural Prozac! Pleasure offers what seems to be a natural antidepressant in the perfect dose for you with *no side effects*. And there's another important way in which your body's natural Emotional Medicine works better than pharmaceuticals: natural pleasure is a key to opening the door to profound, life-altering spiritual experience.

I Lose a Son and Gain the Universe

When my son, Adam, was 12, he moved from San Diego to Massachusetts to live with his dad. This relocation had been prearranged seven years earlier during our divorce settlement. The plan was that I would have Adam from age six to twelve; his dad would have him from age twelve to eighteen. It seemed reasonable at the time. I had no idea how devastating this would be when it was actually time for him to go, even though I knew it was right for Adam. I had thoroughly enjoyed being with my child.

This was the hardest thing I'd ever done. The wrenching grief at the end of my marriage paled in comparison. I knew when my first marriage ended that I'd likely have another one. When Adam left, I knew I would never have another child; this was the end of my experience as a full-time mother.

I had to use all of my Emotional Medicine skills to heal this pain. One particularly hard day, the enormity of the loss was reverberating through every molecule of my body. Adam had been gone about a week. I was nauseated and wanted to throw up. I sobbed and sobbed. I was literally flattened to the floor of my home office like dead weight. During this emotional cycle (which was more like ten minutes than three), I kept riding waves of anguish and asking inside if I was done. I also kept saying to myself, "This will pass." And it did.

Finally, it was over. I was exhausted, but still. At first I felt a kind of nothingness and relieved neutrality. A few moments later, subtle trickles of warmth and well-being pervaded my body. This time I intuitively knew it was important to stay with them, softening and opening to the increasing pleasure. Minutes went by. I became aware that the floor now felt solid and supportive beneath my body.

I heard a bird call outside my window and saw the trees blowing gently in the wind. I saw the blue sky. More warmth and pleasure arose within me. I felt increasingly peaceful. I soon noticed that I no longer missed Adam. I felt connected with the entire universe in a way that filled me completely. I felt that everything was OK ... I was OK ... Adam was OK. The fact that he was gone was irrelevant.

At that moment I was connected to *being* in a way that reassured me to my core. From that point forward, I've carried the knowing of this nourishing *beingness* with me always. I've returned to it again and again. I've rested in it, licked my wounds in it, found my big "S" Self in it. Enjoying these moments of pleasure opened the door for a profound spiritual experience. I am now more capable of letting go in all the ways that life demands.

Of course, this kind of awakening doesn't happen at the end of every emotional cycle. But it often does. I don't want you to miss out.

Here's a "Good to Go" (or "Go to Good") guide to help you extract every bit of soul-satisfying pleasure available at the end of emotional experience. You may want to read through this next section a couple of times so it'll be easier to remember next time you're at the end of an emotional cycle.

Go!

First, as always, when you find yourself at the end of an emotional cycle, keep your awareness in body sensations. It may help to close your eyes. Remember, it's normal if the first sensations you experience are not those of overwhelming pleasure. Don't despair. Be present with what *is* there. It is typical to move through a few moments of tiredness, fatigue or a kind of "nothing's happening" neutrality as you settle down. Not to worry. This is often how pleasure starts.

After about a minute, if you are not yet experiencing any sensations of pleasure, start looking. Scan your body for *anything* that feels good. Look for warmth, coolness or a pleasing temperature in your body. Check your lungs to notice how you are breathing. Remember, you're looking for *subtle* shifts from the swift action of coursing emotion to the peace of slowly spreading pleasure.

Check your hands and feet. See if you feel sensations of well-being spreading across your shoulders or down your spine. Back and shoulders are often repositories of good feeling after emotional release. Look for tingling, pulsing, flowing, relaxing or gurgling sensations anywhere in your body.

Eyes Focused Down Left

You'll be able to dwell in pleasure more fully if you keep your eyes focused *down and to the left*. Whether open or closed, the important factor here is to shift your outer or inner gaze down into your body by moving your eyes down and to the left of your eye sockets. Neurolinguistic programming researchers have determined that when your eyes are focused in this way, you are most likely having an internal, body-focused experience in the present moment.

Take your time. Explore the pleasure you do find. Ask yourself, If these sensations were a color, what color would they be? If you get a sense of a color, allow that extra dimension to deepen your experience. If you don't get a color, just return to your body sensations and enjoy.

This is how natural pleasure begins – small and subtle. These gently spreading sensations are signals that endorphins and dopamine are flowing through your body. Once you're sufficiently shifted, surrender to it. Give in. Indulge. This is as good for you as chocolate (if not better) and it's not fattening. It may help to ask inside, "Is there more?"[9] to support you in continuing to look for pleasure in your body. (This is the reverse of the "Am I done?" question to help you get through pain quickly. Here you want to slow down and luxuriate.)

If you find yourself drawn to thoughts again of what isn't good, gently bring your focus back to what feels good here and now in your body. This is normal. It is just your analytical mind doing what it does best: configuring opposites. For your linear mind, the thought of one category intrinsically includes its opposite. *It doesn't mean anything.* Pay it no mind.

Happily, your body doesn't live in the realm of analysis, opposites, guilt or shoulds. Focusing on bodily experience brings you to a steady green light, beckoning you to cross over safely to pleasure, encouraging you to go for it!

Three minutes seems to be a minimum threshold for pleasure to deliver pharmaceutical-like benefits. Once you **focus on pleasure for three minutes** you'll typically find your thoughts *automatically* gravitate toward optimistic things. Rewarding memories may spring forth spontaneously. Loving thoughts or recollections of people or activities you enjoy often arise effortlessly. If you've got a little time on your hands, try focusing on feeling good for ten minutes or more. The more time spent focusing on pleasure, the more you'll groove your mind for the positive.[10]

After three or more minutes, begin some sentences aloud with, "Right now I am feeling _____" and fill in the blanks. It may seem difficult to put your experience into words, but it's important to do so. Giving voice to your experience grounds and makes it accessible in practical ways. Articulating your experience is also a way to bring ineffable, transcendent experience down to earth. After all, the Bible tells us "In the beginning was the word." Finding words to express what you are feeling is also a way of supporting communication between your left and right brains for a whole bodymind experience.

Expanding Pleasure Pathways in Your Brain

Your right brain is the part most capable of accessing feelings and emotions in your body.[11] It is comfortable with images, sensations and feelings. Your right brain feels the "sense" of things. Your left brain is the part comfortable with analysis and words. In a moment of embodied pleasure, it may seem almost impossible to put words to your experience. This is where multimodal awareness is essential. You can hold the space for dual modes of awareness: profound embodied/energetic experience, and the language that makes it real.

Be on guard, though. Any time you venture into language, your left brain automatically attempts to hijack your experience. No blame. It's just being a good left brain – turning everything into something to be analyzed and categorized, something you are separate from. For this reason, as you articulate the words, "I am

_____," it's important to make a concerted effort to keep your awareness focused *also* on the feeling experience of the pleasure you are describing. This may take some practice.

One way to stay connected to embodied experience is to create an imaginary mouth that can talk and imagine placing it on the body sensations of peace, calm or warmth you are feeling. Using an image in this way gets your right brain involved. It's then easier to circumvent left-brain control and access information and wisdom from your bodymind directly.

For example, if your heart is feeling full and warm, you'd imagine placing an imaginary talking mouth right on your heart. Then ask, "If you, heart, could talk right now, what would you say?" and listen for an answer. When you do this, be prepared for surprises … and when you are surprised by what your heart, gut or knee is saying, you can be pretty sure your left brain is not in charge.

If you keep your awareness in your body with your eyes focused down left, while simultaneously attempting to put words to your experience, at the very least you are having a bilateral brain experience. You are, all at once, having a body experience, aware of having a body experience, and actively working to bring in the dimension of language. This is a pioneering practice. It is the form of meditation I call "living emotion meditation."

Research on meditation suggests that this kind of multilevel, multimodal awareness can actually change brain structure. In any case, when you use your big "S" Self to stay fully connected to the experience of pleasure as well as letting those good feelings come out in words, you'll increase your subjective sense of well-being and mastery.

I Am that I Am: Connecting to Spirit

Feeling pleasure, focusing on body sensations and expanding awareness to include words set the stage for you to have an exquisite experience of Spirit, in whatever form that arises for you. When you begin sentences with the words "I am," you are invoking one of the most ancient calls to prayer of all times: "I am that I am." The phrase "I am" seems to summon Spirit.

I have been stunned by the potent connections accessible by completing this simple phrase: "I am_____." I have heard people say, "I am One." Some say, "I am seeing Jesus." Others have said, "I feel connected to the divine mother, Mary." People have called in a meaningful connection to Buddha, the Archangel Michael, their "Higher Selves," and/or all manner of Native American spirit guides by speaking this potent phrase after a few minutes of focusing on pleasure. If you are not a person whose imagination tends easily to visuals, you'll more likely sense or feel your connection to Spirit rather than envision it. No comparisons! It's all good.

Creating Loving Pathways To, From and By Your Self

Just as importantly, completing the "I am" phrase presents an opportunity to express an empowering experience of confidence in your big and/or small self. The most common phrases I hear when this happens are "I am OK," "I am confident," "I am strong." I also hear laughter, gut gurgles, burps. I see bright eyes, vibrant faces, easily breathing lungs, relaxed, energized limbs, upright, flexible spines, and grounded feet. When people get to this moment of Emotional Medicine healing, I feel I am in the presence of competent, open-hearted beings delighting in and loving themselves.

Learning What Self-Love *Feels* Like

Rosa was referred by a colleague because she was terribly depressed. A 38-year-old single mother with her own website optimization business, most days she had to drag herself out of bed to work. She was in the midst of a complicated custody case with her former husband, Miguel. Miguel had walked out on their marriage two years earlier to start a new life with *Rosa's sister.* To make matters worse, Rosa's own father was taking sides with Miguel and her sister. Rosa said she couldn't stop thinking about the unfairness of it all.

In our sessions, Rosa was relieved to learn she could turn her attention away from endless thoughts of unfairness and victimhood and focus instead on what she was feeling – anger at her father's and sister's betrayal and ongoing grief about her early childhood loss of her mother, the only one who had ever protected her. Rosa quickly learned to allow her emotions to move through their natural cycle. She knew she felt better when she was done, but she didn't want to dwell on that.

Rosa said she didn't want to focus on feeling good. She had little experience of pleasure other than sex (and, she said, she preferred her sex on the rough side). She didn't have any memories of sexual abuse, but lots of memories of childhood whippings. She also had no memories of a loving relationship with her father.

Rosa had always prided herself on her stoicism. Although the custody crisis and family betrayal had precipitated her depression, I believe Rosa would have faced this meltdown sooner or later. There is a limit on how long you can push yourself before your body says, "No more."

One day, I asked Rosa whether she would like to try a little experiment and use the good feelings she'd generated through brief emotional release to create deeper healing. As I knew Rosa was a serious student of metaphysics, I upped the ante by letting her know that people often had profound spiritual experiences when they allowed and enjoyed the pleasure and peace that follows emotional release.

I would guide her, I said, and we could stop whenever she felt too uncomfortable. She agreed. Gently I invited Rosa to tell me what was happening in her body. At first all she noticed was how tired she was. "I'm so fatigued," she said. "Do you feel safe enough to allow that?" I asked. "Yes." She was silent for a few moments. I invited her to notice her breathing. "It's easier," she sighed. Rosa became even quieter. She next became aware of her slow, steady heartbeat. Her muscles were relaxing, she said. I guided her attention to her hands, which were placed in a prayer posture. They were warm and tingly. I suggested Rosa look inside and see if the tingling energy had a color. "Pink," she said. "Soft pink." I guided her to feel an infusion of soft pink energy in every muscle and molecule in her body.

A few minutes passed. I invited Rosa to begin some sentences with "I am _____" and fill in the blanks. "I am ... OK," Rosa said slowly. "I am ... peaceful," she continued. "I am ... *loved*," Rosa said and burst into tears. These were happy tears, she explained. "For years I've read how important it is to love yourself. I never knew what that meant. It was just words. Now, for the first time in my life, I know what they're talking about. Finally, I know what it feels like to love myself. I can't believe it."

Rosa was radiant, vibrating with love and light. We spent a few more minutes enjoying this experience. I guided her to feel this self-love in every muscle, every joint and every organ in her body. We focused on each of her body systems, feeling this infusion of love, OK-ness, and peace.[12]

"Imagine you are in a cocoon," I suggested, checking first to be sure this would not evoke claustrophobic feelings. (Some people prefer to imagine floating on the warm sea.) "Inside this cocoon, you are totally safe and can dissolve. Like the caterpillar, you can let your molecules be rearranged and transformed. Let go and allow this love to infuse every aspect of your being." Rosa sighed deeply. "I am in bliss," she said.

I continued by asking Rosa to imagine sending a beam of this energy out into her future to guide her back to loving herself again whenever necessary. Consider, I said, that this current beacon of love could find her in any future sad, mad, or scared feelings and bring her back to bliss.

I then suggested that we send a beam of this love back through her past (through the way her past pain still lived in her present body-mind) as a beckoning whisper not to give up. I invited her to consider that sending this love back to herself in the past might be part of the reason she survived her nightmare childhood as well as she had.

Towards the end of our time together, I asked Rosa if she were ready to make a choice, a conscious decision, to invite this kind of love and pleasure into her life. I assured her it was OK if she was not ready for that decision – she needed to be true to herself, to her own timing.

Well, she was ready, all right. Rosa had entered the Promised Land and tasted the milk and honey. She had discovered a route to the love she had been looking for all her life. That route went down into her body, through her emotions and up into an experience of real, embodied love. Rosa said, "I need more of this love in my life. I need to create time to allow myself this experience more often."

In closing, I let Rosa know she could tap into this healing energy for guidance about any issues in her life. She could use profound inner experiences as a conduit for God, her Higher Self, the Holy Spirit, spirit guides, etc. Focusing on pleasure could lead her to a wise energy source she could turn to in coping with any literal or metaphorical trials and tribulations.

I invited Rosa to take a moment to look into this good feeling now for some guidance about the upcoming trial. The guidance was simple: disengage. Rosa became clear that she needed to let go from obsessing about this truly unfair, dreadful situation.

Weeks later, Rosa reported she was finding it increasingly easy to step away from the hurtful family dynamics. She refused to allow herself to think endlessly about the injustice. Rosa said she now felt stronger in standing up for herself and her daughter. She could now see how she had allowed her family to victimize her. She was no longer afraid to speak her truth.

Further, she said she could see that she had been continuing to reach out to her angry sister, father and former husband hoping to find love and connection. She didn't need to do that anymore, because she'd found a connection she needed inside herself.

Beam Me Up!

Another way to increase the power of feeling good is to imagine sending a beam of the good, self-loving energy you feel out into your future, waiting for you anytime you need it. For this kind of future focusing, it works best to direct your gaze up and to the right.

If it sounds strange to send a beam of feel-good energy into your future, consider the fact that most healers work exactly this way – through intention. You can send good energy to your future[13] simply by intending to do this. You intend it to be so and it is so.

So, once you've cooked up some self-love and self-confidence, you can imagine sending a beam of that good experience through time and space. Send this imaginary beam into your future as an invitation to bring you back to yourself and/or to Spirit again. No matter what storms are raging, this beam, like a lighthouse ray, can cut through darkness and help you find your way home, back to feeling good again. If you'd like, place your hands together in prayer or on your heart to anchor healing in your body.[14]

In the future, whenever you arrange your hands that way on your body again, it will help you recall that you can move through any turbulence and survive, even thrive. Each time you remember that healing beam, let it symbolize your constant access to an inner guiding light. You can ride that ray home to peace and self-love again and again.

You can also send an imaginary beam of feeling good to your past as a lifesaver when you were so down and weary you thought you'd never find a way out. Though this may sound like "airy-fairy" nonsense, in quantum physics the past, present and future don't always line up in the familiar order. Going "back to the future" is at least a theoretical possibility.

Focusing on feeling good enables you to take deep inner healing and wholeness back into daily life. Loving and accepting your whole self – good, bad and ugly – enables you to reappraise your situation and access the guidance within. In the next chapter, you will learn how to do that and more. You'll also discover how feeling good is the best time to reveal affirmations, set intentions and envision optimal outcomes for your life.

THIRTEEN

Take it Back to Daily Life

Happiness, vitality and peace make life more fulfilling and enjoyable in and of themselves. Even if you just experience feeling good for a few minutes every day, there is no doubt you'll be healthier and happier. However, as a therapist, I know you need to take these good feeling experiences back into your everyday lives and dilemmas or they'll lose power to enhance your transformation.

After you've taken the time to really luxuriate in and be fully present with the good feelings following emotional release, there are five things you can do to make sure you get the most out of your positive experience:

1. Love and accept your whole self
2. Reappraise your situation
3. Look for your part in any problem
4. Look for forgiveness
5. Ask for your next step
6. Set affirmations and intentions

1. Love and Accept Your Whole Self

The first thing you can do to take your good feelings back into your daily life constructively is to use that positive energy to embrace your whole self, strong and weak, generous and selfish, etc. Remember that list you made back in Chapter Two, that "Self at Best" list? Remember, too, that list you made in Chapter Nine of your "Shadow Side/Self at Worst" qualities? These lists feature prominently in the following Action Tip:

ACTION TIP: LOVING YOUR WHOLE SELF

Get your lists out and reread them. Take a new piece of paper and draw a line down the center of the page. On one side write a list of what is kind, strong, brave and positive about you. As you write, use your multimodal awareness to sense how authentic it feels in your body to love and appreciate yourself at this moment. Place your hand over your heart. Ask your heart to tell you what it loves about you today. Be prepared to be surprised. Feel the truth of how your heart loves you.

Next, on the other side of the *same* sheet of paper, list your "dark side" qualities. Ask your heart what it has to say to the part of you carrying your wounds, your shadow. Imagine putting your arm around your worst self. Breathe. Sad, mad, scared emotions may arise. Your loving heart is big enough to include all aspects of who you are. Be gentle.

Finally, look at the sheet of paper that lists your "Self at Best" and "Self at Worst" qualities on the same page. Feel the authentic truth of having best and worst qualities. You are all of this and more. Place your arms around yourself and imagine embracing your whole, terrific, terrible self. You are not alone. Everyone you know – indeed, everyone who's ever lived, carries a similar list in their own hearts. Everyone is a mix of light and dark, healing and wounds. Welcome yourself to the human race.

2. **Reappraise your Situation**

The other day I listened to a message on my answering machine that was very upsetting. I felt immediately pissed off. I could feel the heat of my anger rise up my neck into my face. I yelled a cuss word at the machine and realized I had time to take some Emotional Medicine. No one else was home, so I didn't have to worry about making noise.

I went to my home office, got out my tennis racket and began shouting anger at my perceived perpetrator. For a minute or less I let my body lead me through my anger. Whack and curse and whack, and furthermore…! When I was done, I took another few minutes to focus on the good feelings coursing through my body.

I felt warmth spreading through my shoulders and arms. My belly felt soft; the soft rhythm of my breath filled my lungs. I burped a bit and made a decision to focus on the good feelings for several more minutes.

As I was doing that, I noticed some interesting thoughts about the situation that triggered me. I began to get a sense of what might be going on for the person who pissed me off. Out of the blue, I remembered a situation in which I had done something very similar to what that person was now doing with me. Hmmmm.

Because I am interested in my soul's growth, at some point in any emotional upset or relationship upset, I turn my attention inside. I look for what my participation in any upset might have been. I look for whatever learning is there for me. Granted this sometimes happens later than sooner, but I am always committed to look.

In this case, although I didn't come to any firm conclusions, I noticed that I was calm and resourced. I left my office and went back to listen to the phone message. It didn't sound like the same message. I listened to it a couple of times, trying to hear what had triggered me just moments earlier. Although I could hear hints of prickly energy that I might've perceived as upsetting, this voice-mail now landed entirely differently. Isn't that something?

When you get triggered – and who knows what's responsible for your reaction: your blood sugar or testosterone levels, menstrual cycle, earlier upset, or the wings of a butterfly in South America – your perceptions are altered. You see things through a distorted lens.[1]

This doesn't mean any anger or grief that got triggered might not be true and important responses to the situation, or that your response doesn't have something important to teach you. It just means that reality is usually a projective test. You can't help it that your brain is programmed to filter the present moment through past experience. Sometimes that means your sad, mad, scared responses are bigger (or smaller) than the current situation requires.

Emotional Medicine can help you connect with clearheaded wisdom by moving you through any negative emotional responses that were triggered back to good feelings in minutes. Once filled with self-love and self-acceptance, you are in a good position to look for your part in any problem.

3. Look for Your Part in Any Problem

I've been surprised by clients sometimes when I ask them, once they're feeling good, if they want to take another look at the problem that triggered their upset only to have them reply, "What problem?" This is half a joke and half not.

It is true when you feel resourced, connected with your best self *and* accepting of your worst self, problems often do not seem like problems anymore. Your experience of your self has changed so much that you feel like you can handle almost anything!

However, if you have tendencies toward avoiding problems, it may help to remind yourself you'll feel even stronger and more masterful if you look for your part in any problem. Taking responsibility is the primary antidote for victimhood.

ACTION TIP: TAKING RESPONSIBILITY

Review the triggering situation and your behavior from your now clearheaded perspective. No matter who started it, begin looking for what subtle (or not-so-subtle) part you may have played in the upset. Look for what you might do differently in the future. It's important to realize that sometimes you might not have needed to do anything differently, that just sticking to your guns is the responsibility you need. Sometimes you might discover you need to shift inner attitudes about the upset more than any outer behavior.

There is immense power in taking responsibility in this way, *as long as you do not blame yourself.* Taking responsibility is not about blaming or shaming yourself, it's about seeing what part, if any, your actions played in the problem. If you can't explore inside yourself without blaming or shaming yourself, stop looking until you feel some baseline of self-acceptance.

4. Look for Forgiveness

The same goes for forgiveness. Post-emotion peace may be a good time to look for forgiveness within yourself or others for intentional or unintentional wounding behavior. This is tricky, though, because there are levels of forgiveness. Sometimes getting to authentic, heart-opening, body-based forgiveness takes months or even years of anger medicine.

After my mother died, I was surprised to find anger arising briefly and sporadically for several years. I had worked through grief (and asthma symptoms) in the first months after her death. Although I had a strong intention to forgive her and had done so at spiritual levels, my actual, embodied, human heart was still angry with her.

I was embarrassed about this. For heaven's sake, I was a therapist who knew about Emotional Medicine. Surely I "should" have healed this by now. I had worked on my relationship with my mother for 40 years – therapy, workshops, journaling, the est training, Emotional Medicine. I'd completed four years of postgraduate Family Systems training in my search for healing. As a result of that training, I had taken a family-of-origin road trip to meet all her relatives and learn more about her life. I continually worked for compassionate understanding of her wounding behavior.

As I stayed present with sporadic anger arising for my mother, it didn't help that an acquaintance of mine working in the field of human transformation whose neglectful, alcoholic mother died the same day as mine, claimed she had completely forgiven her in one month. You can imagine I had to work hard to stay out of my self-judgment about that!

Because I believe in "letting the body lead," I couldn't pretend my heart felt truly forgiving of my mother when it didn't. I just kept on moving through brief embodied anger (sometimes it was just a cuss word or shake of the fist), and brief embodied embarrassment about that anger. I continued my exploration of developing compassion for her emotionally hurtful dynamics and waited. I did lots of waiting.

Three years and three potent dreams later, I underwent a profound inner healing with my mother – body, heart and soul. I am so glad I waited and let my body lead. I have not had this kind of ongoing anger arise about her since that time (though sometimes I wish she were here to hear our latest news). Of course I also occasionally grieve the missed opportunity for sharing love with her in this lifetime, in the flesh. I have a loving picture of her above my computer as I write these sentences. I feel her love for me and mine for her.

5. Ask for Your Next Step

When I initially invited people to use their post-discharge good feelings as an opportunity to ask for inner guidance, I was continually astounded with the advice and suggestions they would discover in themselves. While I might have an idea or two about what steps or directions clients could take to heal themselves, people would come up with things I could never think of, even hearing advice in languages they hadn't spoken since childhood!

As a therapist, this definitely took the pressure off any tendencies I had to try and solve anyone's problems. Today, I rarely feel compelled to tell clients what to do because I am clear that my advice would pale in comparison to their idiosyncratic inner wisdom. I see my job now as helping people get to that core state of happiness, confidence and peace so they can ask themselves for guidance.

ACTION TIP: ASKING FOR YOUR NEXT STEP

First, look inside to see if you have expectations of what your next step should be. Ferret them out and let them go. Plan to be surprised. Next, find the places in your body where you are feeling the most good feelings, wherever they are – heart, gut, shoulders, knees. Imagine putting a mouth on those good feelings and let that mouth talk to you. You may get images, words, songs, poems. Take what you get.

If you get an answer that doesn't immediately make sense, take time to be with it … hours, days, weeks, months. Ask for a dream about it. If you don't get any guidance, just notice the quality of the good sensation, e.g., calm, relaxing, pulsing, powerful. Let that quality of energy in your body be the guide for your next step. Play with this.

Of course, it is always possible that the next step you need to take is not to take a step. What you may need most in your daily life is downtime, R&R. You may already be spending too much time taking steps, moving forward too fast, assuming too much responsibility for every situation. Open yourself to the possibility that the guidance may be to do nothing … lay fallow… and wait. You know who you are!

6. Set Affirmations and Intentions

The "I am" statements described in the last chapter are budding affirmations. Sometimes "I am" statements are the only affirmations you'll need. You can take them back into your daily life and use them like prayers, mantras, beacons to bring you home to what's evolving within.

At other times, you might want to use your good feelings to go beyond those simple "I am" statements to words that reflect a more complete pronouncement of your next steps. Here's how a potent affirmation emerged for me.

One month before I completed this book, I sprained my ankle on a trip to LA. My ankle hurt so much that I was fearful I'd be laid up for weeks. As soon as I got home I checked Louise Hay's little pamphlet, *Heal Your Body: Metaphysical Causations for Physical Illness.*[2] (I've carried this pamphlet with me for over 30 years!) Foot problems, she says, are the result of "fear of the future and of stepping forward in life." She got me on this one. I knew that stepping out into the big world with my book was scary for me.

Louise's pamphlet also offers "New Thought Patterns," affirmations to help you mitigate whatever troubling body situation you have been experiencing. The "New Thought Patterns" for my situation were: "I stand in Truth. I move forward with joy. I have spiritual understanding." Although I saw that those words were potent and on target for me, I was too filled with sad, mad, scared feelings and physical pain to relate to them. At that moment, they did nothing for me.

I knew I needed some Emotional Medicine. I asked Arturo to be with me. I was so sad that I was losing my footing! I sobbed, furious that my momentum for birthing this book would be interrupted this way. I pounded my fists on the bed. (At that time I couldn't feel the fear, as it was overshadowed by grief and anger.)

After a few moments, I felt a little peace and calm flow through my bodymind. Although it was hard to focus on the good feelings because of the throbbing pain, I used VIVO to move back and forth between the pain and peace. This all helped. I was no longer emotionally distraught and the pain was somewhat diminished. After a few minutes, I took some anti-inflammatory medication and finally got to sleep.

The next morning when I awakened, my ankle felt much better. It was still tender. I knew it would be some days before I could exercise again. I also knew it was not as bad as I had feared. I moved gingerly through my morning ritual and went to my meditation chair.

Lately, I'd been ending my meditation with five minutes of visualizations about Emotional Medicine reaching a wide, responsive audience. This morning, when I began that process, I felt a familiar tinge of fear arise. I let myself be present for the fear and trembled for a few moments, breathing until it subsided.

In the very next moment, I heard/felt/experienced the words, "I stand in truth," and they hit me like a lightning bolt carrying me to the center of the earth. I repeated the sentence out loud: "I stand in truth.[3]" I felt strength coursing through my ankles and feet. I added the other affirmations: "I move forward with joy. I have spiritual understanding." Each sentence filled my entire bodymind with courage and confidence. Though my ankle took a week to heal completely, my soul continues to be healed by this affirmation.

I'm sharing my process to give you a sense of how to look for and receive affirmations at the end of an emotional cycle. It is really important that you feel complete and resourced when you look for affirmations within yourself or your experience. Although my "standing in truth" affirmation came to me from a source outside of my experience, I know that the Universe was guiding me to Louise Hay's words.

Notice, however, when I was filled with unexpressed grief, anger and fear, those words did not touch my soul. They didn't have real power. After discharging my emotions, I was open to receive them as deeply empowering guidance.

Notice, too, that I describe affirmation as involving a process of *receiving*. I believe the most potent, earth-shaking affirmations are those that arise organically out of an emotion-based life process. When affirmations are revealed in this way you can feel them in your bones, your heart, your gut and soul.

ACTION TIP

The next time you are searching for an affirmation, your first step is to allow it to be a process. Find a quiet space. Make yourself comfortable and drop into your good feelings. Ask for guidance. Begin some sentences either silently or aloud with "I affirm that _____" and see what you get. It's OK if you get nothing. Ask for a dream. Take time to let your affirmations reveal themselves to you. It's also OK to wait for hours, days, weeks to receive the affirmation that will quicken your spirit.

Setting Intentions

The process of setting intentions is very different. If affirmations are a right-brain, bottoms-up, feminine process, intentions are a left-brain, top-down, masculine process. We need both!

I recommend you refrain from engaging in either affirmations or intention setting unless you're feeling good. Setting intentions, however, is something you can do by decision! You can make a decision to align your will with a particular outcome.

The technology described in the book *The Secret*[4] involves imagining positive future outcomes for yourself. The author of this book as well as the Abraham channel declare that it's important to *feel* into the happiness, confidence and peace you'll have when your intentions become a reality. They make the specific point that that is one of the keys to manifesting intentions.

Well, isn't that convenient for you as a practitioner of Emotional Medicine? You now have the technology to use life's trials and tribulations to propel yourself into feeling good fast – and making yourself a hothouse of intention setting.

I have some concern that setting intentions for only good things may rob you of spiritual openness for the profound healing disaster often brings. It's important not to blame yourself or anyone when intentions aren't manifested or misfortune falls.

You can't tell whether your life or someone else's life is on track by how much good fortune is present. Your ego cannot imagine the deep soul growth that might arise from tragedy. Do you think Christopher Reeves (the actor who played Superman) would have *intended* to fall off his horse, break his neck and be paralyzed for the rest of his life? Heck, no. Do you remember how much good his accident did for the cause of spinal cord injury research? Did you see or hear his post-accident interviews in which he radiated peace and beneficence? He seemed to be completely at home about his life, grateful even for the terrible gifts it bestowed.

The Choice is Yours

The fact that you are ultimately, solely, completely responsible for your own happiness no matter what happens to you is one of the more ironic aspects of becoming a human adult after a long, dependent childhood. While it's not very fair that the buck always stops with you, it *is* empowering. The choice is always yours as to whether you want to take steps to transform your life. The choice is also always yours as to whether you use Emotional Medicine to enhance your life in a significant way.

I know, even after all these pages testifying to the great boons and blessings Emotional Medicine brings, it's still not an easy choice to make day in and day out. I know this because it is sometimes still difficult for *me* to feel my emotions. We need to be gentle with ourselves. Please have compassion for yourself and others, knowing how difficult this can be.

Why Deciding to Feel Your Emotions is So Difficult

There are at least five reasons it's hard to make the decision to feel:

1. As a child you were not supported to safely feel your feelings.
2. When sad, mad, scared feelings arise you assume it means there's something wrong – with you, with life, with God.
3. It never seems like the right time or place to let your body express emotion.
4. Sad, mad, scared feelings don't feel good.
5. You don't want to lose control.

1. It's Not Safe to Feel

When you were very little and terrible things happened which you couldn't control, weren't equipped to handle and didn't have the parental support to get through, your organism benevolently helped you cope through mechanisms of denial and repression. Denial and repression helped you survive your childhood. They were necessary, skillful defenses to keep your physiology and psyche from being overwhelmed by what your undeveloped nervous system identified as a life-threatening stress.

The result is that you, like all of us, have an *automatic habit* of pushing painful feelings down and out of consciousness. This habit was useful when you were a child but is not so useful now. (Though in times of great disaster and loss, it still functions as a kindly antidote to the full horror of what you're going through until you're prepared to feel and heal.)

Furthermore, because you pushed down emotions when you were so little and they seemed so big, whenever an emotion tries to rise through your experience now, it often feels like you are, once again, so vulnerable in relation to those big feelings. While you now have a brain and nervous system capable of cooperating with what your body is trying to accomplish without harming you, you can still get caught in avoidance, even before you are aware that's what is happening.

2. If I were Really OK, I Wouldn't Have these Emotions

Now, that you're a grown-up, you may have adopted the idea that if you were really "together," mature, spiritually advanced, hip, etc. you wouldn't have to deal with sad, mad, scared feelings. Since your culture (family, school, religion, society) hasn't welcomed emotions, you've assumed they must be bad, and decided that if they arise, you must be defective.

Every time a painful emotion tries to poke its head through the crust of your habitual patterns of not feeling, your first thought is, "What's wrong with me?" A second thought often follows closely: "What's wrong with life?" In a perfect world, you think, you just shouldn't have to deal with these painful feelings. According to Tom Lutz's book, *Crying: The Natural and Cultural History of Tears*[5] before the Industrial Revolution it was apparently common for *both* men and women to cry in public.

Lutz reports that when the famous medieval warrior Roland died, 20,000 knights wept so copiously that many fell from their horses and fainted! (Obviously, they didn't know about stopping when done.) He theorizes that as factories increasingly needed steady, diligent workers, not emotionally responsive weepers, people stopped crying so much. Eventually crying became something one did in private. Children were soon taught that tears themselves were a problem, not the result of a problem.

3. It Never Seems Like the Right Time or Place for Feelings!

Let's say you're at work, just about ready to leave for the day, and your boss hands you an assignment which must be completed before you leave. Your body might be instantly ready to shake a fist and vocally curse this injustice, but you wisely restrain yourself because it wouldn't be appropriate in the work setting and you can't take the chance of getting fired.

Or suppose you're at a fancy social gathering and someone makes a cutting remark which takes your breath away. Your heart starts racing. Your jaw is charged for you to talk back angrily in your own defense. Your hands, too, may tremble with preparedness to strike. You might feel like bursting into tears, but again you don't do any of these things because you wisely discern it wouldn't be safe or appropriate.

By the time you get to your car, home or office, you have pushed down your natural emotional responses so well that you just don't feel like feeling them. It's all too easy to move on, ignoring any residual charge in your body waiting to complete an emotional cycle. However, if you have an unwitting spouse or pet waiting for you, you may find yourself snapping at them for no good reason.

4. Feeling Sad, Mad, Scared Doesn't Feel Good

Sad, mad and scared feelings often feel awful – temporarily. Sadness may bring a *temporary* sense of helpless despair. Mad may bring powerful *temporary* feelings of rage accompanied by a gripping fear of the anger itself. Scared may *temporarily* bring terror and a sense that your very survival is threatened. Why on earth would you want to move toward something you know doesn't feel good?

Since you, as a human, have a highly developed cerebral cortex, you think you should be able to make rational decisions about emotions, instead of having them control you. Because you haven't been taught how important (safe and appropriate) emotional expression is for health and well-being (not to mention the fact that it's impossible to make rational decisions without emotional input), you may end up deciding to avoid emotional pain at all costs. Couple this with the fact that you as a human are designed to seek pleasure and avoid pain, and you've got a perfect storm of emotional avoidance.

However, there's an interesting paradox at play here: Yes, you are innately programmed to avoid pain as much as possible. That is natural. But, if you're like most of us, you've done many things in your life that didn't feel good in the short run because they were good for you in the long term. In your best-case behaviors, you avoid overindulging in food, drink, shopping, etc., because you want more sustained pleasure than a quick fix can provide.

It's painful to resist that cookie and go for the carrot. It's painful to resist those cocktails when you have a big day tomorrow and don't want even a tiny hangover. It's painful to resist buying that sweater which would look so perfect with your new pants. And yet, many times, you do it. I do it.

I have always been baffled when I see clients who are committed to their exercise workouts, who are willing to suffer enormous bodily pain to whip their physiques into shape, forcefully resist three minutes of acute sad, mad, or scared emotional pain. This is all the more perplexing because, while it takes months to see the results of often-painful weightlifting, you see the results from feeling your emotions in minutes!

I've come to the conclusion that it isn't really the emotional pain that is so noxious and that evokes such resistance. Rather, I suspect that what really gets our jaws in a jut is the loss of control that feeling sad, mad, scared (and yes, even glad) evokes.

5. "I Don't Want to Lose Control"

Perhaps you are telling a very close friend about how terrible you felt when a new love interest stopped returning your calls, or are describing this humiliation to your therapist or pastor. You feel emotions rise within you as you tell your story but you resist them. You say, "I swore I wasn't going to cry about this," "I'm just not going to give him/her the satisfaction of letting this get to me," and "I'm still in charge."

Of course you resist this way! Remember in Chapter Two when I reminded you that your "in-chargeness" is actually a helpful resource in any new learning? It's healthy to have an ego, a sense of self that wants to be in charge. Since you know too well that you're not in charge when terrible things happen, at least you should be able to decide whether or not to let those terrible things affect you after the fact.

The problem is that, while you are capable of being in charge, *in the short run*, of many areas of your natural, animal functioning, you can't stop your body's response to emotions once they are evoked.[6]

Emotional energy doesn't just disappear. The scientific jury is in on this one. Pushing down, avoiding and denying your emotional responses are not good for health. They may go underground for a while (as they did when you were little), waiting for you to find the resources to handle your distress. But sooner or later, if you don't attend to your emotions, something's going to give. And that something is usually your physical and/or mental health.

When you make the choice to allow the *temporary* pain emotional flow evokes, you'll gain *permanent* benefits. Learning to honor and cooperate with your body's natural emotional responses in a skillful way gives you back yourself, your power and your peace – body and soul.

Aurora's Story

Aurora is a successful ebony-skinned fashion designer specializing in clothing made from ecologically sustainable, organic fabrics. Her clothes have been featured in important runway shows across the nation. She is never happier than while letting her creativity lead her through the mounds of natural fabrics she assembles into gorgeous ensembles which feel great to wear.

Aurora came to me because she was depressed. She had tried antidepressants a couple of times but didn't like the side effects, which for her were lack of sexual desire and a certain sense of "distance" from life. When she was on meds, she said, she couldn't feel her creative juices the way she needed to.

Aurora proved to be an avid and quick learner of Emotional Medicine methods. We worked through her numbness and posttraumatic reactions to childhood molestation by an uncle, the death of her mother when she was a teenager, and the recent death of her brother from AIDS. This took some time, but Aurora soon knew how to seek safety inside and out. She was soon able, with coaching in our sessions, to cry when she was sad, stomp when she was mad, and stop when she was done. She made healthy changes in her eating habits, switching to a low-glucose diet to keep her blood-sugar levels from wild fluctuations and avoid undue emotional stress.

We were well on our way to completing our work together when we encountered a problem. Although Aurora was always able to find confidence and peace at the *end* of each session by letting her body lead through her emotions, we had to work through the same old resistance to feeling at the *beginning* of each session. Each time a current incident triggered grief about another aspect of her enormous earlier traumas or losses, she would be annoyed that she had to go through this again, that she had to grieve again, feel again.

Aurora had learned all the Emotional Medicine remedies required to wrangle as much happiness and peace as possible from life in a human body on planet Earth. But, she hadn't made a true commitment to use these remedies on a daily basis. Aurora kept getting derailed by her belief system that something must be wrong if she was in pain. Every time new tears appeared outside of sessions, she had to go through minutes, hours, days or weeks of resistance, and thoughts such as "I shouldn't be feeling this way," or "Not this again," before she would allow herself the simple remedy of feeling tears, crying, stopping, and finding peace.

"Why isn't it over already?" she would moan. "I'm tired of crying. If I were a better client or if you were a better therapist, I wouldn't be having these feelings." Or she'd get caught in self-doubt, saying, "There must be something wrong with me to have grief and anger keep arising in my life."

Even though Aurora would always feel peaceful and strong at the end of an emotional cycle, she had not accepted life as it was: happy/sad, glad/mad, full/empty, peaceful/stressed. She had not made a decision once and for all to feel whatever she felt as she lived her life. This was a spiritual crisis for her.

I asked Aurora if she were angry at God. "Why yes, as a matter of fact I am!" she responded. "I'm furious with God. This isn't right." We soon moved from anger at God to anger at those early gods in her (and everyone's) life – parents.

As we explored this, Aurora moved into wrenching rage and grief that her parents hadn't protected and taken better care of her. She stayed present with her feelings until she cried out her inner child's longing and need to be taken care of. She was then emotionally done, relieved, and finally peaceful.[7]

The next session, Aurora arrived looking visibly happier and brighter. She'd had an epiphany as she was walking along the beach, she said. She realized that she had been caught in thinking that if God, her parents and her therapist really cared about her, if she were truly a good person, they would take away her pain, once and for all ... that she'd never have to feel sad, mad or scared again.

Aurora then had a flash of insight: she realized that feeling emotions was a normal part of life. It didn't mean anything bad about her, God, her imperfect therapist, or her imperfect parents. Aurora saw that if she stopped spending so much time resisting her emotions, she actually knew how to take care of herself effectively. She knew how to use her emotions to support her in feeling peaceful and happy. All she needed, she said, was the will to do it. And now, finally, she had it. Hallelujah!

When people have a breakthrough such as Aurora's, I like to note the date and invite them to make it a red-letter day – the day they decide permanently to honor themselves or their emotions. If, and/or when, you decide to make such a commitment, note the date. Make it a red-letter day. Let's take a look at what it's like to actually let your body lead you through sad, mad, scared and glad emotions.

I remember the day I decided not to stay stuck in thinking I was a bad person: November 22, 1974. It's not that I haven't ever gotten caught in that self-hating territory again. But once I made an irrevocable decision *not to stay stuck* in self-hatred, I took action as soon as I was aware it was happening. For me, it's axiomatic: whenever I think I'm a bad person, it means I've got anger stuck in the buildup part of the emotional cycle (or that I've eaten too much sugar). I don't waste time debating as to whether this time I really AM a bad person. I just immediately ask myself who or what I am mad about, notice my body's response, do some anger releasing and feel good fast. (Or, I'll eat some smoked salmon or sardines, wait 20 minutes and feel better.)

How Will Friends and Family Respond Once You Start Feeling Your Emotions?

You may also be wondering what will happen in your relationships once you learn to cry when you are sad, stomp when you are mad, and shake when you are scared. Perhaps you're concerned you'll be a drag or a burden if you become emotional in someone's presence. You may be surprised to know it's good for people to be around authentic emotion, but *only if they've indicated they're ready for it.*

It is always a good idea to ask people's permission before launching into your feelings, no matter how short and ultimately sweet they may end up being. I didn't do this one very stressful morning (I was jet-lagged, hungry, and cold) when I was first getting acquainted with my son's fiancée (now wife and mother of my first grandchild). Lorien appropriately called me on it, I apologized, and we had a good, relationship-building conversation.

When you have people's permission to allow emotions to move in their presence, anyone with you gets a free ride on the increased life energy that emotional release brings. Like walking near the water of a moving sea or bubbling brook, moving emotions refresh those around you. When your bodymind energy is humming along unobstructed, you will have a positive impact on others.

Explaining Emotional Medicine

Once you've learned to cry when you're sad, stop when you're done, and feel good fast, you will most likely want to share this with loved ones above and beyond any FGFFs you've found. People not reading this book might not understand you at first. They might try to interrupt you, shush you, and stop you from feeling your feelings. They don't know what you know. They might need some experience seeing how you can move through your emotions to get back to feeling good fast before they can trust you and emotional experience in general.

Once you show them how Emotional Medicine works a few times, they'll be better able to be with you as you complete an emotional cycle without thinking they have to do something to take care of or fix you. It's important to let loved ones know they don't have to do anything except be there with a nonjudgmental presence. Explain that their compassionate presence and the healing power of emotion is all you need to feel good fast and be peacefully present for them and your relationship again.

Bye for Now!

Dear reader, we're coming to the end of our journey together in this book. I am honored that you have opened your mind, heart, and soul to the information I've shared with you. I dearly hope this is not the end of our relationship. I hope you will log on to my blog, sign up to follow me on Twitter, receive my newsletter, email me with your questions and comments, and tune in to my weekly web radio show, "Transformational Talk Radio." There you can connect with other people using Emotional Medicine and share your experiences and discoveries as you work with this method. Please check our website, www.emotionalmedicine.com, for books, downloads and other resources to support you on your journey to happiness, vitality and inner peace. I also look forward to meeting you in person at one of my talks or workshops.

As we say goodbye for now, I want you to know I love you. I send you support on the inner journey for crying when you're sad, stopping when you're done, feeling good fast.

Acknowledgements

I could not have started or finished this book without my husband, Arturo. I wish for everyone such a partner, who is always there beaming love and providing support, wisdom and steamed veggies (except when he's not, or I'm not and even then he's always willing to do what it takes to get back to love).

I could not have written this book without my FGFFs (Feel Good Fast Friends): Lynn Pollock (my Gayle), Shana Stanberry, Jan Murph, Leila Stuart, Rebecca Speer, Donna Ray and Deborah Smaller. Not only are these women emotionally supportive, they have also served as intelligent, insightful sounding boards for the ideas that went into this book.

This book could also not have been written without my writing coach, Hal Zina Bennett. For six years, Hal has been metaphorically at my side, helping corral my discursive mind and translate my often inchoate knowing into accessible prose. And I definitely couldn't have finished this book without the superb editing help of Roberta Werdinger, who not only helped cross all "t"s and smooth errant phrases but also gave me the gift of truly appreciating my content.

My son, Adam Hellman, has provided wise counsel throughout this book and offered his tender heart for Emotional Medicine. Watching Adam and his wife, Lorien, act as emotionally sensitive parents to our grandson, Ezekiel, makes my heart soar. My stepson

Tony Andrade and stepdaughter Maria Andrade show me in small ways and large how Emotional Medicine matters to them. My bonus sons, Brick Rucker and Javier Rivera, as well as Liz Cheung, Dave Kebo and JD Lopez, have shared their brains and talents in many useful ways that keep me from getting too old school.

My parents, Martin and Betty Jane Young, were models of humor, intelligence, and unwavering commitment to social justice. I am grateful for their gifts, and for my brother, Craig Young, whose work as a water steward reflects our shared devotion to cooperating with natural resources.

The monthly Poetic Medicine group run by John Foos and Rebecca Speer (with occasional visitations from founder John Fox) provided me a safe place to share profound life journeys with others and grow as a writer.

I found Peter Levine in a footnote in 1993. Personal work and training with him saved my nervous system and gave me an important piece of the Emotional Medicine puzzle.

Conversations with my Zen priest friend, Nicolee Miller, have been clarifying and important support for distinguishing Emotional Medicine and Buddhism.

I am grateful for the revisioning efforts of Psychosynthesis pioneers John and Ann Firman and for Diana Fosha's brilliant work on AEDP and her "celebration of transformational journeys" (note the plural). Many other mentors, teachers, guides and friends have helped me formulate Emotional Medicine, more than I can name here. Thank you all, and know you live in my heart.

Dr. Aline Fournier, my extraordinary Osteopath, and Dr. Oommen George, my wise Homeopath, keep me flourishing. Thanks to Jeannene Lee at Kemp Homeopathic Pharmacy in San Diego, CA for carrying the torch for Homeopathic Medicine and for great service. Feldenkrais sessions with the incomparable Donna Ray never fail to leave me moving effortlessly. Thanks to Dr. CJ Regala for healing hands and workout coaching par excellence. Decades ago, neo-Reichian therapy with Dr. David Cornsweet gave me a valuable foundation for honoring emotions, sexuality, and myself. Dr. Barbara Thomson has provided a touchstone as a fierce defender of emotional healing for 20 years.

Pantea Hadaegh, my ggs (Greek goddess sister), whose sustained interest during book-in-process conversations reaffirmed my faith that Emotional Medicine is relevant for smart young women.

I'm grateful to Gita Morena for leading the way to self-publishing autonomy with assurance and grace.

Louise and Gaetan Chevalier have provided years of ongoing encouragement as well as support for researching VIVO Oral Focus.

I thank Barbara Neighbors Deal, whose early faith in my manuscript bolstered my belief in the importance of my work.

Thanks to Steve Hays, Editor of The Life Connection, for providing me a platform for my Transformational Talk Column since 1998.

My beloved clients: I am honored to be part of your lives in such profound ways. I am moved and touched by your courage, your resilience, and your trust. Thank you.

Finally, my great-aunt, Ruth Forbes McLeod, still a pistol at 100 years of age, encourages me to let go and let God. She invites me continually to allow the effortless flow of spirit in my life.

May all beings be happy, may all beings know peace.

Resources for Your Emotional Medicine Journey

Emotionally Supportive Therapy

To find an AEDP therapist near you, see the AEDP (Accelerated Experiential Dynamic Psychotherapy) directory at www.AEDPInstitute.com.

To find an EFT therapist near you, see the ICEEFT (International Center for Excellence in Emotionally Focused Therapy) directory at www.iceeft.com.

To find a Bioenergetic Analyst near you, see the NANZIBA (North American and New Zealand Institutes for Bioenergetic Analysis) directory at www.nanziba.com.

To find a Pathwork helper near you, see the Pathwork directory at www.pathwork.org.

Trauma Healing

For information about Pat Ogden's comprehensive trauma healing program and to find a practitioner near you, check the www.sensorimotorpsychotherapy.org website.

For information about SE (Somatic Experiencing) and to find a practitioner near you, check the SE website at www.traumahealing.com.

Psychosynthesis
For information about Psychosynthesis, publications and finding a practitioner near you, go to the Association for the Advancement of Psychosynthesis site, www.aap-psychosynthesis.org and www.psychosynthesisresources.com.

Additional US Psychosynthesis resources are www.synthesiscenter.org and www.psychosynthesispaloalto.com. Helpful sites in England are www.psychosynthesis.org and www.sueholland.net. In Italy go to Italy www.psicosintesi.it. "Down under," check www.psychosynthesis.co.nz and www.psychosynthesis.net.au. Check the web for all other countries.

Homeopathy
Visit the National Center for Homeopathy website: www.homeopathic.org. Also visit www.hahnemannian.com, www.discoverhomeopathy.com, and www.homeopathy.com.

For mail and phone order homeopathic remedies: Kemp Homeopathic Pharmacy, 619-234-2166.

Osteopathy
To find an Osteopathic physician near you, go to the American Osteopathic Association at www.osteopathic.org.

Nutrition
Check out the Rosedale diet at www.drrosedale.com for a diet that supports vitality, reduces inflammation and calms your nervous system.

Feldenkrais
Look for a practitioner and learn about the healing potential of the ATM (Awareness Through Movement) system developed by Moshe Feldenkrais at www.feldenkrais.com. You can also find beneficial CDs for home practice at www.feldenkraisway.com. This method

helps increase functionality with structural as well as nervous system issues.

Poetic Medicine
The website www.poeticmedicine.com lists classes and workshops for John Fox's profound method of using group support and unfiltered poetic writing to support personal transformation and healing.

Meditation
Learn about meditation in the tradition of Thich Nhat Hanh at www.deerparkmonastery.org.

For Vipassana or Insight Meditation training, go to www.dharma. org or www.shinzen.org.

The Mindfulness Based Stress Reduction (MBSR) website at www. umassmed.edu can help you find a nearby training program.

American Zen Teacher Nicolee Miller McMahon developed the practice of immediacy to help develop awareness for cooperating with creative flow in all art forms. www.practiceofimmediacy.com.

Particularly Informative, Inspiring and/or Soothing Books
Woman by Natalie Angier

Your Body's Many Cries for Water by F. Batmanghelidj, M.D.

Lifestreams by David Boadella

Talking Back to Prozac and *Your Drug May Be Your Problem* by Peter Breggin, M.D.

Radical Acceptance by Tara Brach

The Unfolding Self and *Growing Whole* by Molly Young Brown

I Ching Optimism by Theo Cade

Feeling Good is Good for You by Carl Charnetski and Francis X. Brennan

The Yeast Connection by William Crook, M.D.

The Brain that Changes Itself by Norman Doidge, M.D.

The Chalice and the Blade, *Sacred Pleasure* and *The Partnership Way* by Riane Eisler

Going on Being and *Going to Pieces without Falling Apart* by Daniel Epstein, M.D.

Intrinsic Freedom by Peter Fenner

What We May Be, *Inevitable Grace*, and *Beauty and the Soul* by Piero Ferrucci

My Life So Far by Jane Fonda

The Journey Through Cancer by Jeremy Geffen, M.D.

Eat, Pray, Love by Elizabeth Gilbert

Blink, *The Tipping Point*, and *Outliers* by Malcolm Gladwell

The Seven Principles for Making Marriage Work and *Raising an Emotionally Intelligent Child* by John Gottman, Ph.D.

Healing Depression and Bipolar Disorder without Drugs by Gracelyn Guyol

The Miracle of Mindfulness by Thich Nhat Hanh

Get Out of Your Mind and Into Your Life by Steven C. Hayes

Hold Me Tight by Sue Johnson

Memories, Dreams and Reflections by Carl Jung

The Dance of the Dissident Daughter by Sue Monk Kidd

Traveling with Pomegranates by Sue Monk Kidd and Ann Kidd Taylor

Broken Open by Elizabeth Lesser

Waking the Tiger and *In an Unspoken Voice* by Peter Levine

A Gradual Awakening and *Who Dies* by Stephen Levine

Embracing the Beloved by Stephen and Ondrea Levine

Joy: The Surrender to the Body and to Life and *Pleasure* by Alexander Lowen

When the Body Says No by Gabor Maté, M.D.

The Wisdom of Oz by Gita Morena

Women's Bodies, Women's Wisdom and *The Wisdom of Menopause* by Christiane Northrup, M.D.

New and Selected Poems by Mary Oliver

Fearless Nest, edited by Shana Stanberry Parker

The Heart's Code and *A Healing Intimacy* by Paul Pearsall, Ph.D.

Molecules of Emotion and *Everything You Need To Know To Feel Go(o)d* by Candace Pert

Divining the Body by Jan Phillips

A Heart as Wide as the World, and *Faith* by Sharon Salzburg

If the Buddha Came to Dinner by Hale Sofia Schatz

Long Life Broth by Steven Schatz

Making a Literary Life and *Dreaming* by Carolyn See

The Instinct to Heal by David Servan-Schreiber, M.D.

A Fine Romance by Judith Sills, Ph.D.

The Omega-3 Connection by Andrew L. Stoll, M.D.

When God Was a Woman by Merlin Stone

The Power of Now by Eckhart Tolle

Gesture of Balance by Tarthang Tulku

The Soul of Money by Lynne Twist

Light in the Mirror by Barry and Joyce Vissell

In My Own Way by Alan Watts

One Taste and *Grace and Grit* by Ken Wilber

Novels Filled with Emotional Medicine

All books by Isabel Allende

Cellophane by Marie Arana

The Language of Flowers by Vanessa Diffenbaugh

Ex Libris by Anne Fadiman

Water for Elephants by Sara Gruen

Loving Frank by Nancy Horan

All books by Sue Monk Kidd

All books by Barbara Kingsolver

All books by Billie Letts

Leaving Mother Lake by Yang Erche Namu

Ahab's Wife and *Four Spirits* by Sena Jeter Naslund

All books by Lynn Pollock

All of Ruth Reichl's autobiographies

All books by Marisa de los Santos

All books by Lisa See

All books by Luis Alberto Urea

A Short History of Women by Kate Walbert

The Wife by Meg Wolitzer

Endnotes

Introduction

1 I did not have any experience with Arthur Janov and his Primal Scream therapies at that time except through John Lennon's music. In the years I was doing research for this book, I encountered his latest book, *Primal Healing: Access the Incredible Power of Feelings to Improve Your Health*. My reading of his material is that he is not focused on letting the body lead. He describes hours of ongoing catharsis for clients. In my experience the body is way too smart to use its resources in that way. It's very efficient.

2 Currently there is a focus in some mindfulness and somatically based therapies to experience emotional flow inside yourself quietly and subtly. While I'm grateful for any focus on emotional experience, however subtle, I believe this misses the physiological, state-shifting importance of allowing the (safe and responsible) external expression of emotion – vigorous movement of arms and legs, voice, the heaving sobs of the chest, etc.

3 Beginning in the late 80s, some clinicians were experimenting with using MDMA for therapeutic purposes. I was intrigued but wanted to have personal experience with the drug before attempting to use it with my clients. Unfortunately MDMA catapulted me into a panic disorder. Fortunately, this gave me an opportunity to learn how to help myself and others recover from anxiety disorders.

4 James J. Gross (2007), p. 87.

5 In a seminal essay in *The New Yorker*, "The Truth Wears Off: Is There Something Wrong with the Scientific Method?" (2010), Jonah Lehrer discusses how the scientific method does not value disproving theses as much as it values proving them. As a result, researchers are forced to go for the glamorous, breakthrough study, which is not always what is needed or even what is true!

6 Diener et al., 2007.

7 For results of EFT research see Greenberg and Johnson (1988), p. 51. For results of Gottman Institute studies see Gottman (1998), pp. 38-39.

8 Davidson (2000), pp. 1196-1214; Davidson and Kabat-Zinn (2003), pp. 564-570.

One: Emotional Medicine

1 Antonio Damasio, *The Feeling of What Happens: Body and Emotion in the Making of Consciousness* (1999), p. 127. I highly recommend this remarkable book.

2 Oatley, Keltner and Jenkins (2006) describe how contempt, embarrassment, shame, pride, love, desire and sympathy may also be considered primary emotions (p. 93). Jaak Panksepp (1998) describes seven "Blue Ribbon, Grade A Emotional Systems": seeking, fear, rage, lust, care, panic and play (p. 52). For simplicity, I'm going to stick with Paul Ekman's original six (2003, Chapter 1).

3 This quote is from Dr. Pert's brilliant book, *Molecules of Emotion* (1997), p. 289.

Two: Find Resources Inside and Out

1 Dr. Daniel Siegel (2010) proposes that our awareness can even function as an unconditionally loving presence for ourselves. He suggests that we use any awareness practice to enhance our sense of self-acceptance ... following the nonjudgmental lead of the "as is-ness" of awareness.

2 Lieberman et al. (2007)

3 Although some neuroscientists and philosophers propose that free will is an illusion because *all* action is initiated in the brain milliseconds before you become conscious of it, it is important to recognize that awareness gives you, if not willpower, then "won't" power. You can always stop an action once initiated. From my personal and professional experience, I know human beings can make deliberate choices to change patterns and create happier lives. And Antonio Damasio delivers even better news in his latest book, *Self Comes to Mind*. An ingenious study conducted by Dutch psychologist Ap Dijksterhuis indicates that "nonconscious processes are capable of some sort of reasoning, far more than they are usually thought to be and that this reasoning ... may lead to beneficial decisions." (p. 274)

4 This "Shifting Focus" exercise is adapted from a "Disidentification Exercise" described in John Firman and Ann Gila's remarkable book, *Psychosynthesis: A Psychology of the Spirit* (2002), p. 95.

5 In severe cases of posttraumatic stress, some people have also experienced an unplanned emergence of anger as their nervous system unwinds. When awareness is used to distinguish the anger as a simple (albeit strong) body experience as distinguished from a narrative-driven acting out, this anger moves briefly through the emotional cycle without harm and leads to the same kind of relief as any embodied Emotional Medicine.

6 Of course, if you've been suppressing too much for too long, or a really devastating event comes along, you may not be able to stop your emotions from leaking a little. I read an account of a famous journalist who gave a newspaper interview soon after her mother died. While talking of her mother (with whom she'd been very close), the journalist tried her best not to cry. However, a few tears rolled down her face anyway (noted by her interviewer). She chose to ignore them, maintained her composure and continued the interview as if nothing had happened. In a male-dominated field, she was likely concerned that tears would have deemed her weak and ineffective. I suspect she completed her grieving in a safe and private space.

7 I am indebted to Diana Fosha who developed the notion of "self at best" (as well as the concomitant "self at worst") in her AEDP (Accelerated Experiential Dynamic Psychotherapy). Diana added an additional conceptual framework to the Psychosynthesis notion I had previously used in my own practice and life: keeping connected with the qualities and resources we have available through our selves at best. "Self at best" resonated for me through my Psychosynthesis training, which views every individual as an amalgam of unconscious drives (sex, death, aggression) as well as the "self at best" superconscious forces (love, altruism, intuition, courage, etc.).

8 Psychosynthesis was founded by an Italian psychiatrist, Dr. Roberto Assagioli, a contemporary of Jung and Freud. Assagioli developed counseling methods focused on the synthesis of all aspects of human experience: body, emotions, mind, spirit. He developed methods for using notions of the transpersonal Self, the personal and transpersonal will, and subpersonalities or "parts" work to support people on a path of personal and transpersonal Psychosynthesis.

9   I wanted to be sure that an endogenous (natural) experience of pleasure through natural stimulation and focus on endorphins wouldn't stimulate a craving for the exogenous pleasure (morphine) this client had been addicted to.

10 While Anne's growth did turn out to be cancer, after surgery to remove the growth and kidney, lab tests indicated that the cancer had not spread. She remains committed to a healthy lifestyle (including taking her Emotional Medicine).

Three: Get Out of Your Head

1   Sometimes there are other causes of head trips in addition to trapped emotions. You may also experience obsessive head trips as an allergic reaction to food or drink that doesn't agree with you. The allergic reaction sets off a sympathetic nervous system reaction which your mind may mistake for emotional or mental distress.

2   Although, for serious Buddhist scholars, there are important distinctions in definitions of mindfulness in various traditions, I'm using the word here colloquially to refer to an ability to be aware of an ever-changing flow of body sensations, emotions and thoughts in present moment experience, while at the same time maintaining contact with a distinct and unchanging sense of awareness and witness.

3   Although it may be confusing to talk of using "mindfulness" techniques to "get out of your head," it may help you to think of mindfulness as "bodymindfulness." The latest research indicates that the human mind is located not just in the head but throughout the body. I even imagine, were Buddha alive today, he would be comfortable with the coinage "bodymindfulness."

Four: Make Friends with Your Body

1 Antonio Damasio (2001), p. 35.

2 This experiment is detailed in another of Antonio Damasio's seminal books, *Descartes' Error* (1994), as well as Timothy D. Wilson's wonderful *Strangers to Ourselves* (2002), and Malcolm Gladwell's compellingly readable *Blink: The Power of Thinking Without Thinking* (2005).

3 The key word here is unexpected. We are gluttons for punishment when working out with a no-pain-no-gain attitude. We can push ourselves on a 10-mile hike, a 25-mile bike ride, a grueling free-weight regimen. This is pain we have under our control, if you will. It is predictable and seems normal.

4 If your religion prohibits masturbation, as does the Mormon Church, you'll need to turn to myriad other outlets for health boosting such as exercise, dancing, good nutrition, prayer.

5 Mark Epstein (2001), p.161.

Five: Learn the Language of Your Body

1 Concentrating on warming your hands is also good medicine for alleviating migraine headache pain.

2 Interestingly, scientists have found the neuropeptides associated with the process of thinking in the gut! In his book *The Second Brain* (1998), Michael Gershon describes this in detail. If Marta knew how to communicate with her gut when she first experienced butterflies in her stomach, she would have known that she was both excited and scared. When the gut is "thinking," those thoughts are more likely to reflect bodily wisdom and guidance for healing than any mental assessment of patterns of thoughts. Marta's patterns of thoughts about men not being trustworthy are what got her into trouble.

3 Breaking emotions down only into a series of discrete sensations can diminish emotional impact if you don't allow yourself to take the ride with the rolling flow of sensations. Unfortunately, I've seen some in the Somatic Experiencing community do just that. Emotional impact is greater than the sum of its parts.

4 Looking for evidence of pleasurable sensations is particularly helpful with children. Since you may want to teach them how to cry when they're sad and stop when they're done, it is important to help them discover how their bodies soothe and settle down after an upset. For example, when a child scrapes his/her knee, you can support strong, healthy crying; then when you, the grown-up, notice the body is done and is shifting to calm, soothing sensations, you can draw attention to the peacefulness that is taking place.

5 My husband Arturo designed an ingenious oral anchor to go with the VIVO process called Oral Focus. You can learn more about the complete VIVO Oral Focus kit and our year-long research with this technology on our website, www.emotionalmedicine. com. However, you can get all the safety benefits you need just from using the VIVO protocol I outline here.

6. The VIVO Oral Focus (VOF) kit was tested in a pilot research project at the Sanoviv Medical Institute in Baja, California, Mexico in 2008 to determine if VOF was useful in decreasing pain, reducing anxiety and increasing happiness and optimism. In an experimental group, ten subjects used the VOF kit for five days. Ten control group subjects spent a similar amount of time listening to classical music. Both groups were tested at the beginning and end of the five days on four instruments: 1) Short Form McGill Pain Questionnaire, 2) Hamilton Anxiety Scale, 3) Oxford Happiness Inventory, and 4) Seligman Optimism Test. T-tests were used to compare mean values before

and after five days of utilization of VIVO Oral Focus sessions for each of the four instruments. Results indicated that the group using VOF were happier, less anxious and in less pain than before the utilization of VOF. The control group did *not* report any significant change in pain after listening to music for the same duration but they still felt happier and less anxious. However, the level of significance obtained for happiness and anxiety with group using VOF was higher than for group listening to music. Research was conducted by Jude Gladstone Cade, Ph.D., Director of Psycho- Spiritual Programs at Sanoviv Medical Center, and Gaetan Chevalier, Ph.D., Director of Research at Psy-tek Laboratories for Thermal Imaging, and Director of Research for the Earthing Institute in Encinitas, CA.

7 It is important to set intentions in the present rather than the future. Healing takes place in the present moment.

8 This stuck quality of depression and anxiety lead many to antidepressant medications for relief. This can be a humane solution for chronic, deeply grooved patterns of depression and anxiety. Eliminating sugar, alcohol and adding Omega-3 oils to the diet, exercising daily and getting enough sunlight can also help maintain biochemical well-being. Emotional Medicine is an excellent adjunct to any medication protocol.

Six: Attend to Anxiety and Depression

1 Yes, even good events like love, marriage, and job promotion create a stress response in the body. These stresses are technically known as "eustress" (a term coined by famed stress researcher Hans Selye) to distinguish them from *dis*tress. But eustress needs to be managed just as much as distress because both are equally taxing on the body and cumulative in nature. The body itself cannot tell the difference between nervous system activation for happy or terrible events. Both register as stressful.

2 Rao et al. (2009), discuss their conclusions that taking probiotics for two months significantly alleviated anxiety and depression in the journal *Gut Pathogens,* pp. 1-6.

3 Babyak et al. (2000), pp. 633-638.

4 Check out Michael Otto and Jasper A.J. Smits' extremely useful book (2011), *Exercise for Mood and Anxiety: Proven Strategies for Overcoming Depression and Enhancing Well-Being.*

5 The question of how much sugar, alcohol or drugs is too much is an individual one. However, if you are anxious or depressed it's a good idea to start by eliminating these first and seeing if you notice any improvement. Unfortunately, one rule of thumb that has proved true for me is that if I'm really *craving* something on a regular basis, I'm probably allergic to it.

6 Laura Blue (2010), Time.com.

7 The Heel Company of Germany is a leader in peer-reviewed double-blind studies about the effectiveness of this true "energetic" medicine.

8 By trauma I mean everything from smaller, yet often devastating, events such as being lost at a store as a child, not having the correct answer when called on at school, to big, disastrous events such as losing loved ones, losing a home to fire or flood, or being injured in violent or nonviolent incidents.

9 The most lethal response to trauma is the complete collapse of body systems in severe shock. While a person in severe shock may appear to be frozen, there is no sympathetic nervous system underlay to the overriding parasympathetic freeze. In this

case the parasympathetic nervous system brings visceral body functioning to a halt. Without medical intervention, death would follow. In the freeze I am describing the viscera are intact, still able to mobilize life energy to run away once the threat has passed.

10 You will find domesticated animals suffering anxiety disorders when they are removed from natural lifestyles, isolated from owners or other animals and not given enough freedom, exercise or proper nutrition. Animals living near construction zones where natural habitat is being destroyed may also exhibit panic symptoms.

11 I wrote this "Shake, Rattle, and Roll" subheading in 2009. Imagine my surprise when Peter Levine's new book, *In an Unspoken Voice,* arrived on my doorstep in October 2010 with the exact same phrase. Great minds think alike (especially those baby boomers' minds familiar with Bill Haley and the Comets)!

12 I do not encourage people to apply mantras or "positive thinking" as band-aids over numb or frozen (or sad, mad or scared) body states. The most effective use of affirmations occurs when the body is consciously recognized as having positive flow and embodied resources. Since the VIVO and Emotional Medicine protocols typically deliver some level of well-being in minutes, it's a good idea to use those first before applying affirmations. In the case of acute panic, while the Calming Protocol might take longer, it is still a good idea to use the mind initially to generate positive images or memories rather than affirmations. These images will likely lead to concomitant positive body sensations. It will then be possible to generate the kind of embodied well-being that makes affirmations a potent tool.

13 Taking no action because you've talked yourself out of an instinctual fear response is different than the inaction of the freeze response. If you have time to talk yourself out of an instinctual fear response, you have a choice. With the freeze response, you have no choice.

Seven: Cultivate Multimodal Awareness

1 Although we're on our way to more relational, compassionate, bodymind-oriented parent-child relationships, we're still impacted by the poisonous pedagogy of "children should be seen and not heard."

2 The original Psychosynthesis "Disidentification Process" invited people to consider: "I have a body but I am not my body. I have my feelings, but I am not my feelings. I have a mind, but I am not my mind. I am a center of pure self-consciousness and will." As a spiritual seeker, I was uneasy with how the "I am not" language separated me from my basic human experience and often unwittingly led me to feel somewhat disassociated. My concerns with this dualistic metaphor and theory almost led me to leave the Psychosynthesis community. John Firman and Ann Gila revised this process and invited people to say instead: "I am distinct *but not separate* from my sensations. I am distinct *but not separate* from my feelings. I am distinct *but not separate* from my thoughts." I am grateful for their insistence on a nondual framework for consciousness.

3 I am using "Spirit" here to refer to that mystical assemblage of feelings, images, thoughts, purposeful visioning and experiences you may call God, Higher Power or Great Spirit, and to which you may feel more or less connected at any given moment.

4 I am grateful for the brilliant American meditation teacher Shinzen Young for this insight. Shinzen was a mathematician

before becoming a meditation teacher. Mathematically, the distance between zero and one is infinity. This notion has helped me be gentle with myself when I have time for only the briefest meditation practice.

5   If you've missed out on loving parental attention, you typically learn early on to fill a relationship void with your self. You learned very quickly *not* to look at others' reactions to protect yourself from a caretaker's vacant, inattentive or angry gaze. Other types of childhood wounds may lead you to fill parental voids by focusing almost exclusively on others' needs. It is as if you believe you can fill the void by doing for others what you would like to have done for you. Fortunately, you can learn to undo this behavior in the present moment.

6   A little more understanding and integration of Freudian notions about the unconscious, transference, projection and other defense mechanisms would have been useful in the early Psychosynthesis movement. Later work by Psychosynthesis theorists and trainers John Firman and Ann Gila in their books, *Revisioning Psychosynthesis*, *The Primal Wound* and *Psychosynthesis* provides a foundation for integrating the wisdom of both Freud and Assagioli.

Eight: Align with Your Big "S" Self

1   In their book *A Psychotherapy of Love: Psychosynthesis in Practice* (2010), John Firman and Ann Gila discuss why they don't like to use the possessive pronouns "your" or "my" when describing Self. They posit that Self is "not an object of consciousness but the source of consciousness ... not 'a being' but the Ground of Being ... so Self can be termed 'NoSelf.'" (p. 27) Although I like the way their thinking integrates Psychosynthesis with Buddhist notions, I'm going to continue to use the possessive pronouns as an interim way to strengthen the more intimate connection you (and I) may gain by doing so.

2   I'd like to make it clear that even though your small self and big
     Self may sometimes seem like separate entities, your big "S"
     Self is always present regardless of whether you're consciously
     aware of and aligned with it or not.

Nine: Accept Your Shadow

1   Although these "shadow" aspects of human experience are in-
     evitable, you can mitigate and minimize their intrusive power
     by proper self-care – attending to healthy diet, exercise, rela-
     tionship building, and Emotional Medicine. The "black holes"
     of dark moods and thoughts following overindulgence of sugar,
     alcohol and recreational drugs are often fueled by the resulting
     biochemical imbalances.

2   Freud postulated that innate human drives of sex, death and
     aggression bumping against the constraints of civilized culture
     were the source of unconscious "shadow" conflicts. However,
     following Dollard and Miller's Frustration/Aggression theory,
     I too don't believe death or aggressive drives are separate from
     drives of self-preservation and/or self-gratification. I am more
     comfortable with the position that shadow thoughts and ac-
     tions arise from blocked developmental/relational/familial
     needs bumping against normal, but unmediated, childhood
     aggression and self-centeredness which arise when trying to get
     those needs met.

3   If you are actually acting out shadow impulses such as hitting
     your spouse or child, or cooking the books at work, you need
     professional help ASAP. Please find a therapist, clergyperson,
     doctor and/or lawyer to help you.

4   Dr. Hayes' book, *Get Out of your Mind and Into Your Life* (2005),
     is the brother book to *Emotional Medicine Rx.* Highly recom-
     mended!

Ten: Let Your Body Lead

1   Kottler (1996), p. 62.

2   Dr. Janov's primal therapy processes have been controversial for over 30 years. While I have not had direct experience with his methods, my reading of his ideas indicates that he has discovered something essential about the connection between emotional release work and healing. I have, however, serious concerns about the ongoing intensity of the work he does with clients. I cannot tell from his writing whether he makes the distinction between restimulating primal pain as a result of over-focus on releasing previously repressed material and true body-led emotional processing. In one of his books he mentions clients needing to experience their neurobiologically devastating birth traumas up to *one hundred times*. This seems wildly excessive and raises serious concerns, for me, that primal therapy could be unwittingly grooving pain circuits more deeply without the balance of increasing and strengthening awareness of and tolerance for pleasure circuits.

3   Arthur Janov (1991), p. 319.

4   Alexander Lowen (1995), p. 293.

5   Mark Epstein (2001), p.161.

6   Kottler (1996), p. 132.

7   Most of this fascinating information about brain chemistry, tears and gender difference comes from Jeffrey A. Kottler's wonderful book, *The Language of Tears* (2001).

8   Gabor Maté (2003), p. 99.

9 I am aware that in the little microcosm of my relationship with Arturo, the problem of men not honoring, listening to, or supporting women was being healed. He was a man and he was listening to and supporting me. In that sense, history was changed by the way we were in partnership at that very moment!

Eleven: Stop When You're Done

1 I didn't mention to Eve that since her crying led chronically to hysteria and anoxia (lack of oxygen), this pointed to the possibility that the situation was triggering birth trauma. That would be something we could cope with once she was stabilized.

2 Nico Frijda (2007), p.186.

3 Nico Frijda quoted in Scherer and Ekman, eds. (1984), pp. 319-344.

4 Ibid., p.190.

5 Ochsner and Gross, in J.J. Gross (2007), p.105.

6 In fairness, Ekman's claim that true emotion lasts only seconds was made in one of his earliest works (1984). In a 1994 essay, "All Emotions Are Basic," in Ekman and Davidson (Eds.), *The Nature of Emotion*, p. 17, Ekman states that emotions generally are characterized by quick onset, brief duration, and voluntary nature, without quantifying "brief duration."

Twelve: Focus On Feeling Good

1 I have contacted numerous neuroscientists to alert them to my clinical discoveries. I have offered to demonstrate the remarkable results I see in my therapy office every week. Since I have a scientific orientation, I would love to see exactly what is happening to patients' endorphin, dopamine, and serotonin levels

to produce the results I reliably see. So far no one has taken me up on this.

2 Many times it's important to first establish a baseline of resourcefulness and good feeling before exploring sad, mad or scared emotions. The pleasure seems to support the organism in safely revealing and healing deeper wounds.

3 Dr. Mehmet Oz (2005).

4 Dacher Keltner (2009), p. x.

5 Mary Oliver (1992), p. 110.

6 Riane Eisler (1995), p. 328. I am grateful that Riane has been a champion of pleasure and partnership her entire literary life.

7 Charnetski and Brennan (2001).

8 Deva and James Beck (1987), p.105.

9 I'm indebted to Diana Fosha and AEDP for phrasing this question so simply and beautifully. It's always a good idea to look for more good feeling, and to keep asking yourself that question until you're really filled with it.

10 Studies show that we have an innate tendency to remember negative experience over positive. Speculation is that remembering negative experience held more survival value when early man faced a host of natural dangers.

11 Current trends in neuroscience tend to see the whole brain as multidimensional with the right/left brain division no longer as important. It is useful for our purposes here to talk about differ-

ent kinds of brain activity operating every moment. I'm going to continue using this colloquial right/left brain language to help delineate the two kinds of awareness being bridged or manifested, regardless of where exactly in the brain they have originated.

12 I have devised a pleasure-deepening guided meditation that moves awareness through all the body systems, imagining them infused and suffused with healing sensations. I do this specifically to bring healing down into bone marrow and molecules. This is designed to heal any body/spirit split. Please check my website, www.emotionalmedicine.com, to download this meditation.

13 Whether you are actually sending energy to your "future" or anchoring a current positive experience in your brain for recall in a future moment is debatable. In any case, you have more power to influence yourself in the future than you may have realized.

14 In Emotional Medicine sessions, the hands often spontaneously move to positions of prayer and supplication during healing experiences.

Thirteen: Take it Back to Daily Life

1 Of course, there is a good case to be made that we are always seeing things through a distorted lens, whether triggered or not. Certain familial, social, political and historical constructs are so deeply embedded that it takes years of meditation practice to become like the experienced Zen meditators whose brains demonstrate that each moment has the freshness of something they've never experienced before.

2 Louise L. Hay (1979), p. 6.

3 Notice that I am not using capital "T" Truth here. Although I know Emotional Medicine to be truth for myself and my clients

for these past decades, I also know there are many truths available for people … and even parallel realities. There are many transformational journeys, many paths. I stand in an open embrace of all possibilities.

4   Rhonda Bryne (2006).

5   Tom Lutz (1999).

6   Of course there are some advanced yogis who can regulate their autonomic nervous systems. But unless you've been hooked up to a machine to determine that you are controlling your gastric secretions, blood pressure and galvanic skin response, it's probably wiser to assume you are not capable of this, even though you may be an experienced meditator. Another way to test for your ability to control what are typically unconscious regulatory body processes it to take an honest measure of your health. Embodied emotional expression and vitality go hand in hand. If you regularly stop emotional flow, you also stop healthy body functioning. (A caveat: Many apparently robustly healthy people are shocked when they discover they have cancer; the body has done such a good job of containing the cancer until it becomes systemic. Although the jury is still out, the onset of cancer may be as influenced by chronically containing emotional expression as are other chronic diseases [fibromyalgia, Epstein-Barr, gastritis, etc.]).

7   In a big breakthrough like this, you may experience waves of deepening feeling. You may complete one emotional cycle, experience peace and bliss, and then find your body ready to go for a deeper experience of emotional pain, followed by more peace and bliss. It is very important to be on guard for head trip restimulating, but to also stay open for organic waves of emotional cycles. In this case, a profound emotional release may last longer than the three minutes or so of everyday-type Emotional Medicine.

Bibliography

I am including here books cited in the text as well as others relevant for Emotional Medicine.

Allione, T. (1984). *Women of Wisdom*. London: Arkana Paperbacks.

Anderson, S. & Hopkins, P. (1991). *The Feminine Face of God: The unfolding of the sacred in women*. New York: Bantam Books.

Andrade, P. (1988). Family of origin: Land of opportunity for transpersonal therapy. In Weiser and Yeomans (Eds.), *Readings in Psychosynthesis: Theory, process and practice*, Volume 2 (pp. 6-14). Ontario, Canada: Ontario Institute for Studies in Education.

Andrade, P. (1992). Right feeling: Doorway to transformation. *Energy and Character, the Journal of Biosynthesis*, 23 (1).

Andrade, P. (2006). Choosing Embodiment. In *Conversations in Psychosynthesis: Psychosynthesis and the body* (pp. 90-104). Albany, CA: Association for the Advancement of Psychosynthesis.

Batmanghelidj, F. (1992). *Your Body's Many Cries for Water: You are not sick, You are thirsty!* Falls Church, VA: Global Health Solutions, Inc.

Assagioli, R. (1965). *Psychosynthesis: A collection of basic writings.* New York: Penguin Books.

Assagioli, R. (1973). *The Act of Will.* New York: Viking Press.

Babyak, M., Blumenthal, J., et al. (2000). *Exercise treatment for major depression: Maintenance of therapeutic benefit at one month.* Psychosomatic Medicine, 62, pp. 633-638.

Beck, D. & Beck, J. (1987). *The Pleasure Connection: How endorphins affect our health and happiness.* San Marcos, CA: Synthesis Press.

Berntsen, D. (2002). Tunnel memories for autobiographical events: Central details are remembered more frequently from shocking than from happy experiences." *Journal of Memory and Cognition,* 7, pp. 1010 –20.

Blakeslee, S. (1996, January 23). "Complex and hidden brain in gut makes stomachaches and butterflies." *New York Times.*

Blue, L. (2010, June). Is exercise the best drug for depression? Time.com.

Boadella, D. (1987). *Lifestreams: An introduction to biosynthesis.* New York: Routledge & Kegan Paul, Inc.

Boyesen, G. (1982). The primary personality. *Journal of Biodynamic Psychology, 3.*

Brach, T. (2003). *Radical Acceptance: Embracing your life with the heart of a Buddha.* New York: Bantam Dell.

Breggin, P. (1994). *Talking Back to Prozac: What doctors aren't telling you about today's most controversial drug.* New York: St Martin's Press.

Breggin, P. and Cohen, D. (1999). *Your Drug May Be Your Problem: How and why to stop taking psychiatric medications.* Philadelphia, PA: Da Capo Press.

Brown, M. (1983). *The Unfolding Self: Psychosynthesis and counseling.* Los Angeles: Psychosynthesis Press.

Brown, M. (1993). *Growing Whole: Self-realization on an endangered planet.* New York: Harper Collins.

Bryne, R. (2006). *The Secret.* New York: Atria Books/Beyond Words.

Cade, Theo. (2011). *I Ching Optimism.* Bloomington, IN: Xlibris.

Charnetski, C. & Brennan, F. (2001). *Feeling Good is Good for You: How pleasure can boost your immune system and lengthen your life.* Emmaus, PA: Rodale, Inc.

Chopra, D. (1993). *Ageless Body, Timeless Mind: The quantum alternative to growing old.* New York: Harmony Books.

Chodron, P. (2001). *The Places That Scare You: A guide to fearlessness in difficult times.* Boston: Shambhala Publications.

Coren, S. (1996). *Sleep Thieves: An eye-opening exploration into the science & mysteries of sleep.* New York: The Free Press.

Crenshaw, T. (1997). *The Alchemy of Love and Lust: How our sex hormones influence our relationships.* New York: Pocket Books.

Crook, W. (1983). *The Yeast Connection: A medical breakthrough.* New York: Vintage Books.

Csikszentmihalyi, M. (1990). *Flow: The psychology of optimal experience.* New York: Harper Collins.

Damasio, A. (1994). *Descartes' Error: Emotion, reason and the human brain.* New York: Putnam & Sons.

Damasio, A. (1999). *The Feeling of What Happens: Body and emotion in the making of consciousness.* Orlando, FL: Harcourt Books.

Davidson, R. (2000). Affective style, psychopathology, and resilience: Brain mechanisms and plasticity. *American Psychologist,* 55, pp. 1196-1214.

Davidson, R. and Kabat-Zinn, J., et al (2003). Alterations in brain and immune function produced by mindfulness meditation. *Psychosomatic Medicine,* 65, pp. 564-570.

Damasio, A. (2003). *Looking for Spinoza: Joy, sorrow, and the feeling brain.* Orlando, FL: Harcourt Books.

Damasio, A. (2010). *Self Comes to Mind: Constructing the conscious brain.* New York: Pantheon Books.

Diener, M., Hilsenroth, M., and Weinberger, J. (2007). Therapist affect focus and patient outcomes in psychodynamic psychotherapy: A meta-analysis. *American Journal of Psychiatry, 164,* pp. 936-941.

Doidge, N. (2007). *The Brain that Changes itself: Stories of personal triumph from the frontiers of brain science.* New York: Penguin Books.

Dollard, J., Miller, N., Doob, L., Mowrer, O., & Sears, R. (1939). *Frustration and aggression.* New Haven, CT: Yale University Press.

Easwaran, E. (1978). *Meditation: An eight-point program.* Petaluma, CA: Nilgiri Press.

Eisler, R. (1987). *The Chalice and the Blade: Our history, our future.* New York: Harper and Row.

Eisler, R. (1995). *Sacred Pleasure: Sex, myth and the politics of the body.* New York: Harper Collins.

Eisler, R. (1998). *The Partnership Way: New tools for living and learning,* 2nd ed. Brandon, VT: Holistic Education Press.

Ekman, P. & Davidson, R. (Eds.) (1994). *The Nature of Emotion: Fundamental questions. Series in Affective Science.* New York: Oxford University Press.

Ekman, P. (2003). *Emotions Revealed: Recognizing faces and feelings to improve communication and emotional life.* Revised edition. New York: Owl Books.

Epstein, M. (1999). *Going to Pieces without Falling Apart: A Buddhist perspective on wholeness.* New York: Broadway Books.

Epstein, M. (2001). *Going on Being: Buddhism and the way of change.* New York: Broadway Books.

Fenner, P. (1994). *Intrinsic Freedom: The art of stress-free living.* Newtown, Australia: Millennium Books.

Ferrucci, P. (1982). *What We May Be: Techniques for psychological and spiritual growth through Psychosynthesis.* Los Angeles: Tarcher.

Firman, D. (1989). *Daughters and Mothers: Making it work.* New York: Continuum.

Firman, J. (1991). *I and Self: Revisioning Psychosynthesis.* Palo Alto, CA: Self-published monograph.

Firman, J. & Gila, A. (1997). *The Primal Wound: A transpersonal view of trauma, addiction, and growth.* Albany, NY: State University of New York Press.

Firman, J. & Gila, A. (2002). *Psychosynthesis: A psychology of the spirit.* Albany, NY: State University of New York Press.

Firman, J. & Gila, A. (2010). *A Psychotherapy of Love: Psychosynthesis in practice.* Albany, NY: State University of New York Press.

Fonda, J. (2005). *My Life So Far.* New York: Random House.

Fosha, D. (2002). *The Transforming Power of Affect: A model for accelerated change.* New York: Basic Books.

Fosha, D., Siegel, D., & Solomon, M. (Eds.) (2009). *The Healing Power of Emotion: Affective neuroscience, development and clinical practice.* New York: W.W. Norton & Co.

Frederick, R. (2009). *Living Like You Mean It: Use the wisdom and power of your emotions to get the life you really want.* San Francisco: Jossey-Bass.

Frederickson, B.L. & Levenson, R. (1998). Positive emotions speed recovery from the cardiovascular sequelae of negative emotions. *Psychology Press, 12*, pp. 191-220.

Frederickson, B.L. (2000, March). Cultivating positive emotions to optimize health and well-being. *Prevention and Treatment, 3,* posted online.

Frederickson, B.L (2001). The role of positive emotions in positive psychology. *American Psychologist, 56,* pp. 218 – 226.

Frijda, N. (2007). *The Laws of Emotion.* Mahwah, NJ: Lawrence Erlbaum Associates.

Geffen, J. (2000). *The Journey Through Cancer: An oncologist's seven-level program for healing and transforming the whole person.* New York: Three Rivers Press.

Gershon, M. (1998). *The Second Brain: A groundbreaking new understanding of nervous disorders of the stomach and intestine.* New York: Harper Perennial.

Gilligan, C. (1982). *In a Different Voice: Psychological theory and women's development.* Cambridge, MA: Harvard University Press.

Gladwell, M. (2005). *Blink: The power of thinking without thinking.* New York: Little, Brown.

Gottman, J., Declaire, J., & Goleman, D. (1998). *Raising an Emotionally Intelligent Child: the heart of parenting.* New York: Fireside.

Gottman, J. (1999). *The Seven Principles for Making Marriage Work: A practical guide from the country's foremost relationship expert.* New York: Three Rivers Press.

Greenberg, L. and Johnson, S. (1988). *Emotionally Focused Therapy for Couples.* New York, NY: Guilford Press.

Greenberg, L., Rice, L., & Elliott, R. (1993). *Facilitating Emotional Change: The moment-by-moment process.* New York: The Guilford Press.

Greenberg, L. & Paivio, S. (1997). *Working with emotions in psychotherapy.* New York: The Guilford Press.

Grof, S. (1985). *Beyond the Brain: Birth, death and transcendence in psychotherapy.* Albany, NY: State University of New York Press.

Gross, J.J. (Ed.) (2007). *Handbook of Emotion Regulation.* New York: Guilford Press.

Guyol, G. (2006). *Healing Depression and Bipolar Disorder Without Drugs: Inspiring stories of restoring mental health through natural therapies.* New York: Walker & Company.

Hahn, T. (1975). *The Miracle of Mindfulness.* Boston: Beacon Press.

Hanson, R. with Mendius, R. (2009). *Buddha's Brain: The practical neuroscience of happiness, love and wisdom.* Oakland, CA: New Harbinger Publications.

Hardy, J. (1990). *A Psychology with a Soul: Psychosynthesis in evolutionary context.* New York: Penguin Books.

Haronian, F. (1967). *The Repression of the Sublime.* New York: Psychosynthesis Research Foundation monograph.

Hay, L. (1976). *Heal Your Body: The mental causes for physical illness and the metaphysical way to overcome them.* New York: Louise L. Hay (self-published).

Hayes, S., Strosahl, K., & Wilson, K. (1999). *Acceptance and Commitment Therapy: An experiential approach to behavior change.* New York: Guilford Press.

Hayes, S. (2005). *Get Out of Your Mind and Into Your Life: The new acceptance and commitment therapy.* Oakland, CA: New Harbinger Publications.

Hilton, R. (2007). *Relational Somatic Psychotherapy.* Santa Barbara, CA: Santa Barbara Graduate Institute.

Janes, J. (1976). *The Origin of Consciousness in the Breakdown of the Bicameral Mind.* Boston: Houghton Mifflin.

Janov, A. (1991). *The New Primal Scream: Primal therapy twenty years on.* Wilmington, DE: Enterprise Publishing.

Janov, A. (2007). *Primal Healing: Access the incredible power of feelings to improve your health.* Franklin Lakes, NJ: New Page Books.

Johnson, S. (2008). *Hold Me Tight: Seven conversations for a lifetime of love.* New York: Little, Brown & Co.

Jung, C.G.(1961). *Memories, Dreams and Reflections.* New York: Vintage Books.

Kabat-Zinn, J. & Chapman-Waldrop, A. (1988). Compliance with an outpatient stress reduction program: Rates and predictors of program completion. *Journal of Behavioral Medicine, 11,* pp. 333-352.

Kabat-Zinn, J. (1990). *Full Catastrophe Living: Using the wisdom of your body and mind to face stress, pain, and illness.* New York: Delta Books.

Keltner, D. (2009). *Born To Be Good: The science of a meaningful life.* New York: W.W. Norton.

Kennedy-Moore, E. & Watson, J. (1999). *Expressing Emotion: Myths, realities, and therapeutic strategies.* New York: Guilford Press.

Kottler, J. (1996). *The Language of Tears.* San Francisco: Jossey-Bass.

Lacks, H. & Leonard, C. (1986). Fear of feeling: Addressing the emotional process during recovery. *Alcoholism Treatment Quarterly, 3,* pp. 69-80.

Lehrer, J. (2010, December.) The truth wears off: Is there something wrong with the scientific method? *The New Yorker.*

Lesser, E. (2005). *Broken Open: How difficult times can help us grow.* New York: Villard Books.

Levine, P. (1977). *Accumulate Stress Reserve Capacity and Disease.* (Doctoral Dissertation.) University of Michigan, Ann Arbor.

Levine, P. (1991). The body as healer: A revisioning of trauma and anxiety. In M. Sheets-Johnstone (Ed.), *Giving the Body its Due.* Stonybrook, NY: State University of New York Press, pp. 85-108.

Levine, P. (1994). *Encountering the Tiger: How the body heals trauma.* Lyons, CO: Ergos Institute Press.

Levine, P. (1997). *Waking the Tiger: Healing trauma.* Berkeley, CA: North Atlantic Books.

Levine, P. (2010). *In an Unspoken Voice: How the body releases trauma and restores goodness.* Berkeley, CA: North Atlantic Books.

Levine, S. (1979). *A Gradual Awakening.* Garden City, NY: Anchor Press/Doubleday.

Levine, S. & Levine, O. (1995) *Embracing the Beloved: Relationship as a path of awakening.* New York: Doubleday.

Lieberman et al. (2007). Putting feelings into words: Affect labeling disrupts amygdala activity to affective stimuli. *Psychological Science,* 18, pp. 421-428.

Lowen, A. (1995). *Joy: The surrender to the body and to life.* New York: Penguin Books.

Lutz, T. (1999). *Crying: The natural and cultural history of tears.* New York: W.W. Norton & Co.

McArthur, D. & McArthur, B. (1997). *The Intelligent Heart: Transform your life with the laws of love.* Virginia Beach, VA: A.R.E. Press.

Marlatt, A. & Kristeller, J. (1999). Mindfulness and meditation. In W.R. Miller (Ed.), *Integrating Spirituality in Treatment.* Washington, DC: American Psychological Association, pp. 67-84.

Maté, G. (2003).*When The Body Says No: Understanding the stress-disease connection.* Hoboken, NJ: John Wiley & Sons.

Miller, A. (1981). *The Drama of the Gifted Child: The search for the true self.* New York: Basic Books.

Miller, A. (1983). *For Your Own Good: Hidden cruelty in child-rearing and the roots of violence.* Toronto, Canada: Collins Publishers.

Morena, Gita. (1998). *The Wisdom of Oz.* Berkeley, CA: Frog Ltd.

Najavits, L., Shaw, S., & Weiss, R. (1996b, June). Outcome of a new psychotherapy for women with posttraumatic stress disorder and substance dependence. Paper presented at the meeting of the College of Physicians on Drug Dependence, San Juan, Puerto Rico.

Najavits, L., Weiss, R., & Shaw, S. (1997). The link between substance abuse and posttraumatic stress disorder in women: A research review. *American Journal on Addictions, 6,* pp. 273-283.

Najavits, L. (2002). *Seeking Safety: A treatment manual for PTSD and substance abuse.* New York: Guilford Press.

Northrup, C. (2001). *The Wisdom of Menopause: Creating physical and emotional health during the change.* New York: Bantam Dell.

Northrup, C. (2006). *Women's Bodies, Women's Wisdom: Creating physical and emotional health and healing.* New York: Bantam Dell.

Oatley, K., Keltner, D., & Jenkins, J. (2006). *Understanding Emotions,* 2nd edition. Malden, MA: Blackwell Publishing.

Ogden, P., Minton, K., & Pain, C. (2006). *Trauma and the Body: A sensorimotor approach to psychotherapy.* New York: W.W. Norton.

Oliver, M. (1992). *New And Selected Poems.* Boston, MA: Beacon Press Books.

Otto, M. & Smits, J. (2011). *Exercise for Mood and Anxiety: proven strategies for overcoming depression and enhancing well being.* New York: Oxford University Press.

Oz, M. & Roizen, M. (2005). *You: The Owner's Manual – An insider's guide to the body that will make you healthier and younger.* New York: Harper Collins.

Panksepp, J. (1998). *Affective Neuroscience: The foundations of human and animal emotions.* New York: Oxford University Press.

Parfitt, W. (1990). *The Elements of Psychosynthesis.* Dorset, England: Element Books.

Parker, S. (Ed.) (2010). *Fearless Nest: Our children as our greatest teachers.* Boulder, CO: Lulu.com.

Paul, D. (1979). *Women in Buddhism.* Berkeley, CA: Asian Humanities Press.

Pearsall, P. (1998). *The Heart's Code: Tapping the wisdom and power of our heart energy.* New York: Broadway Books.

Pearsall, P. (1994). *A Healing Intimacy: The power of loving connections.* New York: Crown Trade Paperbacks.

Pert, C. (1997). *Molecules of Emotion: Why you feel the way you feel.* New York: Touchstone.

Pert, C. (2006). *Everything You Need to Know to Feel Go(o)d.* Carlsbad, CA: Hay House.

Phillips, J. (2005). *Divining the Body: Reclaim the holiness of your physical self.* Woodstock, VT: Skylight Paths Publishing.

Randolph, P., Caldera, Y., & Tacone, A. et al. (1999). The long-term combined effects of medical treatment and a mindfulness-based behavioral program for the multidisciplinary management of chronic pain. *Pain Digest, 9,* pp. 102-112.

Rao, A., Bested, A. et al. (2009). A randomized, double-blind, placebo-controlled pilot study of a probiotic in emotional symptoms of chronic fatigue syndrome. *Gut Pathogens, 1* (6), pp. 1-6.

Rothschild, B. (1993). A shock primer for the body psychotherapist. *Energy and Character, 24*(1), pp. 33-38.

Rothschild, B. (1995a). Defining shock and trauma in body-psychotherapy. *Energy and Character,* 26(2), pp. 61-65.

Rothschild, B. (1995b). Defense, resource and choice. Presentation at The 5th European Congress of Body-Psychotherapy, Carry-Le-Rouet, France.

Rothschild, B. (1999). Making trauma therapy safe. *Self and Society,* 27(2), pp. 17-23.

Rothschild, B. (2000). *The Body Remembers: The psychophysiology of trauma and trauma treatment.* New York: W.W. Norton.

Salzberg, S. (1997). *A Heart as Wide as the World.* Boston, MA: Shambhala Press.

Salzberg, S. (2002). *Faith: Trusting your own deepest experience.* New York: Riverhead Press.

Scaer, R. (2001). *The Body Bears the Burden: Trauma, dissociation, and disease.* Binghamton, NY: Haworth Medical Press.

Servan-Schreiber, D. (2003). *The Instinct to Heal: Curing depression, anxiety, and stress without drugs and without talk therapy.* Emmaus, PA: Rodale, Inc. Originally published in French as *Guerir le stress, l'anxiete et la depression sans medicaments ni pschanalyse,* Robert Laffont, S.A., Paris.

Schatz, H. (2004). *If the Buddha Came to Dinner: How to nourish your body to awaken your spirit.* New York: Hyperion.

Scherer, K. & Ekman, P. (Eds.) (1984). *Approaches to Emotion.* London: Psychology Press.

Schmidt, L. & Warner, B. (Eds.) (2002). *Panic: Origins, insight, and treatment.* Berkeley, CA: North Atlantic Books.

Shannahoff-Khalsa, D. (2003). Kundalini yoga techniques for the treatment of obsessive-compulsive and OC spectrum disorders. *Brief Treatment and Crisis Intervention, 3,* pp. 369-382.

Shear, H. & Aiken, N. (1991). Relaxation-induced anxiety: Clarifying the paradox. *Medical Psychotherapy: An International Journal, 4*, pp. 77-84.

Sills, J. (1993). *A Fine Romance: The passage of courtship from meeting to marriage.* New York: Ballantine Books.

Stoll, A. (2001). *The Omega-3 Connection.* New York: Fireside Books.

Siegel, D. (2010). *Mindsight: The new science of personal transformation.* New York: Bantam Books.

Southwell, C. (1988). Biodynamic psychology – Gerda Boyesen's theory and methods. In J. Rowan and W. Dryden (Eds.), *Innovative Therapy in Britain.* New York: Harper & Row.

Teasdale, J., Segal, Z., & Williams, J. (1995). How does cognitive therapy prevent depressive relapse and why should attentional control (mindfulness) help? *Behav Res Ther, 33,* pp. 25-29.

Teasdale, J.D. (1999). Metacognition, mindfulness, and the modification of mood disorders. *Clinical Psychology and Psychotherapy, 6,* pp. 146-155.

Tolle, E. (1999). *The Power of Now: A guide to spiritual enlightenment.* Novato, CA: New World Library.

Tulku, T. (1978). *Openness Mind.* Oakland, CA: Dharma Publishing.

van der Kolk, B. & Fisler, R. (1994). Childhood abuse and neglect and loss of self-regulation. *Bull Menninger Clin, 58*(2), pp. 145-168.

van der Kolk, B.A. (2001). The assessment and treatment of complex PTSD. In R. Yehuda (Ed.), *Traumatic Stress.* Arlington, VA: American Psychiatric Publishing.

Vissell, B. & Vissell, J. (1995). *Light in the Mirror: A new way to understand relationships.* Aptos, CA: Ramira Publishing.

Wallenstein, G. (2003). *Mind, Stress and Emotions: The new science of mood*. Boston: Commonwealth Press.

Watts, A. (1972). *In My Own Way: An autobiography*. Novato, CA: New World Library.

Wilber, K. (1984). The developmental spectrum and psychopathology: Part II, treatment modalities. *Journal of Transpersonal Psychology,16* (2).

Wilber, K. (1999). *Grace and Grit: Spirituality and healing in the life and death of Treya Killam Wilber*. Boston, MA: Shambhala Books.

Wilber, K. (2000). *One Taste: Daily reflections on integral spirituality*. Boston, MA: Shambhala Books.

Wilber, K. (2006). *Integral Spirituality: A startling new role for religion in the modern and postmodern World*. Boston, MA: Shambhala Books.

Wiley, J. L. (1999). Cannabis: Discrimination of "internal bliss." *Journal of Pharmacological and Biochemical Behavior*, 64 (2), pp. 257- 60.

Wilson, T. (2002). *Strangers to Ourselves: Discovering the adaptive unconscious*. Cambridge, MA: The Belknap Press of Harvard University Press.

Yeomans, T. (2004). The embodied soul: Spirituality in the twenty-first century. In *Conversations in Psychosynthesis*. Association for the Advancement of Psychosynthesis.

Zvolensky, M., & Forsyth, J. (2002). Anxiety sensitivity dimensions in the prediction of body vigilance and emotional avoidance. *Cognitive Therapy and Research, 26,* pp. 449-460.

Index

Penelope Young Andrade, LCSW is a licensed psychotherapist, founder of the San Diego Center for Psychosynthesis, and founder of Transformational Talk Radio. Since 1998 Penelope has written an acclaimed monthly advice column, "Transformational Talk," for *The Life Connection,* a publication that reaches all of Southern California. For more than 30 years, she has been studying and integrating the best of traditional and alternative psychotherapies including Family Systems, Psychosynthesis, Eidetic Imagery, Bioenergetics, Biodynamics, Brennan's "Hands of Light," Somatic Experiencing (SE), and Accelerated Experiential Dynamic Psychotherapy (AEDP.) She has been an adjunct professor at San Diego University for Integral Studies, the University for Humanistic Studies, and the Natural Healing Institute. She and her husband, Arturo, developed and researched the innovative VIVO Oral Focus method for body-oriented self-soothing. Penelope lectures and trains therapists and lay audiences throughout the country, inspiring people everywhere as to the boons and benefits of Emotional Medicine. She enjoys California's sunny outdoor living, hiking in the high desert and high Sierra, swimming, Deer Park meditation retreats with Arturo, and any time at all with her grandson, Ezekiel.